FABULOUS NEW ORLEANS

I love ya
Ralph!

BOOKS by LYLE SAXON

GUMBO YA-YA with Robert Tallant and Edward Dreyer, Pelican 1987
FABULOUS NEW ORLEANS, Pelican 1988
OLD LOUISIANA, Pelican 1988
LAFITTE THE PIRATE, Pelican 1989
CHILDREN OF STRANGERS, Pelican 1989
FATHER MISSISSIPPI, Pelican 1999
FRIENDS OF JOE GILMORE, Pelican 1999

BOOKS about LYLE SAXON

THE LIFE AND SELECTED LETTERS OF LYLE SAXON
by Chance Harvey, Pelican 2003

SOUTHERN LIBRARY SERIES
Published by Pelican Publishing Company

LAFITTE THE PIRATE
CHILDREN OF STRANGERS
OLD LOUISIANA
FABULOUS NEW ORLEANS
END OF AN ERA: NEW ORLEANS, 1850-1860
LOUISIANA HAYRIDE
MARDI GRAS . . . AS IT WAS
GUMBO YA -YA : FOLK TALES OF LOUISIANA
MARDI GRAS: A PICTORIAL HISTORY
OF CARNIVAL IN NEW ORLEANS
NEW ORLEANS AS IT WAS
THE PIRATE LAFITTE AND
THE BATTLE OF NEW ORLEANS
EVANGELINE AND THE ACADIANS

Fabulous New Orleans

By

LYLE SAXON

Illustrated by
E. H. Suydam

PELICAN PUBLISHING COMPANY
GRETNA 2004

First published by The Century Co. 1928
Published by arrangement with The Century Co.
  by Robert L. Crager & Co. 1950
Published by arrangement with Robert L. Crager & Co.
  by Pelican Publishing Company, Inc. 1988

Pelican paperback edition
  First printing, December 1988
  Second printing, November 1995
  Third printing, April 2004

Library of Congress Cataloging-in-Publication Data

Saxon, Lyle, 1891-1946.
  Fabulous New Orleans.

  Reprint. Originally published: New Orleans: R. L. Crager, 1950.
  Bibliography: p.
  Includes index.
  1. New Orleans (La.)--History. 2. New Orleans (La.)--
Description. 3. Carnival--Louisiana--New Orleans. I. Suydam, E. H.
(Edward Howard), 1885-1940. II. Title.
F379.N557S29 1988   976.3'35   88-25480
ISBN 0-88289-706-3

Printed in the United States of America

Published by Pelican Publishing Company, Inc.
1000 Burmaster Street, Gretna, Louisiana 70053

For
GRACE KING

INTRODUCTION

THE very name "New Orleans" brings to mind a Mardi Gras pageant moving through the streets at night: crowds of masqueraders, rearing horses, great decorated floats glowing with color and glittering with gold-leaf. Aboard the swaying cars are centaurs, mermaids, satyrs, gods and men, illuminated by flaring torches carried by strutting negroes robed in red.

This book is rather like a Mardi Gras parade—a series of impressions. Each chapter is like a decorated car which tells a story. Some of the stories are brave and courageous, others are informative, or musing, or bizarre, or fantastic, or cruel; but they are all interlocking stories—a pageant of a city. But if some of the floats seem tawdry, or if the gilding is awry, or if the faces of the satyrs seem to be only of papier mâché, then you must blame me for lack of skill as a decorator, rather than any lack in the stories themselves.

It is at Carnival time that natives of New Orleans abandon themselves to a festival in which the beautiful and the grotesque are strangely mingled; it is at Carnival time that the city is most typically itself. So, in writing this book, I have described Mardi Gras first; then a description of the city itself in order that the reader may understand why such a mad revel is the city's characteristic gesture toward the world. I have not attempted to write history in its strict sense although the main events of the French, Spanish and American Dominations are outlined and several chapters on the new New Orleans have been added.

Many people have given me assistance. I wish to thank Mr. Henry P. Dart, editor of the Louisiana Historical Society Quarterly, for permission to use the records dealing with criminal procedure in eighteenth-century New Orleans; Miss Carrie S. Freret, librarian for the Louisiana Historical Society, for assistance in research; Miss Josie Serf, who has charge of the English documents in the Cabildo, for helping search out several diaries and records. Most particularly, I wish to thank Mrs. Cammie Garret Henry of Melrose Plantation for the use of her library of books dealing with Louisiana, and for the use of her scrapbooks which she has spent thirty years in compiling. And I am grateful to Miss Mercedes Garig of the Louisiana State University for suggestions and assistance in collecting source material.

A condensed version of the first portion of this book, called "Mardi Gras," has appeared in the *Century Magazine;* the episode "Voodoo" was first printed in the *New*

Republic; "Gallatin Street," "An Afternoon Walk" and the chapter dealing with the French Opera House appeared first in the New Orleans *Times-Picayune.* I wish to thank the editors of these publications for permission to reprint them here.

To me the illustrations seem particularly fine. Mr. Suydam has captured the real spirit of the old New Orleans and I consider myself fortunate indeed to be allied with him in attempting to present an impression of the city between the covers of a book.

L. S.

INTRODUCTION

LYLE SAXON came down the river to New Orleans from the town of Baton Rouge, Louisiana, a few years before World War I. For years he worked as a newspaper reporter for a living, but his real occupation was absorbing the city. It is doubtful that any man ever loved a city more, or became more closely identified with one. More than thirty years after he had come to New Orleans to live Saxon used to say, "Now I've become a folk character. They've made me Mr. New Orleans." It was quite true. *They* had.

From the time this book first appeared many visitors to the city thought of Lyle Saxon when they thought of New Orleans, and often they came to see him, almost as they came to see the French Quarter courtyards, and he knew it, and it both pleased and amused him, for he found humor in everything. Yet perhaps not even he realized how closely he was identified with the city he loved, and perhaps only a fraction of the horde of visitors who sought him out through the years actually knew how much he had contributed to the city, not only by publicizing New Orleans in his books, but

also by working and fighting for the preservation, even for
the restoration, of that which he thought most vital to its
individuality and charm.

When, in his early twenties, Lyle Saxon strode through
the Vieux Carré's narrow streets and saw the frightful and
chaotic state of decay into which the neighborhood had
fallen, he knew what it was he wanted to do. He was a young
man in love. His friends tried to dissuade him, but he rented,
as he later said, "a sixteen-room house for sixteen dollars a
month," in Royal Street, furnished five rooms of it, which
were all he could afford to furnish then, and opened his house
to anyone who cared to come and particularly to the writers,
artists and musicians living in, or visiting in, the city. And
for thirty years he maintained his salon—in other houses,
in Vieux Carré apartments, from time to time in a cabin at
Melrose Plantation in northern Louisiana, finally in a huge
room at the St. Charles Hotel in New Orleans. For thirty
years he was the pivot about which literary New Orleans
turned.

Leasing that Royal Street house and moving into the
French Quarter as it was then was startling, even shocking,
to a degree that may seem incomprehensible now. Some old
people, descendants of the Creoles, still clung with a kind
of grim tenacity to a few of the old homes, but all the
other buildings were occupied by the extremely poor, often
by criminals. After dusk few respectable persons ventured
into the neighborhood. Thugs waited in dark alleyways.
Prostitutes stood naked behind shuttered doors and windows. The courtyards, once so beautiful, were often filled
with refuse and incredible filth. Saxon was told he would be
murdered. Once this almost happened. Three ruffians broke

into his Royal Street house, bound him with wire and tortured him with lighted matches and cigarette stubs and kicked out two of his teeth, all in an effort to make him tell where his valuables were concealed. "All I had," he told me years later, "was some family silver and my grandpa's gold watchchain."

But he remained in his house and began to coax his friends to move into the French Quarter, which was no easy task. At first they came only to visit. Sherwood Anderson, spending some time in the city, came every day for lunch. Soon he bought a house a few blocks away. An Ohio schoolteacher who wanted to paint the Vieux Carré, Alberta Kinsey, was convinced by Saxon that she should not return to her small town, but should settle here. She had only a few dollars, but Saxon found her a room in the neighborhood and then brought his newspaper friends to see her pictures, which she sold at first for two dollars each. Now Miss Kinsey owns a house in Royal Street herself and heads the city's art colony. "But then," she will tell you, "if I went to the corner to mail a letter after dark I would run both ways." It was that kind of neighborhood.

The group of writers and painters who found what they sought in the French Quarter grew rapidly. Roark Bradford, then also a newspaper reporter and Saxon's closest friend, lived only a block or two away. William Faulkner, Edmund Wilson, John McClure, Oliver Lafarge, Edith Davenport and many others lived nearby. All came to Saxon's salon. New York friends were invited for visits. They came, and many either remained in the Vieux Carré, or the Vieux Carré, as seen through Saxon's eyes, fastened itself so to their memories that they returned often and sent their friends. Gradually the neighborhood became more and more an art colony, less an underworld. Saxon talked to the owners of buildings and convinced them that these buildings could and should be restored to their former elegance. Then he convinced "uptown" acquaintances that they should move to the French Quarter. Today it contains some of the most valuable property in the city and the popularity of the section as a residential one is still growing. Once Lyle Saxon pointed out to me a vine that is famous in the Vieux Carré. "Look," he said, "I planted that in my courtyard in Royal Street. Now it covers five houses."

Saxon worked first for the *New Orleans Item,* then for the *Times-Picayune,* where he remained for years. In 1927 he resigned to write his first book, *Father Mississippi.* He was in New York when it appeared. His publishers presented him with a copy when he walked into their offices a few days before the publication date. He walked over to Washington Square in the Village, sat down on a bench and looked at it. A few days later he boarded a train and came back to New Orleans. The next year *Fabulous New Orleans* appeared. *Old Louisiana* followed, then *Lafitte the Pirate* and *Children of Strangers.*

Through the years Saxon fought incessantly for what he wanted New Orleans to become. Never rich, he gave away nearly everything he earned throughout his life. No one knows how many young writers he helped—with advice, with encouragement, with money. And it was not always writers that he helped. When the French Opera burned in 1919 he began a long struggle to have it rebuilt. In this he never succeeded, but he never ceased to dream that New Orleans might again become the musical center of the nation it had been a century before. At the time of the fire he wrote in his newspaper account, "The heart of the old French Quarter has stopped beating." When Saxon died another reporter, in another paper, commented, "The heart of New Orleans stopped beating last night."

Not long ago a friend and I were discussing the current vogue for books about New Orleans, and we decided, inevitably, that although much had been written about the city before Saxon was even born, it was Saxon who was in one way or another responsible for the literary interest in New Orleans so prevalent for the past twenty years. Part of this, we decided, was due to his own books, principally *Fabulous New Orleans,* but much was also due to the impact of his own personality and the effect it had upon all those who met him, even during the last few years of his life, when he was ill.

For Saxon was always more interested in living than in writing. He loved to talk and he was perhaps one of the most brilliant raconteurs of his time. If he had not chosen to spend nearly all his life in New Orleans and had lived it in larger places there is no doubt at all but that this would be more widely recognized. It is unfortunately true that some of the best of his stories never reached paper. He talked them. When he was sometimes asked why he didn't write a certain book of which he talked, his reply was often, "You write it." Frequently this was done, and no one knows how many visiting authors left his company with an entire book whirling in their heads. Now and then he later read one of his own stories in print, signed by some writer who had visited him. He would laugh and say nothing worse than that they had not put it down quite right.

Usually the people surrounding Saxon were an incredible mixture. A typical gathering might include an internationally famous author, a cowboy star in New Orleans on a personal appearance tour, a complete stranger who had wandered into the room and seemed to want nothing but a touch for five dollars, a nervous young writer with a manuscript, a couple of hotel bellhops, a waiter who had come up to borrow a book, and nearly anyone else. All met on an equal plane. In Saxon's salon there was no caste or color. All received what they came for—encouragement, money, amusement, and drinks poured by Joe Gilmore, his valet, right hand and close friend.

In another of the conversations his friends often had about him after he was gone, I asked why those of us who knew him well thought Saxon so important, more important than his writing. "It was because he *created* people," was one reply. "No one knows how many people he did create. He could take the dullest persons and bring out whatever latent charm or talent they possessed, and if there was really something there—some real talent, for instance—somehow it came to life after they had known Saxon for awhile, and they were never the same again." I am positive that is true, and that that was Saxon's most important work. No one knows—possibly not even those who were thus influenced—how many people Saxon did thus create. Certainly Saxon never knew.

Until the last journey to the hospital, sick and weak, but still tall and straight, wearing the huge, wide-brimmed, planter-style hat he always wore, carrying, through necessity now, one of his collection of walking sticks, Lyle Saxon strolled every day that he was able through the Vieux Carré, looking at everything he passed with interest that had never diminished, approving of this, disapproving of that, still absorbing it all, stopping to smile at the vine that covered five rooftops, talking to shopkeepers, bartenders, friends on the street, then returning to the big room at the St. Charles Hotel to entertain the people who always awaited him there. The last few months of his life made this exercise almost more than he could bear, and he would return exhausted of strength, yet the last remnants of his strength were given the Vieux Carré as had been so much of his young energy.

For the last three years he suffered a premonition of death, that was persistent, constant and fearful to his friends. He talked of it often, always adding, "I've had a wonderful time. Don't grieve for me." During those three years he spent six long periods in hospitals, without ever receiving a satisfactory answer to what was wrong with him physically. Always a good drinker, now he drank more because he felt so ill, and life became a vicious merry-go-round.

He sat out on a balcony before the St. Charles Hotel on Mardi Gras 1946 and described the first Mardi Gras since the beginning of World War II over a national radio broadcasting chain. A few days later he was back in the hospital. This time he was told he had cancer. He joked about it. "There's no answer to cancer," he would say. Then, as well as he was able, until he fell into a final coma, he proceeded to conduct his salon in his hospital room, entertaining the staff and visitors, with privileges probably never accorded another patient. Friends kept trying to encourage him by telling him he would go home, even that he would recover, but he never believed them, not for an instant. "Stop worrying about me," he kept saying. "I've had a wonderful time."

Death came on April 9. He was fifty-four years old. There were still a dozen books he might have written. There were still countless people he might have *created*.

ROBERT TALLANT

New Orleans, 1949

CONTENTS

PART I

Mardi Gras

PART II

French Town and Spanish City

Contents

PART III

Gaudy Days

PART IV

These Times

ILLUSTRATIONS

ILLUSTRATIONS

• PART I • MARDI GRAS •

Chapter I

TO MARKET, TO MARKET!

IT is the first hour after sunrise in New Orleans. Tall old houses, not yet awake, are tight-shut and mysterious, and the shadows of their wrought-iron balcony railings lie blue and lacelike in the narrow streets. An old gentleman and a small boy are going together to the French Market for morning coffee. They have come from aboard a Mississippi River steamboat which is tied up at the wharf just outside the levee. Already the boy is intoxicated with the scent of the city, strange after the sweet familiar smell of country lanes and new-turned furrows. He sniffs delightedly, wrinkling his nose.

The uneven cobblestones make it difficult for him to walk sedately beside his grandfather; he slips and stumbles instead. As they approach the market he looks curiously at the squat, slate-covered roof supported by tapering pillars of masonry. Under the arcade he sees a moving mass of men, and the building buzzes like a hive of bees.

Wagons pass by, creaking under the weight of cabbages,

of carrots, lettuce, of red and shiny tomatoes. Drivers shout and beat their horses. Whips crack. Men and women line the curb, bargaining with those who sell vegetables and other produce. Old negro women with bright-striped *tignons* on their heads and with baskets on their arms, wander about buying a little of this and a little of that. Fruit is piled high; globes of color, red, green, orange, and clusters of purple grapes. Two nuns, wearing dull blue robes and stiff white head-dresses, are buying a bunch of bananas.

A negro man passes bearing upon his head a flat basket filled with pink roses; the basket bobs in the air above the crowd, and the man whistles as he goes by, a trill of clear, liquid notes.

An old Indian woman, wrapped in a blanket, is selling baskets striped red and green; and near her two Italian children crouch beside a pillar of crumbling masonry warming their hands over a charcoal furnace. A lean black dog runs by with a piece of raw beef in his mouth, and a yellow cat with a little bell at its throat puts up its back and hisses like a snake.

"This isn't a bit like the plantation," says the boy.

And there, in the midst of all this confusion, is the coffee-house, tucked away between the stalls of fruit and vegetables. The old gentleman and the boy sit upon stools, drinking hot, black coffee together—and there are little cakes flavored with honey, still warm from the oven. The grandfather smiles and nods contentedly over the rim of his thick cup, but the boy is solemn. His eyes are wide as he watches and listens. Around them the market men drink coffee and discuss the affairs of the day. The boy hears the

OLD FRENCH MARKET NEAR THE LEVEE

A JUMBLE OF NEW ORLEANS ARCHITECTURE
ON DAUPHINE STREET

rapid trilling of French, the soft slur of Italian, and the easy droning of negroes' voices. It is all new and strange and delightful.

When the cups are empty the man and the boy continue on their way. They go past butchers' stalls with their slabs of bloody beef, and furry, disemboweled rabbits hanging upside down. They cross a narrow passageway and enter the fish market, where thousands of fish are hanging on hooks and piled in baskets, quivering, red and blue in their iridescent coloring. Great baskets of plaited osiers are filled with crabs, blue and green, their claws waving ceaselessly; other baskets are piled with translucent, sea-gray shrimp. Some of the crabs have escaped and are moving about the floor. From time to time a boy in a dirty white apron catches them up with a pair of tongs and throws them back into the baskets. A man comes by, bearing upon his back some twenty red fish, each one strung through its mouth with a bit of green palmetto leaf; as he enters the fish stall he throws his shuddering burden on the flagstones. (*Plop! Plop!* go their flopping tails.) The boy's nose is wrinkled more than ever.

"Oo-o! What a *fishy* smell!" he cries out.

"It's a paradise for gluttons," says his grandfather.

Outside on the sidewalk is the flower market with its hundreds of potted plants: roses, ferns, little trees filled with blood-red peppers, gay in the gray street. At this end of the market many of the negroes and some of the white men have flowers stuck behind their ears or in their caps.

An old beggar woman with wild white hair reclines upon the stone floor leaning back against a pillar, her crutch beside her. She is eating a bunch of grapes and spitting out the seeds at a white rooster which lies there, its feet tied together with a bit of red rag, a rag which is also tied to the stem of a large yellow rose. So witch-like the old crone appears that the boy comes close, staring with all his eyes, half hoping, half fearing that she will suddenly ride away on a broomstick.

He is quite near before the old woman looks up and sees him. Then she smiles broadly:

"Well, young man," she cries in a gay, quavering old voice, "and where did *you* come from all of a sudden?"

The boy answers politely: "I came from up the river . . . I just got here."

"Well," she chirps, "and you don't happen to have a nickel for *me*, do you?"

The old gentleman drops a coin into her hand. She looks at it, smiles, and says carelessly, "May all the saints bless you for it," and then in a confidential tone to the little boy: "I hope you enjoy yourself. Have a good time while you can. . . . That's what *I* always say!"

"Thank you," says the boy, and with a child's optimism he adds, "I will."

And this is my first impression of the fabulous city, when I went there with my grandfather for Mardi Gras, twenty-five years ago. But I have never forgotten the gay old beggar woman, for her voice might have been the voice of the city itself. It has always seemed that New Orleans cries out: "Have a good time while you can. . . . That's what *I* say!"

Chapter II

CREOLE COURTYARD

WE did not return through the square, but went down some narrow street leading away from the river, toward the center of the old city. The sunlight was sliding down the walls, and in the open windows and doors women were gossiping. Parrots in cages hanging in upper windows screamed with raucous voices. Boys whistled as they passed carrying baskets. Heavy doors swung wide on protesting hinges, showing long dark passages with sunlit courtyards beyond, where flowers grew and festoons of vines clung to mouldering walls.

As we passed through the street the negro women were washing the *banquettes* by the simple expedient of pouring pails of water in great swishes, careless of the legs of passers-by. Other negro women were scrubbing staircases with pounded brick dust—"reddenin'" they called it. An old negro woman passed by, dressed in blue and wearing a stiff white apron. She carried a covered basket, and as she walked she cried monotonously: "Callas! Callas!"

Somewhere in Orleans Street, just off Royal Street, my grandfather paused before a heavy door set flush with the sidewalk in the high façade of an old house. He raised the iron knocker and let it fall. And together we waited in the street, while the echoes died away. Orleans Street was a little wider than the streets which we had just traversed, and the houses stood shoulder to shoulder, each one with balconies of ornate ironwork which repeated themselves in shadows against the gray brick walls.

As we were waiting two nuns passed by, walking slowly along, their heads bowed down, but as they reached us, one of them raised her face and I saw that she was black—her face seeming doubly dark against the white coif which surrounded it. Seeing my wide eyes fixed upon her face, she smiled at me with a sudden flash of white teeth.

At that moment I heard the shuffling of feet beyond the great door, and I heard, too, the muffled muttering of a voice. I kept my eyes fixed upon the door, expecting to see it move, but to my surprise a small door, cut within the paneling of the larger one, swung smartly open, and framed in the narrow aperture stood an old negro woman, very trim and trig in her guinea-blue dress, her voluminous apron stiff with starch, and a yellow, red, and blue *tignon* upon her head. She stood aside that we might enter, and in we went, stepping high over the door sill.

The passage into which we had come was fully fifty feet long and perhaps fifteen feet wide. It was paved with blue-gray flagstones and the long unbroken walls were of mouldering plaster which had been tinted green at some past time, but which were now peeling off in places, showing purplish patches, and here and there a space where the bare red bricks could be seen. The ceiling was high above my head and was crossed at intervals by large beams. At the end of the passage, seen through an arch of masonry, was a large courtyard in which bamboo was growing and where tall palm-trees waved in the sunlight. The court was surrounded by the walls of the house, and a balcony extended around three sides of it at the second floor. There was a fountain in the center with a number of small pots of flowering plants ranged around its brim. A tall white statue stood ghostlike at one side, surrounded by a tangle of vines. The space between flower beds and fountain was paved with the same blue-gray flagstones that lined the porte-cochère, flagstones wet with the moisture of early morning, except in those spots where the sun shone directly down.

Across the courtyard, at the back, a narrow flight of stairs rose full three stories, stopping now and then at small landings, then curving and continuing upward. The railing of the stairs was of faded green, and was twined from bottom to top with a magnificent wistaria vine, covered with purple flowers. The whole court was full of color, but so subdued these colors seemed against the vast gray walls that the whole was as dim as some old print that has mellowed with the years.

And near the fountain—I had not seen him at first—sat an old gentleman in black, beside a small breakfast table laid in the open air. The sunlight glimmered on the silver coffee-pot, and upon his crest of white hair, and upon a goblet which stood on the white cloth beside his plate. Upon the edge of the goblet sat a green parrakeet, dipping its bill into the water.

The old gentleman cried out in amazement upon seeing

my grandfather, and embraced him—which I thought extremely odd, never having known Creoles before—and in a
moment they were deep in talk. I stood looking on, less interested in the man than in the parrakeet, that small and
demonlike bird which stood still upon the goblet's rim with
cocked head, and regarded me with bright and wicked eye.

The old woman who had let us in came out of the house
bringing another chair. She was followed by a very black
negro man who carried a smaller chair for me. He was the
very ugliest negro that I had ever seen; his skin was so
black that it seemed almost blue, and the whites of his half-
closed eyes were yellowish. His arms hung nearly to his
knees and he walked with a shuffling gait that was like the
slinking of an animal, but when he spoke his voice was so
meek and childlike that I nearly laughed aloud.

"Ah may be wrong," he said, "but doesn't yo' wan' a
fresh pot a-coffee?"

The old gentleman answered in French, and to my further amazement the negro replied in the same tongue, his
voice rising and falling like a boy's. In another moment he
had gone back across the flagstones and had disappeared
into the house. I heard grandfather explaining that we had
stopped at the French Market for coffee a few minutes before, but our host silenced him with a gesture and the three
of us sat down at the table beside the fountain.

I cannot remember now what the men talked about, and
I hardly listened, so interested was I in the courtyard, and
all the unfamiliar things around me. The fountain was
teeming with goldfish which swam among fronds of some
swaying water-plant. The wistaria swayed back and forth
in the soft-moving air, and from time to time a few purple

petals fell noiselessly to the flagstones. Looking up I could see, high over my head, the fan-shaped windows of the old house, open to catch the sunlight and morning breeze.

The old woman who had admitted us was now cleaning the long passage with a mop, and after the negro man had brought the coffee-pot, the thin cups, and the brioche, he went through an archway and began polishing the head of a brass newel post at the foot of the wide stairs which curved upward into the house proper. I watched him, fascinated by his ugliness, and from time to time he would lift his head and regard me solemnly, a long, fixed stare full into my eyes, as though we two shared a secret all unknown to the others.

Coming back to the conversation of the two men, I found that they were speaking of me. Something unfortunate had happened, I gathered, which was like to spoil the pleasure of my first Mardi Gras.

"The children and their nurse have been gone for an hour—and they will not be home before dark. I have no way in the world of finding them. Otherwise, of course, he could have gone with them."

And they continued to talk more about the children and their joy in masking for the Carnival, until I began to understand that even now at this early hour the children—whoever they might be—were abroad with mask and domino mingling with the other maskers in the streets, and that I was left behind. There was some talk of my grandfather taking me to see the parades, but the old man was firm. No, the boy must mask, and he must see the thing in the way it should be seen. Every child should have that pleasure once at least. He himself had masked in his childhood. It meant everything. Give him time to think and he would work out some plan.

As they continued to talk, I looked away, feeling somewhat embarrassed, and found myself looking again into the eyes of the negro who polished the newel post. And, our eyes meeting, he smiled suddenly, a wide smile which exposed two gleaming rows of white teeth. He rolled his eyes so comically that I nearly laughed aloud. But the next moment—as though nothing had occurred between us—his head was bent again over the shining brass.

Almost at that moment the old gentleman called, "Robert!" trilling the *r* . . . "*R-r-o*-bear!"

"Yassuh!" The negro dropped the rag and came close to us.

Again the old gentleman spoke in French and again the negro answered. I gathered that they were talking of me, and soon my grandfather explained that Robert was to take me to the center of the city where I could see the maskers and the parades. He was to have charge of me for the entire day, unless I grew tired and wanted to come back to the house. In that case I was to say so. A costume would be provided for me.

So fascinated was I with this unfamiliar world that I would have agreed to anything, and so, after a few preliminaries and another brioche, I was turned over to Robert for the day. He disappeared for a few minutes and returned minus his apron, but wearing a hat and coat. There were admonitions to which I did not listen, and seeing my inattention, my grandfather repeated them to Robert: he was never to let go of my hand for one instant in the crowds, and he was to see that I had a costume that I liked, and he was to see that I had something to eat at intervals. And last came the instructions which had to do with our return after the night parade. At the end my grandfather handed Robert five dollars—which seemed a fortune to me—and we were ready to go.

Just as we turned away, I heard my grandfather ask if Robert could be trusted, and I heard the old gentleman say:

"But of course! *R-r-o*-bear has been with me for years and years—since he was a child, in fact. It was I who named him for the opera by Meyerbeer, 'Robert le Diable'!"

In less time that I have taken to tell it here, Robert and I were walking down the passage which led to the street, my hand held tight in his. As the door opened I saw before us, in the street, a group of children dressed in gay-colored costumes and wearing masks. They came running by, brushing against us, shouting shrilly and tinkling scores of tiny bells that were worn as ornaments upon their dominoes: "Mardi Gras! Mardi Gras!" they shouted.

And as the door closed behind us a great change came over Robert. His meekness fell from him as though it were a cloak thrown aside. He began strutting down the street as though walking in time to silent music: "Us is goin' tuh have us a *time!*" he said.

Enraptured, I trotted after.

Chapter III

TWO RED DEVILS AND A ZULU KING

W E went through narrow streets where cats were sunning themselves in doorways and where masked and costumed children tugged at their nurses' hands urging them along. The shopkeepers ran to their doors to shout greetings and the children responded with shrill cries which echoed in the narrow streets. We went past dim shops where tattered books lay in piles upon tables and where old men seemed to drowse as they examined them; we went past second-hand furniture stores where rocking-chairs seemed strangely at home on the sidewalk, as though inviting the passer-by to be seated; we lingered—or rather I lingered—before a bird store where parrots screamed and alligators and snakes lived in cages, side by side.

In front of the French Opera House at Bourbon and Toulouse streets, men were carrying great gilded statues up the stairs and a group of maskers stood watching, making comments upon the mysterious, glittering figures as they disappeared one after another into the doorway. But

Robert would not stop long to let me observe any of these wonders, and I dragged back hanging upon his hand, eager to go forward, but loath to miss anything by the way. It was not long before we turned into a little shop which seemed quite dark after the sunlit street, but in a moment my eyes had accustomed themselves to the dimness and I was dazed by a hundred new delights. It was a costume shop, and even to-day it seems nearly as bizarre as it appeared then.

There were two rooms opening one into the other by sliding doors; in the first room were counter and shelves, with high-piled green boxes bearing labels. Ghostly figures stood stiffly, wearing doublet and hose and plumed hats—models for displaying costumes. Piled upon tables was a motley mess of armor, shields, sunbonnets, false noses, and women's hats trimmed with daisies. Masks were strung across the shop, masks showing the faces of satyrs, clowns, and monks, demons, grinning skulls, and silly fat girls. From the ceiling depended other and more elaborate disguises: gilded horses' heads, purple elephants in papier-mâché, and even a unicorn's head with a silver horn, that could be fitted over one's own head in such a manner that the wearer was transformed immediately into that fabulous animal.

In the room beyond a faded woman in black sewed like mad on a sewing-machine, while another woman ran about waiting upon customers. Two negro nuns—the same two that I had met in the street—were bargaining for the rental of a red devil costume. I heard a phrase: "Ah, madame, but you should allow us a little off the regular price. . . . It's for the church, you know!"

I thought nothing of it then, but to this day the renting of that red devil costume by the negro nuns has remained an unsolved mystery in my mind. Well, it is useless to speculate now, just as it was unnecessary to speculate then, but nevertheless I wonder to what strange use that gaudy suit was put on that Mardi Gras morning so long ago.

At last it came our turn to be served and again I saw black Robert respectful and servile as he had appeared at first. He told the woman in charge that I must be fitted with a red devil costume, something nice and clean, he said. And a moment later I was being forced into a sort of red union suit over all my clothes. There was a hood from which two horns projected, and there was a grinning devil mask. In another minute the thing was done, the suit was snatched off again, and I saw it rolled into a bundle. But Robert had other fish to fry. He began explaining that a second costume was needed for his employer, "dis chile's brother"— which surprised me, more or less, as I had no brother. But I remained silent and waited while Robert looked at this and that, and finally selected some red silk tights and a few other fittings for this mysterious stranger. At last he received a second bundle and we departed from the shop.

"Where are we going now?" I wanted to know, and Robert explained that we must go to his room near-by so that we could dress for the day. I followed him, hugging the bundle to my breast, and thinking that New Orleans was like some strange dream. We went west this time and it was not long before we came to meaner streets. The houses were as old and large as in the streets just quitted, but here negro women leaned from windows and negro babies played upon door-steps. And through open doors

CANAL STREET

EARLY TYPE OF CREOLE HOUSE IN
ST. ANN STREET NEAR BOURBON

one could see inner courtyards piled high with dirt and rubbish. At last we reached a dwelling with a driveway extending under the house proper to some court beyond, and into this driveway we turned, almost running. In the rear we climbed endless flights of stairs until we reached a balcony just under the roof, and here Robert stopped, put down his bundle and fished a big key out of his pocket. A green batten door was opened and we crossed the threshold. Then Robert locked the door against the curious.

I looked about. This then was Robert's room. It was scrupulously clean and it was furnished well enough. It was quite large. A bed occupied one corner. The walls were covered with pictures of saints in various agonies of torture: Saint Lucy carrying her eyes on a plate, Saint Roch with his sores, followed by a collie that held a cake in its mouth; Saint Somebody Else being burned at the stake. I thought them all magnificent. A crucifix hung on the wall, and beneath it was a sort of altar draped in a white lace scarf and bearing three black candles in small candlesticks. A bunch of artificial flowers stood at the foot of a statue of the Virgin Mary. But Robert had no eyes for any of these things.

"Yah! Yah! See dat, Saint Joseph!" he cried in glee, "I sho' fixed yo' dat time!"

He addressed a small statue of a saint which stood upside down on the wash-stand, propped in this uncomfortable position between tooth mug and soap dish. And to my further amazement, he reached out his hand, righted the outraged saint, and after placing him upon the altar beside the statue of the Virgin, he fell upon his knees and began to pray rapidly, eyes closed, lips mumbling.

And then, as suddenly as he had fallen to praying, he was done and rose to his feet again, addressing the saint with the same familiarity.

"Guess dat'll teach yo' not to monkey wid me!" he said disdainfully.

In response to my questions he told a remarkable story. He had prayed to Saint Joseph that he might have the day off from his work, for he loved the Mardi Gras festivities more than anything else. But it appeared that Saint Joseph did not heed his prayer and he was not chosen as the lucky one that would accompany the children on their all-day wandering. Instead a woman servant had been chosen and to Robert fell the hated task of remaining at home to do the housework. He had learned his fate last night and had decided to take desperate measures. This very morning he had quarreled with the saint, "stomped" his foot at him, and turned him upside down against the soap dish for punishment. And now! Did I not see that Saint Joseph had come to his senses? Robert had known, the very moment that I came walking into the courtyard with my grandfather, that his deliverance was at hand. Saint Joseph had sent me in answer to his prayer. Now he would have a day of pleasure.

Now all of this was not very clear, but I said nothing to the contrary. Saint Joseph and his wonders were unknown to me, but I was glad to be the means of making Robert so happy—realizing that in some mysterious way his happiness would redound to my own. And as he talked to me of the things that he could show a young man like me, I began to glow with pleasure. Yassuh! Robert could show me things that no other man in New Orleans could show half so well. All that was necessary was that I forget it afterward and carry no tales back to his master. In return for this trifling promise, I was to be initiated into experiences of unknown brilliance. And having a love for intrigue, I promised anything and everything.

Now it was time for putting on my costume, and Robert helped me to undress. Coat, trousers, and shoes off, I was forced into my devilish disguise. It is true that it puckered rather badly in places and fitted too tightly in others, but what of that? Who was I to care for such trifles? It was not long before I was transformed completely and I stood before the watery mirror highly pleased with my changed appearance. The glass reflected a small red devil, rather lumpy in spots, a devil with a crimson face and a grinning mouth from which crooked teeth protruded, a devil with real, if somewhat wobbly horns, and with a beautiful pronged tail hanging down behind.

And now it was Robert's turn. The mystery of my "brother" was explained, for it was Robert and none other who was to wear the other suit. He had resorted to this device, he told me, because the shopkeeper would not rent a costume to a negro; but he had triumphed over her just as he had triumphed over Saint Joseph.

He stripped. The bagging clothes which made him appear as other men were cast aside, and a strange creature emerged. His body was unbelievably black, and his arms were knotty with muscles. His legs were thick and bent slightly at the knees, and his hands hung down like the paws of some gigantic gorilla. But for all his brutish appearance, Robert was an artist at heart. The care which he expended upon his toilet would have put Beau Brummel to shame.

First the black legs squirmed themselves into a pair of red silk tights, a dangerous undertaking as the garments were so extremely close-fitting that I expected to see the seams burst asunder at any moment; but once the legs were encased in these tights, the lower part of his anatomy was something wonderful to see. The silk gleamed bright, and there was no wrinkle to be seen. His own tan shoes were put on again. A sort of red silk undershirt was added, and a pair of pleated red and green trunks liberally trimmed with spangles, a pair of trunks from which depended a wondrous tail, also spangled and ending with a red tassel. A hood of red ornamented with a pair of cow's horns fitted snugly upon his head, and his mask and mine were identical. He finished his toilet by producing a pair of white cotton gloves which he put on; and now that none of his skin was visible, no one could tell whether he were a white man or a negro—or a Chinaman or anything else, for that matter. As a final touch of elegance to his attire he took from a wardrobe a woman's silk parasol, baby-blue with many tiny ruffles, which if somewhat frayed still made a brave showing, and with parasol in hand he took various *poses plastiques* before the looking-glass.

A few minutes later two red devils emerged from the courtyard into the street, Robert walking before carrying the umbrella and I walking behind supporting his spangled tail. How grand we were! The negroes on the sidewalk set up a shout of glee and clapped their hands as we appeared. Emboldened by this success, Robert executed a few dance steps, and then started off at a trot down the street, with many a flirt of the blue parasol and many a roguish backward glance.

Two Red Devils and a Zulu King

By the time we reached Royal Street again the sidewalks were full of maskers. All of them were going in the same direction, and the street resounded with their shrill cries and with the tinkling of tiny bells. There were children of all sizes and ages, and here and there in the crowd was a taller figure, or a couple of taller figures, men and women hidden under some comical disguise on the way to join the merrymakers in Canal Street. At each corner more masqueraders joined the throng and somewhere in the distance I could hear a band playing. The shop fronts were decorated with flags and with yellow, green, and purple bunting which the Big Devil explained were the Carnival colors. From balconies of lacelike ironwork and from upper windows men and women cried out after the marching maskers, and the marchers answered with nonsensical squeals.

I had the delightful feeling of being invisible—although the two devils were hailed from all sides—as though I had donned a magic cloak from some fairy-tale and were setting forth for strange adventures. Although I remember thinking to myself that no further adventures could be stranger than this pilgrimage through a strange street in a strange city, toward that far-away music that seemed to promise further excitement.

The devil whose tail I was supporting would turn his head at every third step or so, to see how I progressed, and from time to time he would caper wildly and twirl the blue ruffled parasol. His grinning face seemed unbelievably comic to me, and try as I would, I could not believe that the mask hid the black face of Robert. He seemed so completely a devil. And I felt much in the same way toward the other maskers; I could not believe that these simpering masks concealed the everyday faces of men and women such as I knew constituted the workaday world. Soon I gave it up and accepted the madness as something altogether delightful. And I too began to caper, swinging there on that red tasselled tail.

A clock hanging in the street before a jeweler's shop told the hour; and it was just nine o'clock. But to me, it seemed long past noon, and this variation of the hours was part of the madness. But the distant music was a challenge to lagging feet and, joining in the march of the other maskers, Robert and I bounded along, keeping time with the muffled drumbeats.

As the crowd thickened other maskers came close to us and greeted us. To my amazement I heard Robert reply in a high falsetto voice, which sounded like that of an affected woman, while, to my further astonishment, a large, fat woman, dressed in a trailing gown of white silk, spoke in a deep bass voice like a man. I looked sharply at the woman. Now here was a strange thing! Her dress was elegant—surely she was laced tightly into a corset—and her long golden curls were a wonder to see, as they hung down from under a black hat with purple plumes; but her skirt, held high, exposed a brawny leg encased in a purple silk stocking—and she wore a pair of man's shoes! Also, and this was the strangest of all, through the open lips of her simpering mask, a cigar protruded and from time to time she puffed forth a great cloud of smoke.

"Who's that lady smoking a cigar?" I whispered shrilly to Robert, and the "lady" hearing, responded in her bass voice, "Dearie, I'm your grandmother!" and punched me in the ribs.

Then she cried out: "Ho devils! Whither away?" and took Robert by the arm. We made an imposing picture, I think, the three of us as we entered Canal Street, bounding into the center of a group of maskers who danced while six other maskers with mandolins and guitars played some popular tune. Two ballet girls were bounding about upon their toes, their gauzy skirts rising and falling around them, while two other girls, dressed as men and wearing huge black mustaches and false red noses, endeavored to lead them away. Four men with faces blacked and wearing old clothes to which playing cards were sewed at intervals, swaggered along, saw the four girls, embraced them, were repulsed, and finally the eight of them joined hands and went skipping off. A pirate came up to us and lured our fat lady away; she waved her cigar and departed, holding her dress high about her purple legs.

And now, in the midst of the crowd, I looked about. Canal Street was extraordinarily wide, and at the moment there was no traffic upon it, no street-cars nor carriages were moving along; instead ropes had been stretched across all side streets leading into it, and the whole thoroughfare was given over to the maskers, and to those other pedestrians who walked back and forth mingling with the masqueraders. So tight packed were the sidewalks that the maskers paraded in the double roadways or in the neutral ground which lay between. Across the street I could see windows filled with people, and balconies with tiers of seats where men and women were seating themselves to witness the revel in the streets below. People, people everywhere. I had never seen so many, and there was a hum of voices in the air, punctuated with cries and laughter, and by the cries of the vendors of peanuts and popcorn, and by the calls of men who sold tiny whips and bright-colored feather dusters and strings of bells.

The sun shone down upon the mass of moving color, lighting a spangle to brilliance here, or shining upon a piece of tinsel there. There were bull-fighters, pirates, nuns, and priests. A snake charmer with a large imitation snake was shaking its hideous head into the faces of the passers-by. A group of ten boys and girls dressed in identical black and white clown suits marched one behind the other, hands upon the shoulders of the one before; they threaded their way in and out of the crowd as they approached us, but when the leader came abreast of the two devils he uttered a shout, and in a moment we were surrounded. Hand and hand they danced around us, shouting: "Dance devils! Dance devils!" And Robert, quick to oblige, executed a ribald dance which drew shouts of merriment from all who watched, while I capered after swinging from his tail.

It was over as soon as it had begun, and again we threaded our way along, square after square, all packed with masqueraders and those who had come to see. I wished to linger, but Robert was firm. We would have to hurry, he told me, if we wished to be in time for the arrival of the Zulu King.

Now the Zulu King meant no more to me than the fourth dimension, but he sounded exciting, so I demurred no longer but hurried after the devil who bounded before me. We dodged through groups of maskers, we ducked under ropes, and finally after traversing several squares, turned from Canal Street into another thoroughfare where a group of negro girls were dancing under an arcade while two negro men picked on banjos. I saw no white maskers here, but there were many negroes in costume who seemed to be holding a Mardi Gras all their own. And here I found that the crowd was moving in another direction, away from Canal Street. We went along the street with them, square after square. Past pawnshops with the three golden balls hanging outside, past cafés, where negroes sat on stools eating while other negroes served them; past saloons which smelled of stale beer and wet sawdust and from which came shouts and curses. At last we reached an open space with a large red railroad station at one side, and with a canal— or what appeared to be the end of a ship canal—directly before us. The banks of the waterway were lined with negroes, pushing and shoving about in order to gain some point of vantage. Some of them were in costume but most of them were in their everyday clothes. They were packed so tightly together that it was almost impossible to force a way between them.

Just as we found ourselves wedged into the thickest part of the crowd there came a chorus of shouts:

"Yon' he is!"

"Yon' he come!"

"Gawd a-mighty!"

"Wha' he is?"

"Da' he!"

We pushed and shoved with the rest, and in a moment actually succeeded in making our way to the water's edge, and here Robert lifted me bodily and seated the little devil on the big devil's shoulder, where I sat, legs around his neck, looking with all my eyes.

The sun shone bright on the strip of water, and there in

the distance I could see a patch of purple and red which was repeated in the water below. It was the royal barge of the Zulu King approaching.

Now there are a great many people who have been born in New Orleans and who have lived there all their lives, but who have never seen the arrival of the Zulu King; and I feel sorry for them, for surely there is no more characteristic sight to be seen in the South. This custom has continued for many years—a sort of burlesque of the grander Mardi Gras of the white people, and it provides the note of humor which is lacking in the great parades.

The Zulu King and his faithful henchmen were approaching slowly, the barge propelled by a tiny puffing motor-boat. The barge itself looked as if it had been rather hurriedly decorated with whatever scraps happened to be at hand. The canopy over the throne was made of sacking, and was supported by rough poles. A bunch of paper flowers adorned its top, and beneath it, in a tattered Morris chair, the king sat. He represented a savage chieftain, but whether from modesty or from fear of cold, the Zulu King wore, instead of his own black skin, a suit of black knitted underwear. There were bunches of dried grass at throat, ankles, and wrists, and a sort of grass skirt such as hula-hula dancers wear, and he wore a fuzzy black wig surmounted by a tin crown. In his hand he carried a scepter—a broomstick—upon which was mounted a stuffed white rooster. There were some tattered artificial palm-trees at the four corners of the royal barge, and a strip of red cloth was draped from palm to palm. Four henchmen, dressed almost exactly like the king—save that they wore no crowns —were capering about beside him. Some red and purple flags were stuck about here and there. And as the barge approached us, the king opened a bottle of beer and drank a toast from the bottle; while negro men and women on the bank produced flasks from their pockets and drank their own.

When they were quite near us, I saw that the king and his followers had improved upon Nature's handiwork by blackening their faces and by putting stripes of red and green paint liberally upon their cheeks and upon their black union suits. These things I noticed as the barge was tying up at the end of the canal quite near me and while flasks on shore were passing from hand to hand.

A delegation of negro men wearing evening clothes and having red and purple scarves draped from shoulder to waist, waited upon the bank, and they kept calling out greetings to His Majesty:

"Wha' de Queen?"

"Ain't yo' brought us no Queen?"

"Ain't yo' lonesome all by yo'seff?"

And to these gibes, the king answered grandly, "Ef I has a Queen she goin' tuh be a man—'cause I'm through wid wimmen!"

This was considered magnificently humorous, for a cry of joy went up from those who lined the bank.

And now came the disembarking. With difficulty the negroes in evening dress opened a way through the crowd and a wagon drawn by mules was brought close to the barge. The wagon was a large, almost square vehicle without sides; only a flat floor over the wheels. At the moment it was bare. But not for long. The king rose, picked up his Morris chair and climbed aboard. The henchmen followed, each bearing a potted palm. The bunting was stripped from the barge and was nailed into place around the edge of the wagon—and the flags and flowers were distributed about. And, with the king and his four followers aboard, it moved along and another wagon took its place.

The second vehicle was much like the first, except that it had a wood-burning cooking stove in the center—a stove in which a fire burned and from the short stovepipe came a cloud of black smoke. An old negro woman stood by the stove, frying fish, and from time to time she would remove a steaming morsel from the pan and pop it into some open mouth that was eagerly upheld to receive it. The negroes crowded around the vehicle, screaming out in delight. Two negro men were seated in chairs near the stove—also aboard the wagon—cleaning fish. And there was a basketful of catfish beside them. Aside from a garland of flowers which adorned the stovepipe, the wagon was undecorated.

The men who had been waiting on the bank now mounted their steeds—mules—and sat there, making a brave show with their white shirtfronts and red and purple scarves. Two of them carried stuffed white roosters on their shoulders. Like the king's, their faces were blackened and painted with red and green stripes. And as the king's chariot moved off from the side of the canal, these out-riders distributed themselves around it—a guard of honor.

Next came the fish-frying wagon, and this was followed by a motley collection of horse-drawn carriages—evidently the odds and ends from some livery stable. They were for the greater part open carriages or victorias, and they were decorated somewhat sketchily with flags and bunting. In these carriages rode various leaders of negro society; heads of lodges and fraternal organizations, wearing high silk hats; heads of negro unions, wearing badges and colored ribbons. A group of marching men followed the carriages— some in costume, some merely dressed in their best—but all highly pleased with the Zulu King and his crew.

Slowly the procession went down Rampart Street—that street which Robert and I had just traversed—and from every store, lunch-counter, billiard hall, and saloon, a crowd came out to see.

Negro women in the crowd called out invitations to the king, shaking their hips and rolling their eyes, and to these love-cries he responded with answers more amorous than delicate, while black girls exclaimed loudly to each other— and to any one else who cared to listen—"Oh, ain't he *some* man!"

The parade progressed at a snail's pace, owing partly to the crowded street and partly to the eccentricities of the drivers of the mules, who stopped here and there to chat with acquaintances along the way. At these stopping points the king rose from his chair, went to the edge of the wagon, and bent down to exchange a resounding smack with some dusky belle who came close, holding up her thick lips. And after each of these salutes, the king would turn about and yell back to the old woman who was frying fish, "Give dis gal a mouf'ful uv fish, sister!" to which the old woman would reply, "Sho' will!" and the damsel would stand beside the second wagon until the morsel of hot catfish was put into her open mouth. And at these signs of royal favor the crowd would cheer afresh.

"Great day!"

"Gawd knows!"

"Look at dat!"

"Well now, *people!*"

"Annie done tempt de king!"

But once the monarch suffered a slight accident as he bent to exchange salutes with a black girl. One of the dark-skinned outriders was directly behind the royal car, and as the king bent forward the hungry mule took a mouthful of the king's grass skirt. There was a sudden tug, a shout, and the king turned to find the entire back of his skirt gone, while only a few wisps of straw were seen hanging from the mule's mouth.

The assemblage burst into a roar of Rabelaisian mirth, and the king planted a well-aimed kick at the mule's head. Then, with more haste than dignity, he seated himself again upon his throne. And the parade moved on.

Robert had pushed up his devil-mask and stood leaning against a post, rocking with laughter. And we remained there while the procession moved away from us down the street while a band boomed out a ragtime march.

Chapter IV

HAIL REX!

It was nearly noon before we reached Canal Street again where the great street pageants were to take place; for Robert's return down Rampart Street was interrupted a hundred times. Rampart is the Broadway of New Orleans negroes and there are many shops, eating houses, and booths which sell those things so dear to the negro's heart, and to the negro's stomach.

After the Zulu King had passed Robert and I stood watching the stragglers who followed in his wake: masked yellow girls dressed as Spanish dancers, wearing high-heeled red shoes, spangled skirts, and black lace mantillas draped over their heads; negro men dressed as Indians with faces painted and feather head-dresses; men dressed in their everyday clothes, or even in overalls, but wearing grotesque masks; negro children of every shade from velvet black to the lightest *café au lait,* screaming and romping in the streets, enjoying the Carnival to the fullest degree. Robert was anxious to keep moving. He mumbled something under his mask to me—something about showing me things—and then ducked between the swinging doors of a negro saloon. It was a long, rather dingy room, with a bar, a watery mirror behind it; the bartender was a negro, and negro men were lined up drinking beer. While Robert quenched his thirst I drank a bottle of red pop which matched my costume, and sitting on a chair against the wall, looked about me. It was the first bar-room that I had ever seen at close quarters, except those aboard the Mississippi River steamboats, and I was interested in the signs and notices pasted on the walls. There was a notice that "The Poor Boys' Social Club" was entertaining with a "Monster Dance" and there was another notice that the "Hot Papa Café" was holding a contest that day for the funniest negro masker. I listened to the conversation, which went something like this:

"How yo' comin', Devil?"

"Po'ly, thank Gawd, an' yo'?"

"Oh, Ah can't complain, but Ah specks Ah'll feel mighty low an' broke down to-morrow. Me, Ah'm goin' tuh have me a *time* tuh-night!"

"What yuh doin tuh-night?"

"Ah'm goin' tuh de Boll Weevils' Ball. Plenty 'ooman, plenty gin."

"Dem wimmin ain't goin' tuh fool wid yo', ugly ole boy!"

"Mebbe not. But Ah sho goin' tuh trip 'em up, ef'n dey don't!"

This was considered very humorous and was greeted with a burst of guffaws. Robert, who had pushed up his mask to drink, looked funnier than ever, so very red and

LOOKING DOWN ROYAL STREET

OLD COURTYARD IN CHARTRES STREET
AT MADISON

black he looked, and the woman's ruffled parasol which he carried closed in one hand gave an idiotic touch typical of the day.

When he had finished his beer and I my pop, we "took the street" again. There were strange things on display in the shops and in the show windows, and particularly in one drug store before which we paused while Robert examined the articles displayed there. He waited so long and looked so intently that I remember the things even now, but it was many years later that I realized their significance—and it is probable that I should have never realized it, had I not seen a similar shop window on Rampart Street a few years ago. Here was piled blue powder, yellow sulphur-like powder, black chicken feathers tied in neat bunches with bits of thread, black candles, small spirit lamps . . . many other seemingly unrelated things. But now I know why Robert stood spellbound contemplating them. These things were Voodoo accessories—the necessary ingredients for conjuring, the implements of devil-worship, the dark factors in a darker magic. I remember Robert's respectful interest, his rolling eyes, his intent scrutiny. And I remember that he vouchsafed no word of explanation to the small boy who stood by, awaiting his pleasure.

Finally, jerking himself away with an effort, Robert continued along Rampart Street toward Canal. It was not long before we caught up with the Zulu King again. His royal equipage stood abandoned in the street, and the royal court had entered a negro "barrel house" for refreshments. There was a burst of music from behind swinging doors, and within we could hear the shouts and guffaws of negro men and women. The saloon was crowded to its doors, and from somewhere in that dense-packed mass we could hear the sound of tinkling guitars and the shuffling of feet. Robert made one ineffectual effort to wedge his way in, but gave it up after a moment and returned to me, and hand in hand we threaded our way through the ever-thickening crowd.

Ahead of us lay Canal Street, now so tightly packed with people that it was impossible to move forward at more than a snail's pace. The wide street was filled with moving figures. About half of them were masked, the others dressed in everyday garb. High above the streets the balconies were massed with spectators, and in every window and even along the roofs of the buildings there were men and women. Flags fluttered everywhere.

If the street had seemed mildly insane before, it was bedlam now. A happy roar hung over the heads of the crowd, a hum of voices, punctuated with sharp cries, whistles, cat-calls. And everywhere the tinkling of tiny bells—an undercurrent of sound infinitely strange.

And color, color everywhere: red, purple, blue, arsenic green, and the glitter of metal head-dresses and spangles in the sunlight. There were clowns, of every size and of every color of costume; there were hundreds of ballet girls, often ten or more in a group, all dressed in black and white, exactly alike. There were animal disguises; men wearing purple elephants' heads of papier-mâché; huge donkeys' heads. Sometimes two men would combine in order to represent a comical horse or a violet-colored cow. A man passed by high on stilts, his pink and white striped coat tails blowing out in the breeze. Two men were dressed in black tights, painted with white to imitate skeletons; they were truly terrifying with their skull faces and macabre aspect. Accompanying the skeletons was a fat woman dressed in the uniform of a United States marine; she dragged a squalling child by one arm: "That's only your papa," she said, indicating the taller of the skeletons, but the child, unimpressed by this information, continued to squall.

There was a burst of music near us and a policeman rode by on horseback, clearing a narrow path through the crowd. Robert and I, crushed back against the curb, were almost under the feet of the marching men who came swinging by. It was one of the so-called "little parades" which amuse the crowds before the arrival of Rex, King of the Carnival. On a purple and gilt banner I could read the name of the organization: "The Jefferson City Buzzards"! And with a blare of cornets, they were upon us. First came twelve fat men dressed as little girls, all in white. Their huge stomachs were draped with the widest of baby-blue sashes, and they wore pale blue socks which ended half-way up their fat and hairy legs. All of them wore long flaxen curls surmounted with baby caps trimmed with blue rosettes. Nearly all of them were smoking cigars. They bowed right and left as they marched along and smiled widely, gold teeth glittering in the sunlight. Their "queen" was an unusually fat man who bulged out of a baby carriage, sucking a large stick of red and white striped candy. Another man—this one with a big mustache—was blacked up to represent a negro mammy, and pushed the carriage, perspiring copiously. The babies were followed by a group of men in white linen suits, each carrying an American flag.

They strutted with the music and kept bowing and throwing kisses to the spectators. A negro band brought up the rear —a band which played the rowdiest and bawdiest jazz that I had ever heard.

The Jefferson City Buzzards had hardly passed before another marching club followed it. This time the marchers were in Oriental costumes—men of the desert and their houris. They carried a banner bearing the name of their organization. A few minutes later another club came by, the men dressed as negro minstrels.

Suddenly I became conscious of a swelling whisper which ran through the crowd. Necks were craned. Maskers stopped their antics and stood on tiptoe, all looking in the same direction. Robert, with his hand on my shoulder, tip-toed too, shading his devil mask with white gloved hand; and then he turned to me and said—his voice muffled behind his mask—"It's de parade!" And then, almost upon us, I saw twelve blue-coated policemen on horseback riding abreast. They came charging down upon the crowd and we moved back before them, falling over each other in our haste.

If the street had seemed tight-packed before, it was even worse now. Elbows came in contact with my forehead, feet smashed down upon mine; I was buffeted about, almost thrown down as the crowd became more congested around me. But Robert dragged me back to him with an effort, and in another moment I found myself seated with my legs around his neck, high over the heads of the others. And as I emerged from that undercurrent which had seemed to drag me down, I had the feeling of a swimmer rising upon the crest of a wave. And there before me, stretched out as far

as I could see, was a mass of maskers, and beyond them a
series of glittering mountains were moving toward me. . . .
The Carnival King was coming.

First came the mounted policemen who cleared the way,
and behind them were masked courtiers riding black horses;
they wore gold plumes on their hats, and their purple velvet
cloaks trailed out behind them over the flanks of the horses;
they wore doublet and hose, and they carried gleaming
swords in their hands. There were perhaps twelve of these
outriders, gaily dressed except for the fact that they wore
black masks which gave a sinister effect. Behind them came
a brass band tooting lustily. Two negroes carried between
them a large placard emblazoned with one word, "Rex."

And now the parade was actually upon us. The first float
in the procession seemed to me the most wonderful thing
that I had ever seen. It was a mass of blue sky and white
clouds surmounted by a glittering rainbow, and under the
rainbow's bridge were masked figures in fluttering silk, men
and women who held uplifted golden goblets. It was the
title car and upon its side was written the subject of the
parade—a subject which I have wholly forgotten to-day,
but which dealt with some phase of Greek mythology. The
glittering float towered as high as the balconies which overhung the street from the second stories of the houses, and
as this gay-colored mountain came gliding past me I was impressed with the fact that the car was swaying and that it
seemed fragile for all its monumental size. It was almost as
though the whole were on springs. The car was drawn by
eight horses covered in white and with cowls over their
heads.

A blaring band followed the title car, then more outriders, dressed this time in green and gold and wearing purple masks; and behind them came a car which was even larger than the first. It was like a gigantic frosted wedding cake and at the top on a golden throne was seated Rex, King of the Carnival. Such a perfect king he was, with his fat legs encased in white silk tights, a round fat stomach under shimmering satin, long golden hair and a magnificent curled yellow beard! His face was covered with a simpering wax mask, benign and jovial. On his head he wore the very grandest crown I had ever seen, all gold and jewels which sparkled in the sun; and he carried a diamond scepter in his hand which he waved good-naturedly at the cheering crowd. Behind him a gold-embroidered robe swept down behind the throne, cascaded over the sloping back of the float and trailed almost to the ground, its golden fringe shaking with the movement of the car. There was gauze and tinsel everywhere and thousands of spangles glittered in the sun. At the feet of the monarch two blonde pages stood, little boys no larger than I, with long golden curls and white silk tights, which were rather wrinkly at the knees. How I envied them!

Robert and I were both screaming with delight, and I clapped my hands. And then a preposterous thing happened —a magnificent thing. The blonde monarch, so high over my head and yet so near me, leaned out and with his scepter pointed directly to me as I sat perched upon the shoulder of the big red devil. He said something to one of the pages, something which I could not hear, and the page with a bored smile tossed a string of green beads to me. It swirled through the air over the heads of the people between us and dropped almost into my outstretched hands; but my clumsy fingers missed and it fell to the ground. Immediately there was a scramble. Robert stooped, I fell from his shoulders, and I found myself lying on the pavement as though swept under a stampede of cattle. Hands and feet were all around me, but somehow in the struggle I managed to retrieve those beads, and triumphant I scrambled up again and Robert put me back on his shoulder.

This had taken only a moment, but during that time the king's car had moved on and another car was in its place. I could see glittering serpents—monstrous golden pythons which twined around white columns, and there were nymphs with green hair who held up bunches of great purple grapes as large as oranges and which glimmered in the sunshine with their iridescent coloring. The float with the serpents and grapes seemed monstrously large to me, even larger than those two which had come before, and it came to a swaying halt directly before us. I had a good opportunity to examine the serpents at close range and was somewhat relieved to find that they did not move but remained twined about the fluted columns.

It was then that Robert pinched my leg to attract my attention. He was pointing toward the Carnival King, whose throne was now a short distance from us. The King's back was turned toward me now, but I could see that he was greeting some one upon a balcony opposite. I had not noticed this balcony before, oddly enough, but now as I looked I was conscious of tier after tier of seats rising from the second to the third floor of the building, the seats filled with men and women, not maskers but ordinary mortals dressed in their best. At the moment their hands were stretched out in greeting, and they were smiling. There in the first row of seats on the balcony was a beautiful girl wearing a big floppy pink hat. She stood with both hands outstretched toward Rex as he sat before her on his throne. They were separated by a distance of perhaps twenty feet, but his high throne was almost level with her, and both of them were far above the heads of the crowd in the street below. They were exchanging greetings. And then from somewhere came a man with a step-ladder which was set up in the street.   Up the ladder a man ran nimbly, bearing a tray with a white napkin over it. He presented the tray to the King. Suddenly a bottle was opened with a loud pop, and I saw champagne poured out into a thin wine glass, champagne which spilled over the edge of the goblet and ran down into the street below. Rex, King of the Carnival, was toasting his queen. Years afterward, I heard the story of this, why it was done and how old the custom was, but then the small boy who looked upon it saw only another fantastic happening in that mad dream of Mardi Gras.

The ceremony was soon over, the step-ladder was whisked away again and Rex on his swaying throne was drawn slowly down the street. I could hear the cheers which greeted him as they grew fainter in the distance, drowned in the blare of bands. One by one the gorgeously decorated floats passed before us, each telling some mythological story. There were satyrs, fawns, mermaids, centaurs, the like of which I had never seen before. Here the whole of fairyland had become a reality before my eyes. I counted the glittering cars as they passed. There were twenty in all and almost as many bands of music. And always that strange, unreal quality, that gaudy, blatant thing which I could not define then and which I cannot define now, except that it gave to me the feeling of seeing a thousand circuses rolled into one.

By the time the last car in the parade had passed the spot in the street where Robert and I were standing, the procession had turned at some distant corner and was returning on the opposite side of Canal Street, and without moving from our position we were able to see the parade again. This time, looking with more scrutinizing eye, I noticed things which had escaped me before—that the beautiful masked women who rode upon the floats were strangely masculine in body, and that the figures of papier-mâché which had seemed so beautiful at first were not quite as realistic as I had imagined. However, I did not look upon the parade with a critical eye, but accepted it for what it was, a gay dream.

The moment that the last car had passed in the street, the crowd began to surge about again. Robert, heaving a sigh of relief, let me slide down his body to the ground, and we tried to make our way into a store where cold drinks were for sale; but every one in the crowd seemed to have the same idea, and we found it impossible to force our way inside. Accordingly we drank pink lemonade which a street vendor was dispensing at the edge of the sidewalk. It tasted only faintly of lemon and sugar, but it was cold and pink and our thirst made us grateful.

Now that the parade had passed by, the maskers had the street to themselves again, and a hundred small festivals were going on. Men were picking upon banjos, men played on accordions, girls beat upon tambourines, and down the street came a small wagon on which there was a piano. One man played while another sang through a megaphone, and those in the street sang too—some popular song.

In the noise and confusion I found myself jostled and bumped at every second step. A large woman dressed as a jockey stepped heavily upon my foot as she strode by, and I wailed in pain; but Robert, hardly noticing my plight, urged that we begin further investigation. And now that the parade had disappeared in the distance he caught my hand and began picking his way through the crowds of maskers again. I asked no question and made no objection but I found myself so tired that I could hardly drag one red leg after the other.

I thought at first that he intended going back to Rampart Street where we had left the Zulu King, but instead he turned north this time and we went down a narrow street beside a railroad station. Just back of the depot we came upon a row of imposing houses built of wood and ornamented with jig-saw towers and useless-looking balconies. The odd thing about these houses was that, although windows were closed and shades drawn down, it was evident that festivity was reigning within, for a stream of men was ascending and descending the steps, as though paying visits from house to house. In one doorway I saw a beautiful golden-haired fat lady who wore a blue silk kimono; she was holding conversation with the gentlemen on the steps. They seemed intent upon entering and she seemed equally certain that they should not do so. As we passed, I saw her smile disappear and she shouted suddenly: "Damn it, I said the house was full and it is full. Now you get the hell away from here!" And then slammed the door—*blam!* But the men did not seem to mind at all, but went on to the next house and rang the bell.

Robert was deaf to my questioning; and he continued to stride along the narrow street. Now we passed cafés from which there came bursts of music and within I could hear the shuffling of feet, the jangling of pianos and shrill cries. What a good time these people were having! I wanted very much to stop and go in at each such café, but Robert said that we'd better not, as negroes were not allowed inside.

We turned a corner and went along Iberville Street—a thoroughfare which ran parallel with Canal Street. Here, more beautiful ladies leaned from windows, calling out greetings in jolly and friendly fashion. They were all a little fat, it seemed to me, and their lips were very red; but they all smiled and held their kimonos around them, and they all kept crying out for the passers-by to come in and see them. Some of the men who were walking slowly along the sidewalk stopped to talk with these friendly girls, and some of them went up the steps and into the doors, closing the doors after them. The structures in this street were very peculiar, I thought; long houses, only one story high, and divided into small apartments. The individual apartments were about twelve feet wide and each had one door and one window. Only pretty ladies seemed to live in them, one in each apartment. And to make it stranger still, many of these ladies had their names painted upon their front doors. As we went along I read the names aloud: "Laura" and "Wanda" and "Anna" and "Bessie," and sometimes the names were prefixed with a sort of title, such as "Chicago May" or "French Marie," and some of the doors had the additional notice: "Come in!" which was very nice and hospitable, I thought. But my grandfather had warned me that morning that the city was not like the plantation, and that I must adapt myself to city ways, so, remembering his admonition, I made no unnecessary comments aside from reading all the names aloud as we passed by. But I remembered it all, and determined to ask questions later.

Robert still wore his mask, as many other men in the street did, and from time to time one of the red-lipped lassies would hail him with a cry: "Hello papa! Showing your boy around?" or they would wave to me and say, "Hey little boy, bring your daddy in to see me!" And I being a polite child, would wave back and say, "You must come see us sometime!"

Finally this square of houses was left behind and we came to another café on a corner where there was even noisier music playing inside and where men and women were dancing to the sound of rattling drums. I squatted down on the sidewalk and peered under the swinging doors, and there I saw a long bar-room with mirrors on the walls and beyond it a dance hall. There were figures moving about in time with the music and it all appeared so fascinating that Robert could hardly drag me away.

Policemen were walking along the streets, and if one of the ladies would come out of her door upon the sidewalk to hail some passing man, the policeman would chase her back into the house again—a thing which struck me as unkind, for the ladies were all so gay and gracious, while the policeman seemed so gruff. One officer spoke to Robert: "That kid is too young to be down here alone," he said, pointing at me with his club. "Is he with you?" And Robert, mustering up his best white-folks' voice, replied from under his mask, "I'm taking him somewhere." And the policeman shrugged his shoulders and walked on.

The second square was like the first one, only the women seemed older and fatter, and not quite so charming. It is true that they made up for these slight defects by being even friendlier than those in the first square. They insisted that we come in, and even cried out: "Please, daddy! Oh, daddy!" or "Sweet papa, I want to tell you something. Oh, wait!" But Robert did not slacken his pace and I followed after.

The third square was almost like the second, except that there were yellow girls at the windows and doors, mulatto girls in light robes or nightgowns, and these were just as polite and gracious to us as the others—the white ones—that we had passed. At one house, which was a little larger than the rest, a large mulatto woman dressed all in red and wearing high-heeled red shoes, stood in the door announcing to any one who would listen that a "show" was going to start in a few minutes, and she urged the passing males to stop and see it. Of course I begged to go, but Robert was firm. No, there were other things to see, he said.

At last we turned a corner and came to a street where there were black women hanging out of the windows and where negro men loitered in the street outside, and after passing for a square or more along this street we came to a café where a big sign announced that this was "The High Brown Social and Athletic Club." And it was into this doorway that we turned.

Chapter V

SPIRIT OF CARNIVAL

THE High Brown Social and Athletic Club turned out to be a negro saloon. By this time I was beginning to feel quite at home in such places and thought this one to be in no way remarkable. But Robert did not linger in the bar-room. After a brief whispered conversation with a sleek, black negro behind the bar, he led me through swinging doors and into a back room where there were tables and where a mulatto man was playing on a jangling piano, while several yellow girls and their dark-skinned boy friends sat at tables drinking together. Nor did we linger here, but going through a rear door we found ourselves in a smelly courtyard. Here two negro men were sitting on boxes and Robert talked with them for a while. They seemed to object to me—for some reason that I could not understand—but Robert explained that he could not let me out of his sight and that I would behave myself and say nothing. After some further argument a gate was opened and we went down an alley and into another house. I was completely "turned around" by this time and felt that if Robert deserted me now, I should be forever lost. Behind heavy doors I could hear the booming of a drum and the whine of fiddles. And when this door was opened the breath of air that came out was so stifling that I fell back for a moment. We went in, but it was like entering an oven.

The room was very large and was tightly closed. Electric lights shone brightly and I saw that the ceiling was a mass of red and green streamers of paper, rather reminiscent of Christmas. The ceiling was all I could see, for the place was thronged with negroes. We made our way through the crowd around the door, and came out upon the dancing floor, where many couples were moving in a slow, shuffling dance; men and women with bodies pressed together so that they seemed one, and many dancing with closed eyes and lunging hips.

And it was then that I saw the Zulu King again. He was lolling on a throne on a sort of dais at one end of the room. He was laughing very loud and showing all of his magnificent white teeth. He lay back in a chair, and upon his knee was a mulatto girl with a short red dress. She was drinking from his glass.

The room smelled of unwashed bodies and stale beer.

Robert led me to a corner and found a chair for me. Then, after telling me to sit there quietly—and cautioning me not to take off my mask—he was gone, promising to return in a few minutes. A little later I saw his red devil costume and realized that he had joined in the dance. With arms entwined around some dusky damsel he was gyrating with the best of them, and his squirms and bumps were something to see!

It was not long before the music stopped and a shout echoed through the room. "Time foh de contes'!" some one cried, and presently the floor was cleared and the dancers ranged themselves around the hall.

And then the members of the orchestra laid aside their instruments and turned about in their chairs in order to watch. All except the drummer. His big drum was moved further out upon the dancing floor and he began beating out a measured rhythm.

To the center of the floor came a woman, a thin quadroon. She began to shake in time with the drumbeats, first a shoulder, then a hip. Then she began to squirm and lunge. At each beat of the drum her position would change, and as the measured beating continued she moved her body with each beat. At last she was shaking all over, head wagging, hips bobbing back and forth. And as the drumbeats became more rapid, her gyrations became more violent. At the end of a few minutes the drumming stopped and she stood limp in the center of the floor.

There was wild applause.

She retired and another girl took her place, this time a black girl. Her movements were more suggestive, more animalish—and pleased the crowd more extravagantly than the first dancer had done. The drumming was done in the same fashion as at first. When she had finished a third girl took her place. I was very bored and wanted Robert to take me away, and I could not understand why the negroes thought this entertainment so fine.

So after a time Robert took me outside into the court-yard again and had a negro waiter bring me a big plate of red beans and rice and a glass of ice water. There in the smelly courtyard I sat on a box and ate my lunch—and realized that I was very hungry. Robert stood watching me until I had finished, then while I waited he ate his lunch. For Robert was a stickler for convention. Never let it be said that he let a white child eat with him. No sir! The little gentleman could not be debased by eating with a negro —but he could be dragged into any sort of den that Robert pleased to enter himself. . . . It was a strange convention, but no stranger than many others that exist.

At last I was ready to enter the dance hall again, and found that the contest was ended and the winner had been acclaimed. She was a large, fat, black girl, dressed in a yellow dress. Her face shone with grease and sweat, but she was proud and happy with her success—for this meant that she should be given the crown of the Zulu King. Some mystic ceremony was performed, with much hugging and buffoonery, and at last the king rose and led his queen to the center of the floor. Some jargon was repeated, and there was loud laughter. And the dancing began afresh.

I sat placidly in my corner, watching. It was pleasant enough to sit and watch, and I rested. I think that the music must have lulled me, for my head drooped lower and lower, and at last I slept.

I woke with a start. Shrieks rent the air. A general fight was in progress. I could not see Robert anywhere. Women were knocked down; men threw chairs. I saw a big negro knock a smaller man sprawling, and the man lay where he fell, his mouth open. And it was at this minute that I saw the Zulu King—a razor in his hand. He was slashing at some man who held a glittering thing high in the air . . . and a moment later I heard a man's scream that ended in a gurgling sound. The tall black man fell backward on the floor . . . and there in the open space stood the king, the razor red in his hand.

Then panic!

Men and women rushed for doors and windows: men knocked each other down. I heard a mulatto girl squall shrilly as she was trampled upon. Within a minute or two more there were only three people in the room: one was the negro who lay with his throat cut, the other was the man who had been knocked senseless a few minutes before, and I was the third—a small and frightened devil, holding with both hands to the chair on which I sat.

Outside I could hear shouting, and the sound of a police whistle blowing. I was terribly frightened. And the dead man on the floor seemed to be looking at me with his wide open eyes.

And it was then that I saw Robert. He emerged inch by inch from behind the piano. He took one look at the men on the floor, then he cried out something which I could not understand. And then he grabbed me and we, too, ran out of the place. We were just in time, for as we ran down a long alley, I heard the whistle repeated and the sound of a door being battered in.

"It's de policemens. . . . We got tuh make haste!" cried Robert as he dragged me along. I could not see one negro that had been with us in the hall. They had disappeared as completely as though the earth had swallowed them up.

We walked rapidly down the street. Robert had snatched off my mask and was carrying it in my hand. His own mask was in place. He did not say a word until we had gone for several squares, and turned four corners. Then he sat down in a doorway and fanned himself with my mask:

"Jeese! Dat wuz a close call!" he said.

It would be impossible for me to tell you of all that happened during that long and gaudy afternoon. It remains a blurred remembrance of mad and futile flights from one part of the city to another. First we went down through the Vieux Carré again and into Frenchmen Street. There the people were having a maskers' contest, and prizes were being offered for the most comical masquerader. I remember standing in the sun and watching a varied crowd pass by a reviewing stand—and the lucky ones carried off such prizes as hams and bunches of bananas and live geese and chickens. There were, I believe, cash prizes too, but I cannot say with any degree of certainty. Robert explained to me that many of these maskers remained in this section of the city all day and never came to Canal Street at all. It was an old custom for the people of Frenchmen Street to stage a festivity of their own. Just why Robert wanted to see it, I am not sure, but see it he did—and I saw it too.

After that Robert took me into the most remarkable places: into the lobbies of big hotels and into sumptuous saloons. At these times he would whisper that I raise my mask, and that, if any-one asked questions, I must reply that we were looking for some one. I obeyed without asking questions—but years later it occurred to me why Robert wanted me to do this. Masked, he could not be distinguished from a white man—if he did not speak—and holding a small white boy by the hand, he could gain access anywhere.

It is highly probable that Robert saw places that day that he had never seen in his life before and never saw again. For I remember that we strolled nonchalantly through the lobby of the St. Charles Hotel, where there were but few maskers and where reigned a dignified grandeur that Robert assured me was "genteel." Across the street from the St. Charles was the old Ramos bar, where twelve barkeepers stood in a line, shaking the silver containers which held the famous gin-fizz—now only a memory. In the Ramos saloon there were many women, beautifully dressed, who leaned against the bar with one foot on the brass rail and who imbibed the fizzes or sipped absinthe.

Later I learned that on Mardi Gras all police regulations regarding bar-rooms were put aside, and on that one day it was permissible for women to go into these places. Many of the most fashionable women of New Orleans went on Mardi Gras to drink gin-fizz at the old Ramos bar— and on that day it was considered a more or less conventional thing to do. One incident remains clearly in my mind, a beautiful, slender girl with a corsage bouquet of orchids called me to her—while Robert stood back modestly—and gave me a sip from her glass. It was the first time I had tasted absinthe, and the flavor made me wrinkle my nose and cry out, "It's paregoric!" This definition was greeted with shouts of laughter.

Half an hour later we were riding on a street-car, bound for a revel in some other portion of the city. This time it was in a rough neighborhood, some twenty squares above Canal Street and somewhere near the river. It was a neighborhood of factories and corner saloons, but there was a carnival going on there, too. Here drunken men lay about in bar-rooms and many fights were in progress. Robert informed me that this was "The Irish Channel"—a bad neighborhood, and that "White mens up thisaway would jes' as soon kill a nigger as eat dinner!" But when asked why he had brought me to such a place, he said that he wanted me to see everything. . . . It was there that we saw a street dance in progress, with a portion of the roadway roped off and many couples bouncing about in the street to the music of a band of coatless and sweating musicians. By this time I was tired out, but Robert kept luring me on from place to place by vague promises of showing me something new. We must have visited half a dozen markets, I am sure, and before each of these markets a neighborhood celebration was in progress. Here was none of the grandeur that I had witnessed in Canal Street, but it was the carnival of the masses—and they seemed to be having as good a time as their more fashionable neighbors.

My feet were lagging and my head hung down by the time we had left the fifth or sixth market and I demanded to be taken home. Robert's pleas were all in vain, for I was firm. My grandfather's admonitions were remembered now —when I had need of them—and finally Robert promised that we should go back to his room and rest for a bit. The night parade was the grandest spectacle of Carnival, he told me, and I must be fresh for that. Accordingly we returned on a street-car to Canal Street and after crossing it —threading our way among the tireless maskers who were still parading about and singing and dancing—we turned into one of those narrow streets of the Vieux Carré and finally arrived at the house where Robert and I had dressed that morning.

Once in Robert's room, I collapsed on the bed, wailing that my feet were killing me and that I didn't intend to stir out of the house again. The sunlight was sliding up the walls of the houses now and it was late afternoon. Robert decreed that I could rest for half an hour, and he kept repeating that he had promised my grandfather to show me everything, and that it would be a shame to disappoint him. Then, when he realized that I was really exhausted, he became solicitous for me. He undressed me, I remember, and let me soak my aching feet in a bowl of cool water. He rubbed my tired legs, gave me a cold drink of orange-flower water and praised me extravagantly. Why, for a young man my age, I had behaved wonderfully and he had never enjoyed taking out another young white man as thoroughly as he had enjoyed escorting me; that he had shown me something that most white men never had seen and never *would* see. But I must promise not to tell a soul. And I promised, gladly. So great had been our intimacy during this incredible day that I had come to believe that Robert and I had been friends for a lifetime. Never had I been waited on so well or so thoroughly—nor had I ever been praised so highly for nothing at all. I could not understand it, and did not try to. But to this day I am grateful to Robert for what I experienced.

Lulled by his promises and physically tired out, I fell asleep, and when he roused me it was twilight and outside I could hear the tramping of feet, an endless shuffling, and the murmur of a crowd moving along. It was time, Robert said, for us to be up and stirring, for he wanted me to see the Comus parade from the base of the Lee Monument, many squares away.

He helped me get dressed again, this time in my own clothes, and the devil suit was laid away in a drawer. I hated to see it go out of my life, and I remember touching it with affectionate fingers while Robert was busy at something else. He too had laid away his disguise, and although the night was warm, he was bundled up in a long overcoat which was buttoned to his chin. When I was ready, we went into the street again.

Twilight was deepening and the narrow street was filled with a moving crowd. Every one was going in the same direction, toward Canal Street. We were forced to fall into step and we went forward slowly. Although many wore costume, there were no false faces in evidence now—for with the first twilight the masks must be laid aside by order of the police. Robert gave me a long and rambling explanation for this in which the words "bad people" occurred over and over. I gathered that the masks had been used to shield criminals in the old days, and that the rule for unmasking with the first twilight was strictly necessary.

Canal Street presented a gay picture. There were strings of electric lights looped from corner to corner, and arches of vari-colored electric bulbs crossed the street at close intervals—yellow, green, and purple lights. From the balconies and from the tops of buildings came long streamers of yellow, green, and purple bunting, doubly noticeable now by the artificial light. Flags fluttered and the bunting billowed in the evening breeze from the river. Waves of pleasant coolness came to our grateful faces.

There were but few negroes to be seen; they had retired to their own quarter in Rampart Street, and those masqueraders who were walking about now were white men,

women, and children. They seemed tired but happy, and
bits of song were heard above the hum of the crowd—and
everywhere the jingling of little bells, that same undercurrent of sound that had pleased me so much earlier in the
day.

The balconies above the streets were filled with people
and I was conscious that every one was getting into a favor-
able place to witness the pageant that was to come. Having
seen a procession by daylight I knew—or thought I knew—
what a night parade was like.

I thought that we would remain on Canal Street as we
had done that morning, but Robert assured me that he knew
a vantage point that was far superior, and accordingly we
went up St. Charles Street for eight or more squares. All
along the street men and women lined the sidewalks. Many
of them had brought camp-stools or cushions and were sitting along the curb; others spread out newspapers and sat
on them. In front of the stores the shopkeepers' families
had gathered and were perched on boxes or tables in order
that they could see above the heads of those on the sidewalk.
In order to walk, we had to leave the sidewalk and move
along the middle of the street. There was no traffic other
than the moving crowd; for this was the route of the parade
and it had been cleared for the coming of Comus.

At last we reached Lee Circle—an open circular place
where St. Charles Street widens out and becomes St.
Charles Avenue, and where Howard Avenue crosses. Here
the ground has been built up into a sort of round mountain,
and at the top of this grass-grown mound there rises a huge
fluted column of stone which in turn supports a bronze
statue of Robert E. Lee. At the base of the column is a

LEE CIRCLE IN ST. CHARLES AVENUE

ST. LOUIS CATHEDRAL FROM ORLEANS STREET

pyramid of stone, like gigantic steps rising one above the other, each step more than a yard high. By scrambling up this giants' staircase, we reached the summit; and there, seated on the edge of the topmost step, we sat leaning back against the stone column which disappeared into the dark, ness above our heads. We were just in time to secure seats, for many others were there already, and within five minutes after our arrival every available inch was filled. The crowd continued to arrive and in a few minutes more the grassy slope was covered. And still they came, crowding the side-walks until there was no more room at all.

From our perch we could see far up the avenue to where the twinkling street lights diminished in the distance. And as I grew accustomed to this godlike point of view, I saw that crowds lined both sides of the avenue as far as eye could see. And the crowd was humming like a swarm of bees. There was the feeling that comes into a theater as the lights are lowered and the footlights flash up, a feeling of joyous expectancy which is also a promise.

As I sat there in the cool dimness, I could hear various sounds rising above the humming of the crowd; the shrill whistle of air escaping from balloons which children had in-flated, the irresponsible whine of harmonicas, jangling of tambourines, the cries of street vendors, the shouts of po-licemen who rode by clearing the street. Near-by I could see half a hundred gas-filled balloons pulling at their strings; in the half-light the gay reds and blues seemed dark, and the globes of color shone with a reflected light, with a luster like that of ripe grapes. Below me, spread out to infinity it seemed, were people, people, people. They did not seem real to me, but rather like figures seen in sleep—dream figures, unreal and impersonal. All day long I had been looking upon masks and now that the masks were gone it seemed that I still looked upon faces that had no connection with their owners. It was a strange sensation of unrealness, as though life itself were changed and material things had no meaning. I felt apart from it all, yet strangely it was a part of me. And always that heart-stirring excitement as though I strained my ears to hear distant music.

There came a whisper which turned into a cry. The parade was coming. I looked with all my eyes up the avenue but at first could see nothing but the flickering rows of lights as they converged far away, but then, after a moment, I was conscious of a red glare in the sky—almost on the horizon it seemed, an aura which seemed to rise from the ground, or to emanate from the air itself. It was something apart from life as I knew it. It was magic itself.

As I looked, smaller lights became visible in the red glare, little twinkling lights of yellow and blue and green, bright pinpoints of flame. Then, as the endless stream of lights moved nearer I was conscious of great wreaths of black smoke which swirled upward into the darkness, smoke which held and reflected the flaring lights and which surrounded this glimmering far-off pageant with a rim of fire. I heard music . . . first just a broken bar, then another, finally a melody, faint and sweet.

We were high above the parade, and it was coming directly toward us, down the avenue. Little by little objects became visible, dark shapes against the flare—men on horseback clearing the route. Then below each glowing point of flame I could discern a red figure—men holding the torches. And always the bobbing of these lights and their

swirling smoke rising toward the dim stars. In the center of
each of these circles of light, masses of pale color became
visible—the floats, pale in the night, yet brilliant too. And
they seemed to glide noiselessly and effortlessly forward;
relentless, like a gigantic dragon bearing down upon the
crowd.

Slowly details became clear—men on black horses, courtiers with plumed hats and black masks. The horses reared
and pranced as though trying to unseat their riders. Music
blared out, muffled as though various bands were trying to
outdo each other, which indeed was true. And from far off
I could hear cheering and rippling applause as those along
the way greeted Comus, the last and most dearly loved of
all the kings of Mardi Gras.

Now the torches were nearer and I could see that prancing negroes were holding the flambeaux. The torches flared,
and the red-robed negroes strutted in time with the music.
Possibly thirty torches were ranged around each float in
the parade. And in addition there were taller, more brilliant
flares of stage fire—red and green and white. These lights
were reflected upon the decorated cars—cars which rose
high in the air and which were shaped irregularly, mountains moving toward us, undulating as they came.

The night parade is a dream festival. Even now, twenty-
five years later, I cannot look upon one of them unmoved;
but to the small boy they were more real than reality.

First came the title car, shimmering with tinsel and
fluttering with gauzy streamers; the torches burned yellow
and blue, and the dancing lights were reflected as though
from a thousand tiny mirrors. In black letters on gold I read
that Comus's whim this year was "Legends of the Golden

Age." Following the title car came Comus himself, riding on his swaying, glimmering throne of white and gold, and to me the king seemed suspended in the air upon his golden chair, suspended there, framed in fire. His crown and jewels sparkled with points of light. He was a blonde and jovial monarch who gestured right and left with his scepter, gestured slowly and with a superb geniality. The sheen of golden satin vied with the glistening of burnished metal. Great golden tassels quivered. And this shimmering, glittering, swaying mass passed slowly by, drawn by eight horses—horses which seemed like mysterious, unknown animals, covered with white—their eyes showing black through eyelets in the cloth. Negro men led the horses, negroes in red robes and with cowls over their heads. And everywhere the prancing negro torchbearers, and the blaring of bands. The undulation, the bobbing lights, the quivering masses of changing color, the unending rhythm, seemed to stir a similar quivering in me.

We were far enough away and high enough above the parade to feel the illusion. This was no man-made thing that came out of the darkness; it was magic.

One by one the floats passed by: Ulysses setting sail in a golden boat while his bare-armed followers pulled at long shining oars; Circe and the companions of Ulysses—great, terrible swine—built no doubt of papier-mâché, which groveled before a beautiful enchantress; Jason and the golden fleece. . . . It seemed as though all the beauty and all the riches of the world had been spilt out to make a small boy's paradise.

Many of the subjects have gone forever from my mind, but I remember one float upon which a titanic ogre stretched a threatening hand over a group of masked men who seemed unafraid, or unaware of their doom, and who danced and blew kisses to the crowd there in the shadow of those terrible clutching fingers. On another float a glittering spider trembled horribly—a spider which seemed as large as an elephant and so realistic that at any moment I expected to hear the screams of those gay maskers who had fallen into its clutches.

One after another the cars went swaying past, each one preceded by a band, and each one framed in a fiery ring of bobbing flambeaux. As the procession reached the mound upon which we sat, it turned, circled the base of the statue and continued behind us down St. Charles Street. As the last car passed, we turned to follow it with our eyes—and there, strung out along the street, we saw the gorgeous spectacle again, the backs of the floats this time—almost equally beautiful, and exhibiting another side, decorated, and sometimes filled with maskers who danced upon the swaying vehicle.

The parade moved so very slowly and stopped at such frequent intervals that Robert and I were able to keep abreast of it, and when we reached Canal Street, where the procession went first up one side of the wide street then down the other side, we were able to see it all again. And again I saw the rainbows, the bolts of lightning, the witches, the ogres, the fairies in their fluttering robes of brilliant color. The maskers on the floats were throwing trinkets to the crowd in the street—beads, tiny bags of sweetmeats, metal ornaments. And upon coming close to one car, I saw that each masker was provided with a silken bag which matched his costume—and it was from these bags that the bagatelles were produced and flung toward the outstretched hands below.

At last the parade left Canal Street and entered Bourbon Street, a narrow thoroughfare which led toward the French Opera House. So narrow was the street that the great decorated cars covered it from sidewalk to sidewalk, and the maskers who rode high on top of the cars were almost level with the balconies of wrought iron which overhung the street. Men and women on those balconies were almost able to touch those masqueraders on the floats. It was here that I realized the hugeness of these moving cars—for, filling the street as they did, and lumbering over the rough pavement, the great glittering masses seemed as incredible as though the very houses were gliding past.

Here the throng upon the sidewalk was massed so tightly that it was impossible to make progress through it, and Robert and I stood jammed back into a doorway while the pageant rumbled past us. And as the last car went by the crowd began to move with the parade—moving solidly— and we were borne along willy-nilly, to the very door of the French Opera House. At the entrance to this beautiful old building each car stopped for a moment and the maskers were helped down—and the empty float continued down the street, while the silk-clad masqueraders climbed the steps and disappeared into the wide doors. In Toulouse Street at the side of the Opera House there was a long line of carriages, and gorgeously dressed ladies and gentlemen were descending from them and entering a side door. The number seemed endless. Gems flashed, there was the scent of perfume in the air. Horses plunged and their shoes struck fire from the cobblestones. And tight-packed everywhere stood people, watching the world of society as it went, laughing, to the Comus Ball.

Looking down the street, I saw the great floats lose their fairy-like quality—for as they passed beyond the door of the Opera House the negroes extinguished their torches, and with the light out, the floats became only dead things— their life and beauty gone. One after another they disappeared into the darkness, gone as utterly as a snuffed-out flame.

Chapter VI

ASH WEDNESDAY

ROBERT and I were turning away, or "fixin' to go," as Robert expressed it, when suddenly some one put a hand on my shoulder. "I was beginning to be worried about you," said my grandfather's voice.

He stood beside me in the crowd, smiling down upon me.

"Have a nice time?"

"Yes, sir."

"See everything?"

"Oh, yes, sir!"

"Enjoy yourself?"

"Yes, sir."

"Ready to go back to the country?"

"No, sir."

"Are you ready to go to bed now, or do you want to see some more?"

A moment before I had been so exhausted that I could hardly stand but at the promise of something else to see, I exclaimed:

"I'm not tired at all."

My grandfather turned to Robert who stood meekly by:
"So you took good care of the young man?"

"Yassuh!"

"And did he give you any trouble?"

"No, *suh!*"

I saw my grandfather hand Robert something, and his face lit up:

"Thank you, *suh!*"

"And now," said my grandfather to the negro, "go on and amuse yourself. Thank you for taking care of the young fellow and showing him everything. I'll take care of him now."

Robert looked at me as though he wanted to ask something of me, but seemed to think better of it, and turned away.

"Good night," he said.

"Thank you a lot . . . if you ever come to the plantation I'll show you things, too." This was the best I could offer. Again Robert said good night and a moment later he was gone in the crowd.

It was then that I saw that the old Creole gentleman was standing at my grandfather's elbow. He too was smiling at me. "Your face is dirty," he remarked as though he were stating a well-known fact. I scrubbed at it with a grimy handkerchief.

"Oh, never mind," he said, "we're going up into the *troisième*. We'll never be noticed. Come along."

I followed the two old men into the Opera House, up long flights of stairs, through great swinging doors and into a foyer with red carpet on the floor and great gleaming crystal chandeliers and mirrors which reflected the people who were passing before them. We climbed more stairs. I was like a child in a dream; everything was vague and a red haze seemed to hang over the lights. At last we reached a balcony high up in the Opera House, and here, after some trouble, we found our seats almost at the back of it. The two men sat down and I squeezed, somehow, between them, disputing with the chair arm for the right of way.

Far, far below me I saw hundreds of men and women moving about. The theater was filled from pit to dome with a mass of spectators—guests at the ball. In the proscenium boxes were women in evening gowns, glittering with jewels. There were flowers everywhere. Below us lay the horse-shoe—we could see part of it—and here again were gaily dressed ladies and black-coated gentlemen. The stage was illuminated and decorated to represent a starry heaven. On a high throne were the King and Queen, as small as dolls, it seemed to me—so high I sat. The proscenium arch curved high above their heads, and before them stretched out a long expanse of dancing floor, a floor which extended out over what had been the parquet of the theater. (It was many years later that I found out that a movable floor was put down over the seats for the Mardi Gras balls, thus transforming the theater into a magnificently large ball-room, and the loges, boxes, and balconies serving for seats for the spectators. But I knew nothing of all this then—and accepted this thing as it was.)

My head drooped sleepily. The red haze around the lights seemed to grow denser. Somewhere an orchestra played softly. The King and Queen were rising and beginning their march around the dance floor. Couples fell in behind them—the men in costume and masked, but the women, with the exception of the court ladies, in conventional evening dress. Behind the King and Queen long gold-embroidered robes swept out—robes supported by pages in white. I recognized, in a dim sort of way, some of the characters that I had seen riding by on the floats earlier in the evening: Ulysses, Circe, and the rest of those masqueraders. But many seemed wholly unfamiliar, as I saw them in that half-trance between sleep and waking.

There had been a series of tableaux before we had entered the theater, my grandfather's friend told me . . . but I did not care that I had missed them. I nodded sleepily, and at last my head went down on my grandfather's shoulder. I must have slept for hours, for when he awakened me it was midnight and the court of Rex had left its ball and had come to join the court of Comus—the climax of the Mardi Gras festivity. I was only conscious of two kings and two queens and two courts . . . more spangles, more glitter, more brilliance. It was too much. I could stand no more.

"I want to go home," I said.

"All right, old sleepy head," said my grandfather, "let us go."

Somehow I staggered down the stairs and somehow I staggered through the dim streets. We went back to the house that I had left that morning—a day, a century ago. The courtyard seemed quiet and ghostly in its peaceful dimness—and the moon shone down on the fountain. Again I climbed many stairs and in a bedroom somewhere in the front part of the house I got undressed and tumbled into a big, four-post bed.

When I awakened it was dawn outside and I could see the red reflection of the sun in the sky. An altercation was going on in the street below and there were bells ringing, church bells, sounding dolefully, mournfully, slow solemn strokes.

I slipped out of bed, went to the window and looked down into the street. Outside a policeman was trying to induce a very tipsy masker to relinquish his hold on a lamp post and go home. But the masquerader insisted that he had to go to Early Mass in the Cathedral. This seemed to disturb the policeman, for he argued long and patiently that such a thing was out of the question. But the masquerader was firm. Finally they departed, the policeman supporting the arm of the tippler.

At the corner this couple came face to face with two nuns who walked at the head of a long procession of little girls—girls all dressed alike in pink dresses—orphans on the way to church. The policeman dragged the reveler to one side and reverently raised his cap as the nuns passed by.

After they had all gone the street was empty again, except for a little woman all in black who hurried along with small, clicking steps following the nuns and orphans toward the church. And the sun of Ash Wednesday rose above the steep roofs of the houses opposite. I yawned prodigiously and turned into the room again. My grandfather lay in another bed, still sleeping. I went back and climbed into my own bed again. How strange New Orleans seemed after the plantation! The day before was a gorgeous dream. It couldn't have happened.

A little later there was a knock at the door and Robert

came in, meek and mild, bearing the tray with the cups of early coffee. My grandfather sat up and took his cup, looking sleepily at me. As I sat cross-legged in bed sipping the warm, sweet drink I said to Robert: "Oh, wasn't Mardi Gras grand? Robert, *do* you remember . . ."

But he interrupted me. "Ah don't 'member a thing about it," he said meaningly.

"Oh!" I said, and was silent again.

• PART II • FRENCH TOWN AND
SPANISH CITY •

Chapter VII

OUT OF THE WILDERNESS

THE city of New Orleans must be forever associated with the Mississippi River, for the city was built to guard the mouth of this great stream and owes its existence to its geographical position. And for this reason it will be necessary to speak briefly of the river itself.

Hernando de Soto, it will be remembered, discovered the Mississippi in 1541, but it was not until 120 years later that La Salle explored the river to its mouth. The French, entrenched in Canada, believed that with the fortification of various strategic points along the Mississippi they would be able to hold forever the lands along its banks. They planned a vast empire for France. The earliest explorers realized that a stronghold was necessary near the river's mouth, and they looked about for a suitable place to build a fort. This was not so easy as it appears, for the land lying near the mouth of the river was low and swampy and was frequently inundated by floodwaters.

The first high land above the river's mouth was the

bluff where the city of Baton Rouge stands to-day—but this was nearly two hundred miles from the mouth of the river. Accordingly the explorers sought the next suitable spot. The land between Baton Rouge and the sea is a low, flat country, a vast delta, built up in long centuries by the Mississippi as it flows to the Mexican Gulf.

A fort was built by the French on the west bank of the river, below the present city of New Orleans, but it proved unsatisfactory. In the records of the time we find many references to a certain portage used by Indians which seemed the most logical spot for the establishment of a permanent French colony—a settlement that was destined from the beginning to become a great city.

In 1697 Iberville was sent over from France to colonize Louisiana and in his diary under the date of March 9, 1699, we find an entry pertaining to the portage which later became the site of the city of New Orleans:

The savage I had with me [he writes] showed me the place in which the savages have their portage, from the end of the bay where our ships are anchored, to reach this river. They dragged their canoes over a fairly good path; we found there several pieces of baggage belonging to people going one way or the other. He pointed out to me that the total distance was very short.

Early the next year Iberville examined the spot, and he writes on January 18:

I have been to the portage. I found it to be about half a league long; half the way being woods and water reaching well up on the leg, and the other half good enough, a country of cane-brakes and woods. I visited one spot, a league beneath the portage, where the *Bayougoulas* [this word in the manuscript has been crossed out and

CHARTRES STREET LOOKING TOWARD THE
CATHEDRAL

OLD INN YARD ON CHARTRES STREET

replaced by *Quinipissas*] formerly had a village, which I found to be full of canes, and where the soil is but slightly flooded. I have had a small desert made, where I planted sugar-canes brought by me from Martinique; I do not know if they will take, for the exhalations are strong.

The portage was rather a dangerous place, it seems, for there are records of many losing their way there, and on a map drawn a few years later we find the trail indicated as "The Portage of the Lost."

Penicaut writes in his memoir that he camped at this place and slept under the enormous cypresses which served at night as perches for innumerable "Indian fowls weighing nearly thirty pounds, and all ready for the spit." He adds that gunshots did not frighten them.

Remonville in his "Historical Letter Concerning the Mississippi," writes on August 6, 1702:

A fort on the Mississippi River eighteen leagues from its mouth on the west side, and which is commanded by M. de St. Denis, a Canadian officer, since the death of M. de Sauvolle (whose place has been taken by M. de Bienville, brother of M. d'Iberville), must also be changed. It should be transferred eleven leagues higher, to the eastward, in a space of land twelve leagues long and two leagues wide (at barely a quarter of a league from the Mississippi, which is very fine) beyond the insulting reach of floods and near a small river. The latter flows into Lake Pontchartrain and, by means of the canal where M. le Sueur passed, joins the sea about a dozen leagues from Mobile. This will make communications much shorter and easier than by the sea.

Remonville in another memoir of 1708 speaks again of the advantages of the portage: "The principal establishment ought to be built on high ground dominating Lake

Pontchartrain, and in the neighborhood of the spot where Iberville built the original fort." And he goes on to mention the fortifications that will be necessary. He speaks of the culture of silk-worms and tells of the fine mulberry trees growing there.

In 1709 Mandeville wrote that it was advantageous to use the portage rather than to try to go through the mouth of the Mississippi "which lies twenty-five leagues down a very difficult country, often flooded and filled with alligators, serpents, and other venomous beasts."

Now in 1697 when Iberville had come to colonize Louisiana, he founded his first colony on the Bay of Biloxi, near the present location of Ocean Springs, Mississippi. Two years later Iberville was made governor-general of Louisiana and brought more colonists over from France. His brother Bienville was his companion and also an officer of the colony, and when Iberville died in 1702, Bienville was left in command. He moved his headquarters to Mobile, but the hostilities of the Indians were such that the colony dwindled. The years dragged on and white men penetrated further and further into the wilderness, but it was a small group at best. In 1712 a census was taken, and the entire population scattered from Mobile, through the vicinity of what is now New Orleans, and up the Mississippi as far as the present city of Natchez, numbered only 324 men. It was in 1712 that the Louisiana colony was turned over to Crozat, and it was in 1715 that Louisiana was brought to the notice of all Europe by the notorious "Mississippi Bubble."

This was John Law's monumental scheme which was started to help the depleted condition of the French treasury. "The Company of the West" was formed in France, and under the leadership of Law a great many emigrants were sent to Louisiana to colonize the country.

The Mississippi Bubble remains one of the most amazing events in American colonial history. It smacks of modern methods, for Law was the first "booster" for America. Nowadays we would call this exploitation of Louisiana a gigantic "development." As a matter of fact, his method of exploitation was a ghastly hoax. Law and his followers pictured Louisiana as a paradise on earth; according to their stories, it was a land of milk and honey. They told stories of gold and silver mines. The Indians were pictured as a simple, friendly race, quick to enter voluntary slavery for the white man. Fortunes awaited every Frenchman who went to Louisiana. For a trifling present, the friendly Indians would pour gold, silver, and gems at a Frenchman's feet.

One curious difficulty presented itself. The Frenchmen objected to the names of the colonies in Louisiana. Mobile, they said, cast reflections on its own stability; Massacre Island was calculated to alarm timid souls; while Biloxi and Natchitoches "struck the Parisian ears as being very exotic!" This difficulty had been noted by Bienville before, and there is a curious record in which he speaks of having changed the name of Mobile to Immobile, and Massacre Island to Dauphin Island.

Nevertheless, John Law and his followers needed a point upon which to focus their efforts, and in 1717 we find the "proposed city of New Orleans" suggested in an official record. Now here was a name to which no Frenchman could find objection, for New Orleans was named for His Royal Highness the Regent of France, the Duc d'Orléans. And in 1718 Bienville and his followers founded the city—there in the wilderness beside the Mississippi. It was formally baptized Nouvelle Orléans.

Immediately purists took issue with the name. There is an amusing comment by Father Charlevoix: "Those who coined the name *Nouvelle Orléans,*" he observes, "must have thought that Orléans was of feminine gender. But what does it matter? The custom is established, and custom rises above grammar." And here, it seems to me, we have a true Frenchman speaking!

The spot which Bienville chose for his city was one slightly higher than the swamps which lay north and south of it. It had an elevation of ten feet above sea level, and was believed to be above the reach of the floodwaters of the river. Then too, the site commanded the whole Mississippi. It was not too far from the river's mouth, yet it was far enough inland to escape the worst of the tropical hurricanes which swept in from the Mexican Gulf. For many years, as we have seen in the documents quoted earlier in this chapter, the place had been used as a portage for Indians. Here, by leaving the river and dragging a canoe a mile inland, one was able to reach a navigable stream, the Bayou St. John—called by the Indians *Tchoupic,* which signified that the water was muddy. By traversing this bayou one could reach Lake Pontchartrain, which connected with Lake Borgne, which in turn connected with the Gulf of Mexico. This "back door" to the city was of great advantage; for it furnished a safer, shorter route to the Gulf coast and the settlements there. The mouth of the Mississippi was a dangerous place and had never been fully explored. In a document quoted elsewhere in this chapter we read of the monsters which were said to dwell near its mouth, and the Indian legends told of other horrors there—of gigantic beasts which waited to spring upon the unwary travelers. And in Father Louis Hennepin's diary, written thirty-six years before, telling of the discovery of the river's mouth, we find him exclaiming, "May God preserve us from the crocodiles!"

In addition to the monsters, there were driftwood and sand-bars. The river divided itself into half a dozen streams before it reached the deeper waters of the Gulf. As only the most superficial soundings had been taken, ships ran aground frequently and there had been many disasters there. Bayou St. John provided a way to the Mississippi which was comparatively safe. Bienville foresaw that the great river would be of vast importance in later years—it was, in fact, becoming more important every year—and he realized that France must have a strong foothold near the river's mouth.

In February, 1718, John Law's first shipload of men, money, and provisions came to the colony and anchored at Dauphin Island. Bienville seized this opportunity for founding the city that had been in his mind for so long. Laborers cleared the wilderness between Bayou St. John and the Mississippi, and the streets were laid out. There was even the ceremony of breaking ground for a church. Rude huts were built, ditches were dug to drain the low spots. A small levee was thrown up along the river front to protect the "city" from the yearly inundations by the river. It was all as crude and as simple as possible. But it was a beginning.

When the ship which had brought the first colonists to New Orleans returned to France, Law's followers began their magnificent propaganda. An old placard of that day has been preserved and its description of New Orleans is truly amazing. The rude settlement has become a great city overnight. It is described as a place of tropical luxury equalling the dream cities of the Arabian Nights. In a land of palm-trees and blue moonlight nights, Frenchmen live like kings. They are surrounded by beautiful, bronze-colored women of great beauty and seductiveness, and they are waited upon by naked Nubian slaves. There is constant talk of gold and silver mines, of vast vineyards, of ease and luxury. One of the placards exhibited at that time in the Parisian cafés bears a fantastic drawing of an Indian giving a white man lumps of gold in exchange for a small knife.

The city in Louisiana, named in honor of the Duke of Orleans, became a byword in the Paris cafés. It was a paradise indeed, and the prices asked for land were astonishingly cheap. Well might the prices be cheap, for Louisiana was a wilderness and nothing else—a wilderness extending away toward the north and west as far as imagination could reach. But the Frenchmen in the cafés did not know this when they sold their holdings in France and invested their money in Louisiana real estate. Many families sold everything and fared forth to this land of promise.

Law and his followers realized that there must be cheap labor in the colony and accordingly the French jails were emptied of their criminals, and these men were brought in shiploads to Louisiana to labor and die under the tropic sun.

There followed a bad time. Shipload after shipload
of men arrived at Dauphin Island and found nothing.
There was no food, no shelter, and no escape. Starving,
heartbroken, they wandered about, tortured by mosquitoes,
blistered by the sun. The ship sailed away and the men
remained to starve. Men went insane. Men died. A shipload of "brute negroes," intended as slaves for the colonists, arrived and the savages were put ashore—to die and
rot unburied on the beach. White men and black perished
together, or fell a prey to malaria or contagious disease.
Hundreds of men died without seeing the lands in which
they had invested all their savings.

But some survived. Some managed to get away from
the island and made their way up the Mississippi, or overland through the swamps to New Orleans. Some even pros-
pered. Lands along the river, above and below New Orleans, were granted out as plantations. Shiploads of negro
slaves brought from Santo Domingo or other West Indian
islands were sold in New Orleans. They were usually sold
on credit and were paid for by instalments. And in the
vicinity of New Orleans began the network of plantations
which was to bring so much prosperity a hundred years
later.

In that bit of wilderness which was now called the city
of New Orleans, the Chevalier Le Blond de la Tour was
made engineer in charge of Bienville's colony. It was de
la Tour who surveyed the city and laid out the streets; and
the old section of the city remains to-day as it was when
first hewn out of the forest. That is, the street names
remain the same except in one or two instances. And as for
the streets themselves, their names give a clear indication of

the spirit of the founders. The town centered around the Place d'Armes, now called Jackson Square. This square faced the river, and on the opposite side, also facing the river, the first rude log church was built. It was simple and small enough, but it sufficed the needs of the colony.

Let us consider the street names for a moment: Old Levee Street was the title given the tree-shaded walk that led along the river bank where a small embankment had been thrown up to keep back the floodwaters of the Mississippi. It was here that the men of the colony gathered in the late afternoons and in the evenings; it was here that they sat and talked of far-off France, as the moon rose above the forest on the opposite shore of the Mississippi nearly a mile away—a bright tropical moon which reflected itself in the broad and rushing stream which lay at their feet. The next street parallel with the river was called Chartres, for the Duc de Chartres, a title of the Orléans family; Royal Street came next, a sort of "Main Street" where the merchants kept their shops; then Bourbon Street, from the royal Bourbon family of France; then Dauphine Street, from Dauphin the eldest son of the king of France, but possibly after the Dauphin's wife, for as *rue* is feminine, the name for euphony's sake became feminine too—but, as Father Charlevoix remarked relative to the city itself: what does it matter? The difference is slight. Burgundy Street was named from one of the royal titles or from one of the provinces of France; Bienville Street was named after Governor Bienville, whose house stood on that street near the river; Conti Street was named for the prince of Conti, illegitimate son of Louis XIV; Saint Louis Street after the French crusader; Toulouse Street after the

Compte de Toulouse, and Dumaine Street after the Duc du Maine, both illegitimate sons of Louis XIV by Madame de Montespan; Saint Peter, Saint Ann, Saint Philip streets, after favorite saint baptismal names of the Orléans family. Barracks Street designated the street where the royal barracks were located, near the levee. Hospital Street, obviously, because the hospital was located there. The main cross street, a little wider than the others, was called Orleans Street, after the Regent, Duc d' Orléans. It was the center of the original city and began just back of the Place d'Armes.

One could walk through every street in the city in two hours' time or thereabouts; for the squares were small and the streets only fifty French feet wide. In 1726, eight years after the colony was founded, the population numbered only 880, in addition to 65 servants and 129 slaves. There were only ten horses in the whole settlement. However, it must be remembered that this was the population of the city proper and that most of the richer men lived on plantations outside the city, and that some of these planters owned individually as many slaves as all those slaves numbered within the limits of the city itself.

Now there are a great many documents in existence which deal with the founding and with the early life in New Orleans, and some of them are very interesting, in that they throw considerable light on the character of the city. For example, there is La Harpe's description of the environs of the town:

It is situated [he writes] in flat and swampy ground fit only for growing rice; river water filters through under the soil, and crayfish abound, so that tobacco and vegetables are hard to raise. There are frequent fogs, and the land being thickly wooded and covered with cane-brakes, the air is fever-laden and an infinity of mosquitoes cause further inconvenience in summer. The Company's project was, it seems, to build the town between the Mississippi and the St. John River which empties into Lake Pontchartrain; the ground there is higher than on the banks of the Mississippi. This river is at a distance of one league from the Lake. A canal joining the Mississippi with the Lake has been planned which would be very useful even though this place served only as warehouse and the principal establishment were made at Natchez. The advantage of this port is that ships of . . . [left blank] tons can easily reach it.

On June 10, 1718, when the city was emerging from the forest, Bienville notes in his diary: "I am grieved to see so few people engaged in a task which requires at least a hundred times the number. . . . All the ground of the site, except the borders which are drowned by floods, is very good, and everything will grow there."

New Orleans did not prosper despite all the advertising that John Law had given to it. There were few enough laborers and the colonists encountered so many difficulties that they were almost ready to abandon the settlement. At the very time of its founding, the river rose and inundated the newly cleared streets; the ditches were filled to overflowing and each square became a small island. To this day there is a Creole word "islet" which signifies a city square.

When the waters had receded the colonists went back to tilling the soil and conducting their business. But luck did not favor them. The spring of 1719 found the Mississippi again in flood and Bienville chronicles in his diary that the Indians "did not remember having ever seen its like." All the citizens of the town began building a levee with

frantic haste. A small embankment had been thrown up in
the beginning—a foot or two high—but now another foot
was added to it. Even Bienville seems to be wavering in
his determination to keep the colony at this spot, for on
the 24th of November, 1721, we find his name affixed to a
document telling of the difficulties of the colonists and of
the ravages caused by the river. There was much jealousy
and dissatisfaction among those who were in charge of
the colony's affairs. We find Hubert—who was at Natchez
—turning the tribulations of New Orleans to his own
account, and we find a document in which he speaks of a
general exodus from New Orleans to Natchez, due to
floods. However, Le Page du Pratz, who was living in
New Orleans at that time, does not even mention the high
water of that year. In 1719, we find a notation by Hubert
stating that "There are in New Orleans but three Canadian houses and a store belonging to the Company, where
we stopped." However, in 1720, we find in another document that "There are stores for the Company, a hospital,
lodgings for the governor and the director. About fifty
soldiers, seventy clerks, hired men, and convicts drawing
wages and rations from the Company. Two hundred and
fifty concession-holders, including their people, are waiting
for flatboats to take them up to their concessions."

We learn from this same document that there are forty
plantations in the immediate vicinity. Among these plantations is that of Bienville "with twenty slaves, blacks and
savages, and six head of horned cattle. He has sowed half
a cask of rice."

Law's scheme had collapsed. The Frenchmen in the
cafés of Paris who had called Louisiana "the new Peru"

the year before, were now bitter in their denunciations of this "barbarous wilderness." Nevertheless every vessel that crossed the Atlantic carried a few men at least to the colony.

The documents of this period are a most remarkable collection and fantastic stories continued to be written of New Orleans. Of course the only writers that we can believe are those who are actually on the ground—and those who had no axes to grind. One man writes that New Orleans contains eight hundred beautiful houses and is like Paris in many respects. And yet Bienville himself assures us that there are not twenty houses in the city proper.

Now in 1703 the King of France had sent twenty-three girls to the colony in Louisiana. These girls were taken from various houses of correction in Paris. As New Orleans did not exist at that time, it is likely that the girls were taken to Biloxi or to Mobile. But in March, 1721, a group of young women were sent to New Orleans in the care of a group of nuns. There is an interesting document in relation to their arrival, dated April 25, and signed by both Bienville and Delorme:

Eighty-eight girls arrived by *La Baleine*. Since the fourth of March, nineteen of them have married off. From those who came by *Le Chameau* and *La Mutine* ten have died. So that fifty-nine girls are still to be provided for. This will be difficult as these girls were not well selected. Could they possibly, in so short a time, have changed to such an extent? Whatever the vigilance exercised upon them, they could not be restrained. Among the three Directresses responsible for their conduct, two have occasioned complaints. Sister Gertrude is ill-natured, she rules sourly and capriciously, and has been guilty of a prank, which cost her the respect of the girls them-selves. Sister Marie has none of the talents required for such responsibilities. Sister Saint Louis has been retained, having a very good character, but the others were sent away.

How tantalizing this is! It gives an interesting insight into the behavior of the girls, but of what prank Sister Gertrude was guilty, the document does not state. It is interesting to note that simultaneously with this shipment of young women, Madame Doville, a midwife, was sent to the colony, her salary fixed at four hundred *livres*. She was nicknamed, we learn, *La Sans-Regret*.

On the 25th of June, Bienville wrote again:

Thirty-one girls have been married off between the 24th of April and the 25th of June. All were from those sent from *La Baleine*. Several were given to sailors who asked insistently for them. These could scarcely have been married off to good residents. Nevertheless they were granted to the sailors only on the express condition that they should settle in the Colony, to which they agreed. These sailors will supply practical navigators to the special conditions of the region, and this was much needed.

Penicaüt was more optimistic about these girls and declares that if Sister Gertrude had brought ten times as many, she would have found no difficulty in placing them. He goes on to tell what the girls brought with them:

"Each one [he tells us] had as a dower for the supposed marriage, two pairs of coats, two shirts and undershirts, six head-dresses, and other furnishings with which they were amply provided so that they might marry with all possible despatch. [And he adds, somewhat gaily]. . . This merchandise was soon disposed of, so great was the want of the country."

Until the end of 1722, vagabonds, deserters, smugglers,

and other jailbirds were deported from France to the colony. A good deal has been written of these rogues who came to Louisiana—and who caused endless trouble there —but very little has been written of those others whom the Regency of France saw fit to deport: for a large number of persons of quality were sent to New Orleans. The reason that it is difficult for the historian to find out who they were is a curious one; their names were not mentioned in the general correspondence of the Colony and many of the records of them seem to have been destroyed purposely. Therefore a letter from Bienville on this subject is of particular interest:

The King's exiles now in the Colony have no independent means of subsistence [he writes]. Several among them are people of distinction, incapable of doing the public labor which supplies others with a livelihood. Something must be done for them. Henceforth, letters written by these unfortunates to their families—who turn a deaf ear and do not answer—shall be addressed to the Company, so that the latter may compel their relations to send necessary relief.

Many aristocrats had asked to go to New Orleans in order to escape incarceration in the Bastille or at Fort l'Evêque. Others had been sent at the demand of relations, or because no one consented to serve them with pensions. On the lists of those deported, marginal notes occur often: "His family wishes him to go to the Mississippi Islands," or "Madame la Duchesse de Lorraine has requested this." The position in which these delicately reared men and women found themselves in New Orleans was pitiable. And sometimes the marginal notes give illuminating glimpses of their mad struggle to escape deportation. Here is one, typical enough: "Made such a rebellion that a coach had to be taken to conduct him to the hospital."

Some of the reasons for sending these aristocrats to the colony seem pitifully inadequate: "Attacked the guard at the Comédie with a drawn sword." For this he—whoever he was—was exiled. Here is another: "He has slain his adversary in a duel." Sometimes they were even simpler: "Went poaching," and there is one which sounds romantic enough: "Took a girl from the archer's hands." One poor woman was simply said to be "outrageously impious," which might mean anything—or nothing at all.

It must not be supposed, however, that only criminals and exiles found their way to New Orleans. Several high-born women came over to join their husbands or their lovers who had gone before to prepare the way. Many a high-bred girl, dragging the heritage of her illustrious name behind her, came to a home in the new colony. And it is recorded that these wives found New Orleans much to their taste. It is true that the houses were plain enough, but there were slaves who did all the work and the lady had only to nod and her bidding was done. The negroes were excellent servants, fine cooks, quick to learn to please. And Louisiana abounded in good things to eat. Wine seems to have been plentiful in the colony, and early shipments record great quantities of brandy. We have records, too, of young women coming over with all their household goods, furniture, silver, and china. Almost from the beginning there was a sort of society—a group of men and women who held themselves aloof from the rabble and who, as best they could, preserved the manners of the court of France.

And it is due to a letter from one of these ladies of quality that we have one of our most exact descriptions of New Orleans, three years after its founding. As her letter is a long complaint against the discomforts she was enduring, it is likely that she did not overestimate the beauties of the settlement in which she found herself. She tells us that the houses are built with a framework of cypress logs and the spaces between these logs were daubed with a mixture of mud and Spanish moss. The houses were whitewashed inside and out, she writes. Each house was set in a garden in which orange trees grew, and the garden was surrounded by a high picket fence, also whitewashed. There was no glass in the colony, but heavy batten doors could be closed against the elements. It was the custom to build but four houses to the city square. By planting a hedge of orange trees within the fence, an almost impenetrable wall was constructed, and so it was possible to leave all doors and windows open on warm nights and one could sleep without fear of intruders. Each square was surrounded by a deep ditch, and the sidewalk between the fence and ditch was known by a Creole word *banquette*. Sidewalks are called *banquettes* in New Orleans to-day.

In another letter one house is described in detail and so rich is its equipment that it seems almost incredible. We are told that crystal chandeliers holding candles swung from rough rafters, and that the floors were carpeted with fine furs "lying so close together that the boards could not be seen." And across the carpet of fur came the wife of the colonist, "dressed in the style of the French Court," and offering a hospitality so simple and so complete that the writer forgot for a moment that he was not in Paris itself!

"In fact," this writer continues, "there is a song in the streets that declares New Orleans to be a little Paris, and beyond that it is impossible to go!"

But another writer, of approximately the same time, tells us that New Orleans is "a wild and desolate place, filled with ruffians and naked savages." As I have pointed out before—it is all in the point of view. It is highly probable that both writers were right, for New Orleans was a strange mixture of elegance and brutality.

But the elegant ones were few and the larger group was a hard-drinking, jovial band of pioneers, men and women to whom the worst had happened already, and who were ready to make the most of the moment. The strong survived and the weak died. And it is probable that New Orleans was neither better nor worse than other settlements in early Colonial America. But it was different. One must remember that there were no Quakers, no Puritans in New Orleans. These were Latins and they brought with them their Latin frankness as to eating and drinking and as to matters pertaining to sex.

And from these first settlers a definite type emerged, a type known a few years later as the Creole.

Chapter VIII

GERMAN PIONEERS

A MAP of New Orleans drawn in 1726 gives a good general idea of the population and arrangement of the town, for the names of the residents are written on the margin, and their houses are indicated on the plan. On Old Levee Street—or *Rue du Quay*—we find the *Direction* or official building, the hospital, the house of M. Pauger, the engineer. Beyond these is located the residence of "M. Trudeau and his six children," and the house of "M. de Noyan, in which resides Petit de Levilliers and his wife and two children," also the houses of the St. Martin family, the Bellairs, and of Marest de la Tour. Further down the street in that part of Chartres which lies below the church and was then called Condé, we find "the small house of Joseph Carriere, where he stops when he comes to town"; and from this, we may deduce that Carriere is a planter who lives for the greater part of the time on his plantation. Near-by are the houses of de Lassus and M. de Brois-briant, commander-general.

Royal Street seems to be well filled with shops: there are carpenters, a wig-maker, cabinet-makers, a cobbler's shop, armorers, and a *chandelier,* or candle-maker. "Jean Pascal, with his fat wife and child," are living in the "large house of M. Chauvin de la Freniere, where he stays when he comes to town." Another planter, evidently. Near-by lives M. Fazende, the councillor, "with his wife, child, mother-in-law, and brother-in-law."

This census is very informal, and in some instances we find nicknames appended. In Bourbon Street, which like Royal seems filled with shopkeepers and their families, we find "la Bouillonerie, called 'La Docteur,' and Joseph Cham, called 'La Rose.' "

Bienville lived in a more aristocratic neighborhood. His neighbors were M. de Chavannes, secretary of the Council; M. Fleuriau, attorney-general; Dr. Alexandre, surgeon-major of the Hospital, and other dignitaries.

The *cannonier* Chesseau lived on St. Philip Street, which appears to be fairly well lined with houses. In Barracks Street, St. Ann, St. Peter, Dumaine, and Orleans streets there are four houses to nearly every square. The population in 1726 was 880 free white men and women, 65 indentured servants and 129 slaves, all living within the town boundaries. There were only ten horses in the settlement, and the number of "horned cattle" is not stated.

By this time New Orleans had become the capital of the Province of Louisiana, with the legal institution of a Superior Council. As we have seen, a convent of Capuchin priests had been established for the education of boys, and in 1727 the Ursulines arrived to open a school for girls.

It can be deduced that a steady stream of men was

pouring into the colony, and no longer the riffraff of the Paris streets. These are sturdy tradesmen, and they are accompanied by their wives.

It was in 1726 that a large number of Germans settled in New Orleans and others in the vicinity of the town.

John Law had realized that he needed good farmers to make his own concessions in Louisiana valuable. In his propaganda-scattering he had not forgotten Germany. There is a pamphlet, printed in German and bearing the date 1720, which gives a good idea of the fantastic lies told of Louisiana. It is probable that this flimsy little book was brought to New Orleans by some of the early German settlers. The following paragraph is characteristic:

> The land is filled with gold, silver, copper, and lead mines. If one wishes to hunt for mines, he need only go into the country of the Natchitoches. There he will surely draw pieces of silver out of the earth. After these mines, we will hunt for herbs and plants for the apothecaries. The savages will make them known to us. Soon we shall find healing remedies for the most dangerous wounds, yes, also, so they say, infallible ones for the fruits of love.

Another description of New Orleans at this time has come to light in an old letter written by a German adventurer to his wife at home:

> I betook myself [he writes] to where they are beginning to build the capital, New Orleans. Its circumference will be one mile. The houses are poor and low, as at home with us in the country. They are covered with large pieces of bark and strong reeds. Everybody dresses as he pleases. . . . One's outfit consists of a suit of clothes, bed, table, trunks. Tapestry and fine beds are entirely unknown. The people sleep the whole night in the open air. Although I live among savages and Frenchmen, I am in no danger. People trust one another so much that they leave gates and doors open.

German historians tell us that as a result of John Law's agitation, more than ten thousand Germans set sail for Louisiana between the years 1718 and 1724. We have seen what happened at Dauphin Island. So inadequately provisioned were many of these German ships that hundreds of these pioneers never lived to reach the shores of America. But other shiploads managed to make their way up the river, past New Orleans and into what is now Arkansas. There they founded a colony of their own on Law's concession. Men from various German towns joined them there, bringing their wives. There were even shiploads of emigrants from Switzerland who settled somewhere near the mouth of the Arkansas River. The Jesuit priest, Father Charlevoix, who came from Canada, down the Mississippi to New Orleans, stopped in December, 1721, at the "mournful wrecks of the German settlement in Arkansas."

The Germans soon became dissatisfied in their settlement and left Law's concession. They built rafts and made *pirogues* such as the Indians used, and floated down the river to New Orleans. Some of them settled in the city proper; others took up their residence on the river bank near the city—still called "The German Coast." Others penetrated the forests which lay near the city and the town of *Des Allemands* remains as a record of their travels. These Germans were a strong, healthy lot—for the weak had died before they reached Louisiana—and incomparable colonial stock they proved. Some of the oldest and proudest Creole families of to-day trace their ancestry back to these stalwart men and women.

It is strange to see how rapidly the German names disappeared—or were altered beyond recognition—in this French world in which these settlers found themselves. One explanation lies in the church records. The priests were all Frenchmen, and it is probable that they found the German names impossible to pronounce or remember. Some of the most peculiar names in Louisiana to-day, names which defy the stranger to guess their origin, are corruptions of those matter-of-fact names of German families.

For example: Weber becomes Webre or Fabre; Kamper becomes Cambre; Kerner is changed to Cairne or Carnel or Quernel; Buchwalter becomes Bouchvaldre; Wichner becomes Vicknair. Waguespack, a family name that frequently inspires questions, was originally Wagensbach. In Louisiana the Tregre family is legion; once they were Traeger. Troxler becomes Trosclair; Dubs becomes Toups, and perhaps the oddest of all is Schexnaydre, a good Creole name which was once Jake Schneider. Zweig was translated bodily and is now Labranche.

As the Germans intermarried with the French, the names began to change and the German language began to disappear. It is said that this happened most rapidly in those families where a German married a French girl. And certainly the old church records seem to prove this assertion true. In one family which I traced through several generations, we find such names as Hans, Otto, Fritz among the boys of the first generation, while in the second generation the names of the sons were Anatole, Marcel, Achille, and Onezime.

"The German Coast" was in reality the bank of the Mississippi River, beginning at a distance of perhaps twenty-five miles above New Orleans and extending for some forty miles on both banks of the stream. The pioneers must have had a bad time in clearing that land, for it was virgin forest. The settlers were furnished with the simplest of implements. Only a pick-ax, a hoe, and a spade! There were no plows to be had, nor horses. The wilderness was a dangerous place. There were leopards, bears, panthers, wildcats, and snakes. And there were hostile Indians. Several years in succession the lands along the German Coast were inundated with the floodwaters of the Mississippi.

And yet, they remained, they stuck it out, and they succeeded. In time gardens emerged from the forest; in time comfortable houses were built. But it was not done in a year, no, nor in five years nor ten. It is probable that the Germans fared worse than the French settlers, for it is natural to suppose that Bienville took care of his own people first. And in all fairness to him let it be said that he was in no way responsible for the Germans' being there.

Law's Mississippi Bubble had burst, and Law had fled from Paris. It took months for the news to reach Louisiana, but the news arrived just at the time that the Germans appeared in New Orleans. They had come to demand that passage be given them to their homes in Germany; but when they found the Company of the West in such circumstances that this was impossible, they remained and made the best of it.

The best was none too good. Through years of back-breaking labor the Germans did what they could. There is a Creole saying still heard sometimes in New Orleans, an expression that is used with reference to any tremendously difficult task: "It takes German people to do that!"

In spite of all the hardships which the pioneers had to endure and the difficulties to be encountered, German energy and industry conquered in the end. Although hundreds perished, the survivors wrested a living from the soil; not only a bare living, for in the course of time they attained a high degree of prosperity. Early travelers who came down the river describe the neat appearance of the little white houses, which stood in "endless numbers" on both banks of the stream. They also tell of the thrifty Germans who rowed down the Mississippi to sell their produce on Sunday mornings in front of the church. Twice, it is said, their produce saved the city from famine.

Strange to think of them there—those flaxen-haired, blue-eyed people, surrounded by a wilderness, defending their homes from marauding Indians; stranger still to think that gradually they were drawn into the French-speaking world around them, so that in time they became a part of it. Strange that historians have neglected them to such an extent—giving only scant notice of the tremendously important part that they played in the colonization of Louisiana, and particularly the important part they played in the history of New Orleans.

Chapter IX

THE OLDEST BUILDING

AT the corner of Ursuline and Chartres streets, in the heart of the Vieux Carré, you will find the convent of the Ursuline nuns—the oldest building in New Orleans, and perhaps the oldest structure in the Mississippi Valley. It was completed in 1734, seven years having been given to its construction; and even now, as it nears the end of its second century of service, it stands firm and secure as though it were likely to endure for another hundred years.

It is a building so characteristic of the city that it tempts one to a detailed description, but perhaps it is enough to say that the structure is a large one, two stories and attic, built of brick and covered over outside with gray plaster; the windows and doors are generously proportioned and are closed with heavy batten blinds of cypress, faded to a bluish green. The steeply-pitched roof, cut by dormer windows, was once of tile but is now of blue slate. It is a solid building, firm and honest. There is no attempt at decoration and therein lies its charm; for it is

so admirably proportioned that it needs no ornament. Inside the building we find floors of wide cypress boards, worn
deep with the tread of nuns who have been sleeping in their
graves for more than a century. The staircase, which rises
in a gentle curve to the second story, is particularly fine,
with its balustrade of hand-hammered ironwork. Like the
bolts, bars, and hinges, this railing was beaten into shape
by negro blacksmiths in the city's forges. These "brute
negroes," as they were called, were masters of their craft,
and throughout the old section of the city, one finds that
the oldest ironwork is the most beautifully wrought.

Within the convent, we find that the windows and doors
are slightly rounded at the top and are deeply recessed,
owing to the thickness of the walls. All beams and rafters
are of hand-hewn cypress logs and the marks of hatchet and
adze may still be seen. No nails were used, but the timbers
were fastened together with wooden pegs. There is an
atmosphere of serenity and peace in the old building, there
in the center of its high-walled garden. Only caretakers
inhabit it to-day and visitors are allowed to pass across the
worn door sill and climb the stairs. And in the dim old
rooms there seems to hang a faded fragrance of other
days—a faint perfume wafted between two centuries.

This building is part and parcel of the history of New
Orleans, for it was here that the Ursuline nuns made their
home for so many years. When they left it for another
convent, the building became the dwelling place of the
archbishop; later still it became a school. Now it stands
empty.

In the last chapter we spoke of conditions in the colony
in the first few years after the founding of New Orleans;

URSULINE CONVENT, THE OLDEST BUILDING

CATHEDRAL ALLEY

we spoke of three groups of girls who arrived aboard ship and who were speedily married off to men in the colony. But there were few enough women at best, and in the old documents we find many curious allusions to this lack. Even Bienville—himself no great lover of women, and rather gruff in his judgment of them, if we can judge by his comments in official documents and letters—regrets that the young men of the colony are misbehaving. "Send me wives for my Canadians," he writes, "they are running in the woods after Indian girls!" And the priests, knowing well the condition in the settlement, wrote: "Let us sanction with religion marriage with Indian girls, or send wives of their own kind to the young men."

In the meantime the children in the settlement were growing up in ignorance, and Bienville realized that schools must be established. A few Capuchin priests came to New Orleans and were given quarters near the church where they offered instruction to boys, and the officers of the colony were anxious for schools for young women. Accordingly the Company of the West, through the Jesuit priest in New Orleans, M. Beaubois, contracted with the Ursulines of Rouen for the establishment of a convent of their order in Louisiana. The convent was founded in New Orleans in 1727 under the auspices of Louis XV.

Fortunately for us, we have a sprightly account of this from the pen of Madeleine Hachard, a young postulant in the Ursuline Convent at Rouen. Madeleine accompanied the mission to Louisiana, and as she was apt with her pen, she was made secretary to Mother Superior Tranchepain (an odd name this—"Slice of bread!"). The Superior dictated detailed letters of the doings of the nuns and of their progress—and Madeleine in her moments of leisure wrote letters home to her father, her brothers, and sisters. Madeleine's family was very proud of her letters—as well they might be—and had them published in 1728. Mother Tranchepain's letters were published a few years later and they are nearly the same as Madeleine's. It is obvious that the young postulant, after writing down the sage wisdom of her superior, turned her attention to her own letter writing, and merely rewrote these letters in her own gay fashion—thus giving life and reality to them. She comments upon everything, gossips a little, and proves such a fascinating correspondent that I wish it were possible to quote her letters in their entirety.

She begins by telling of her trip by stage-coach, with the little group of nuns and two Jesuit priests, from Rouen to Lorient by way of Paris. The party visited Versailles and saw the palace of the king, something which pleased her so much that she has the fleeting thought of "shutting her eyes in order to mortify her flesh." At Lorient Madeleine took the veil, her novitiate having been shortened as a special favor. Henceforth she is "Sister Hachard de St. Stanislas."

Three more Ursulines joined the mission there, which raised the number of the party to eight nuns, two postulants, and a servant. "And as for us," Madeleine writes, "do not be scandalized, my dear father, we are taking a *Moor* to serve us, as it is the fashion of the country; and we are also taking a very pretty little cat that wanted to join the community, supposing apparently, in Louisiana as in France, there are rats and mice."

Only once does she lose her gaiety. The vessel has

come and the nuns are ready to embark. Madeleine's pen falters as she writes that "the voice of God," and only tnat, could have separated her from those she loves so well, and she ends by begging "in mercy do not forget your daughter."

Her next letter is dated in New Orleans, six months later, for the voyage across the ocean took five months to the day. Misfortunes followed, one after the other, until their tribulations become laughable through sheer repetition. First their vessel the *Gironde* struck on the rocks shortly after leaving Lorient, and almost went to pieces. The shock threw the nuns headlong and they thought that their time had come. Shortly after this a terrible storm overtook them. The nuns were packed—all eight of them —into the small cabin, eighteen feet by six. The rolling of the vessel caused them to be buffeted about to such an extent that most of them became seasick. Their food was upset time after time; dishes from the table tumbled into their laps. "But never once," says Madeleine, "did we regret the holy mission that we have undertaken." In fact, they were so long at sea that they learned to joke about their misfortunes.

Another storm struck them and all the live stock perished. Forty-nine sheep and five hundred chickens died "apparently from seasickness." In fifteen days they did not make the progress of three. Finally even bread and water had to be measured out to them.

At last they reached Madeira, where supplies were replenished and here they were invited by the Superior of the Monastery of St. Clare (she was none other than a Portuguese princess!) to visit the nunnery, but the Ursulines refused, "not fancying the quaint Moorish customs of the islanders."

Two days after leaving Madeira, they were attacked by pirates! Immediately preparations were made for a fight. The cannon was loaded. The three secular women dressed themselves in men's clothing and took their places with the sailors. The three priests were ready to offer assistance—"Père Tartarin stationed himself at the stern, Père Doutreleau at the bow, Brother Crucy on the bridge to pay out ammunition to the men. All these warriors, armed to the teeth, were admirable in their courage. . . . As for us, our only arms were the chaplets in our hands. We were not cast down, thanks be to the Lord! and not one of us showed any weakness. We were charmed to see the courage of our officers and passengers, who, it seemed to us, were going to crush the enemy at the first blow."

Madeleine waxes almost regretful as she recounts that the pirate vessel withdrew without firing even a single shot.

Then another storm. The sisters had to tie themselves into their beds in order to remain in them. At last they arrived at Santo Domingo. Here they laid in another supply of provisions. They were warmly welcomed there, and a barrel of sugar was given as a present to each nun and priest. After other adventures in the Gulf of Mexico they reached an island which they thought to be Dauphin Island. The nuns were jubilant, "yielding without restraint to their feelings of joy," when suddenly the vessel ran aground with such a shock that the nuns went sprawling headlong to the deck. "We took our rosaries in our hands and said our *In manus* believing that all was over and that our Ursuline establishment would be made then and there!"

Nothing could dislodge the vessel. In order to lighten the *Gironde* the cannon were thrown overboard. The luggage was to go next, the nuns resigning themselves heartily "in order to endure greater poverty," but it was decided to select the sugar barrels for sacrifice. Splash! And there was an end of all the fine presents from Santo Domingo. Still the vessel did not move and the luggage was doomed again—but in the end the captain threw overboard all the casks of liquor, and the ship floated. Almost immediately they went aground again, this time on a sand-bar, where the vessel pounded so dreadfully that even the captain thought she must break to pieces at any moment.

Every one fell to praying, no matter where, each one making vows to no matter whom—all being in such a state of confusion and alarm that we could not agree upon any particular saint to recommend ourselves to. . . . Most of us were at the feet of our amiable superior, who represented to us that we ought to have less trouble than others in suffering death, since before embarking we had made the perfect and entire sacrifice of our life to the Lord. . . .

Another miraculous escape, and five months from the day the nuns left Lorient, they disembarked in the harbor at Balize, at the mouth of the Mississippi. They went ashore at a little island at the river's mouth where they remained for a week until a boat could be summoned in order to complete their journey—sixty miles up the river to New Orleans. The Superior, Father Doutreleau, Brother Crucy, and five sisters went in a *pirogue,* the others "followed in a shallop with Mr. Massy."

They were seven days on the river and even Madeleine confesses that all the trials and tribulations aboard the *Gironde* were as nothing to this. A *pirogue* is a tricky boat at best—being made from a large tree trunk, hollowed out—as it is even more dangerous than a canoe. The slightest jar is sufficient to upset it. And there were the nuns, crowded with all of their luggage into a *pirogue,* some perched high on top of their trunks, afraid to move a muscle, as they were paddled up the swift and dangerous stream. The sun blistered them; they were cramped and pitifully uncomfortable. Each evening it was necessary to stop an hour before sunset in order to get to bed before the mosquitoes attacked them . . . swamp mosquitoes which cling like a black veil until they are brushed off dead. "Messieurs les Maringouins," Madeleine calls them. Fortunately the oarsmen had brought mosquito nets for the nuns (Madeleine calls them by their Creole term *baire*) and by bending down long canes the netting could be arranged in such a way that they were protected from injury. Twice the mattresses were laid in the mud, and one night such a terrible storm arose that Madeleine declares that the mattresses floated! However this intrepid nun strikes a philosophical note at the end of her letter: "All of these little troubles are trying at the time, but one is well recompensed for it in the end by the pleasure one takes in telling of them."

They arrived in New Orleans very early in the morning. There were very few of the inhabitants astir, and the nuns went through the streets to Bienville's house which had been rented for them and in which they lived until a suitable building was completed.

An old picture, painted at the time of the landing of the Ursulines, is still in existence. It furnishes some amusing detail. Here the nuns are shown in procession as they leave the river bank; they are being received by Father Beaubois who, with a gesture, is introducing them to the Capuchin pastors of New Orleans. With his other hand, Father Beaubois is indicating a group of Indians and negroes near-by, the savages appearing almost "in a state of nature." One negro woman, holding a baby in her arms, looks at the nuns with open mouth. A beautiful bronze-colored squaw, bedecked with sea-shells and beads and surrounded with many fat papooses, reclines seductively upon a log. A gigantic Congo negro looks on from his point of vantage atop a woodpile. Behind the nuns a young girl, Claude Massy, is holding a cat in her arms. (It will be remembered that Madeleine Hachard described this kitten as joining the party at Lorient, and we are relieved to see that it has survived the voyage. A curious note attached to the picture assures us that this cat is "the mother of all felines in Louisiana"!) Several priests are seen emerging from a rude church in the background. The whole group is depicted as standing under immense, moss-draped trees.

In another letter Madeleine describes Bienville's house to her father in Rouen. "It is the finest house in town," she writes, "a two story building with an attic . . . with six doors in the first story. In all the stories there are large windows, but with no glass; the frames are closed with very thin linen, which admits as much light as glass."

Then she describes New Orleans:

Our town is very handsome, well constructed and regularly built, as much as I could judge on the day of our arrival; for ever since that day we have remained cloistered in our dwelling. The streets are large and straight. The houses well built, with upright joists, filled with mortar between the interstices, and the exterior white-washed with lime. In the interior they are wainscotted. . . . The colonists are very proud of their capital. . . . The women here are extremely ignorant as to the means of securing their salvation, but they are very expert in the art of displaying their beauty. There is so much luxury in this town that there is no distinction among the classes so far as dress goes. The magnificence of display is equal in all. Most of them reduce themselves and their family to the hard lot of living at home on nothing but sagamity, and flaunt abroad in robes of velvet and damask, ornamented with the most costly rib-bons. They paint and rouge to hide the ravages of time, and wear on their faces, as embellishment, small black patches.

Before the Ursulines arrived in New Orleans, Bien-ville's enemies and critics had succeeded in having him recalled to France and Perier had been appointed to succeed him as head of the colony. Madeleine tells in a letter—written some time later—of Perier's efforts to improve the city. "He has established a well regulated police," she writes; "he has declared war on vice; he expulses those who lead a scandalous life; corporal punishment is inflicted on girls who lead a bad life; they hang, they break on the wheel for the least theft; the Council is supreme. There is no appeal; they bring cases from Illinois, four hundred leagues distant."

Of the Ursulines who entered Bienville's house in 1727, two nuns and one postulant returned to France, aboard a vessel called, oddly enough, the *Rhinoceros*, in November of the same year. One of the reasons given was that the climate proved unsuited to them.

The nuns had scarcely begun their tasks when the

Indian massacre at Fort Rosalie took place and as a result twenty-four orphans were brought to the Ursulines. A list of the nuns' activities appears endless. They conducted a school for girls, their curriculum including "French and English language lessons, geography, arithmetic, catechism, history, writing, sewing, and housework." They had charge of the hospital until 1770. They established a free orphanage.

In 1734 their convent was completed, costing "one million francs," a huge sum for those days, and on July 24 the Ursulines took possession with great pomp. Bienville, who had been reinstated as governor of Louisiana, was in charge. The description may still be seen in the annals of the order, and it gives a glowing picture of the ceremony:

Toward five o'clock in the afternoon our convent bells rang a merry peal to announce our decision. Immediately the troops ranged themselves on each side of the abode we were about to leave forever. Governor Bienville, Mr. Salmon, intendent, together with the most distinguished citizens and almost the entire population, came to form our escort.

After the Benediction of the Blessed Sacrament, which was given by the Reverend Father Philip, assisted by Reverend Fathers Beaubois and Petit, S. J., all left the chapel in processional order; the citizens opening the march, followed by the children of our orphanage and day school, and over forty of the most respectable ladies of the city, all bearing lighted tapers and singing pious hymns. Next came twenty young girls dressed in white, who were followed by twelve others dressed as angels.

The young lady who represented Saint Ursula wore a costly robe and mantle, and a crown glittering with diamonds and pearls, from which a rich veil hung in graceful folds; and in her hand she bore a heart pierced with an arrow. Her companions were clad in snow-white dresses and veils and they bore palm branches emblematic of victory.

Last of all came the nuns and clergy; the former bearing lighted tapers, and the latter a rich canopy under which the Blessed Sacrament was borne in triumph. The soldiers marched on each side. . . .

As soon as the procession was in sight of the convent some kind friend commenced to ring the bells to hail our arrival; thus we entered the new abode amidst the chiming of bells, the fifes and drums and the singing of hymns. . . .

The Ursulines played an enormously important part in the early history of New Orleans, for it was in their schools that the future mothers of the colony were educated; it was the Ursulines who took care of the orphans and nursed the sick. Year after year they remained, gaining strength with the growing city.

From their convent windows these cloistered nuns looked down upon the changing world. They saw the population in panic as Indian massacres threatened; they nursed the citizens during epidemics which threatened to destroy the colony; they saw O'Reilly's fleet sail up the river as Louisiana passed from the hands of France to the hands of Spain. Near-by in the Place d'Armes, they saw the flag of France lowered and the Spanish flag unfurled in its place. And later they saw the Spanish flag lowered before the tricolor of the French Republic. Last they saw the tricolor as it fluttered down to be replaced by the flag of the United States.

Grace King in her volume, "New Orleans, The Place and The People," remarks: "It must have seemed strange to them—particularly to that one old sister who lived

through it all, to shake hands with Jackson in 1815—that
no government in the community was steadfast except that
of Saint Ursula, nothing lasting in life save the mission of
wives and sisters."

Chapter X

MASSACRE

WHEN the French came first to New Orleans they found the neighboring Indians friendly. This was due to the fact that Bienville treated them as fairly as he knew how and tried to understand their point of view. We find him in constant touch with the neighboring tribes and there are records of several minor disputes which were straightened out during his first term of office. When Perier was appointed to the office of governor-general of the Colony of Louisiana and Bienville returned to France, the Indian troubles began in earnest. More and more white men were settling in the colony and difficulties began to arise from many quarters.

The situation at Fort Rosalie, which stood where Natchez, Mississippi, stands to-day, was growing acute. The Natchez Indians were getting tired of the tyranny and oppression of the French officers of the garrison, who had made many of them slaves and had treated others with cruelty. Accordingly they planned to kill all of those in the settlement at the fort. They carried out their plan to the last detail and the records are tales of bloody horror. Various historians have written of this, but the old documents seem more vivid, and as I shall speak only briefly of the massacre, I shall quote a letter from Diron d'Artaguette to Maurepas. Diron d'Artaguette was prominent in affairs of the early colony, but the name disappears from Louisiana records at the time of Bienville's return to France. Here is part of his letter, translated from among the papers in the Mississippi Provincial Archives:

My Lord:—My duty and the perfect attachment that I shall always retain for your Lordship induce me to relate to you what is happening to-day in this colony of Louisiana.

The Natchez Indians, a nation established ninety leagues above New Orleans, having information toward the end of last November that the French wished to force them to abandon their villages and their lands in keeping with the order of Sieur de Chepart [spelled in other places d'Etcheparre], who was in command at that fort, conspired to slaughter all the French who were established there. For this purpose they used the pretext of forming a hunting party as much for themselves as for the French, because they said that the Choctaws were going to attack them; but as most were without guns they borrowed some from the colonists and then dispersed themselves into each of their houses in such a way that to these in which there were only one or two Frenchmen four Indians went. The chief with several of the Honored People went, about eight o'clock in the morning, to the residence of Sieur de Chepart, who was in command at this post, with some fowls that they wished to trade to him in spite of himself. When they had put the fowls into Sieur Chepart's house this officer wished to throw them out. As he was stooping to pick up these fowls, it is reported that the chief of the Natchez gave his people the signal to fire, which they did at once, killing Sieur de Chepart. The shot was heard by those Indians who were in the other houses of the French. The shot together with the cry of the chief was the signal, and the Indians fired on all sides.

This lasted until four o'clock in the afternoon, when the massacre ended. Then the Indians had all the heads of the French brought into the public square, with the booty that they had taken. The spoils they divided among themselves. As they had spared as many French women as they could during the massacre, they brought them all together and put them into two houses where they are being kept under surveillance. It is feared that the women may be slaughtered before they can be taken from that place. The Indians have likewise taken many negroes and negresses whom they also have with them. . . .

He ends his letter with a plea that soldiers be sent at once in order that war may be made upon the Indians. The force at New Orleans, he says, is inadequate. He criticizes Governor Perier for his lack of decision in attack.

In a report dated June 9, 1730, Father Philibert, a Capuchin priest and missionary, gives a detailed account of those who lost their lives in the massacre at Fort Rosalie. He gives a name and description of each, and to read it through is depressing enough. In all there were 144 men, thirty-five women, and fifty-six children killed. Many of them were mutilated before being beheaded. In the list we find the phrase "burnt and tortured" after many of the names. A few who managed to escape brought back the detailed story to New Orleans.

Immediately the town was in an uproar. The residents were panic-stricken. For New Orleans was without defences. It is true that a palisade of wood surrounded the town, but it was woefully inadequate and the Indians could have burned it easily. To the horror of Indian attack was added the fear of slave rebellion. Planters with their fami-

OLD SPANISH ARSENAL IN ST. PETER STREET

COURTYARD OF THE CABILDO

lies abandoned their homes and rushed into New Orleans for protection. Every day came fresh alarms. Day after day the beating drum caused a frightened populace to assemble in the Place d'Armes, where the men stood guard while the women took refuge in the church.

However, the Indians seemed satisfied with what they had done at Fort Rosalie, for they retreated into the forest, bringing with them the white women and children whom they had captured. There are documents without number, telling of bartering with this group of Indians or that for the possession of a French woman or child. Five years later there is a curious account of a little boy, still with the Indians, a child that the savages refused to give up and who was exhibited scarred and naked to white men near Mobile. What his fate was, we have no way of knowing. However, many of the children were rescued and fifty-six of them were given to the Ursuline nuns. These children constituted the first group of orphans cared for by the colony.

Governor Perier made the grave mistake of trying to inspire the Indians with fear. Arming a group of negroes and promising these slaves their freedom, he sent them against a small group of peaceful Chouachas Indians who lived near New Orleans. Here we have another record of horror.

Soldiers from the New Orleans barracks managed to capture four men and two women of the Natchez nation, and Governor Perier had them burned at the stake on the levee in front of the Place d'Armes. These Indians accepted their fate stoically, and "even the women showed not the least trace of weakness as they were consumed by the flames." The people of New Orleans came out to see the execution and a "considerable concourse of people" stood by. There are, however, records of protest, and Perier was criticized severely by some of his own officers for this piece of brutal stupidity.

Perier's failure to secure the safety of the city was so severely criticized that he was recalled to France and Bienville was sent back to the colony again. But the hand of Bienville seemed to have lost its cunning. His expeditions against the Indians were failures, due principally to his lack of money and men. In the end he returned again to France, broken with grief and disappointment. The Marquis de Vaudreuil was appointed to succeed him.

And now we come to a most amazing development in the history of New Orleans. There came a time of gaiety and luxury in the city. The Marquis de Vaudreuil was typical of the French court of that time. He was very rich. He brought his wife to Louisiana with him. A whole shipload of beautiful furniture and trappings was brought for their use. He established a sort of court in New Orleans. There were balls, with court dresses *de rigueur*. There were dashing officers and jeweled women. This may be said to be the beginning of fashionable life in Louisiana. During de Vaudreuil's régime the first play was produced in New Orleans—"The Indian Father" performed in the governor's house in 1753.

His term of office in New Orleans was a picturesque time, but it was not interesting historically. At the time of the beginning of the Seven Years' War, when French and English fought hand to hand for the possession of Canada, de Vaudreuil was promoted to the governorship of Canada, and M. de Kelerec was appointed to succeed him in Louisiana.

Chapter XI

CRIME AND PUNISHMENT

VIEWED in the light of modern methods, criminal trials in New Orleans during the French Colonial Period were brutal indeed. The accused was locked up in jail, usually loaded down with chains. He was not present when the witnesses were called to testify against him; but after their testimony was heard and written down, he was then brought into court—still wearing his chains—and the record read to him. He could deny the accusations, if he liked, but this did little good, for he was allowed no lawyer, nor was there a jury. The Superior Council listened, decided upon his guilt or innocence, and pronounced the penalty. There was no further appeal.

One of the earliest trials in which there is enough written evidence to give a fair idea of the proceedings, takes place in 1720. This was two years after the colony was founded. We find two men, Jean Baptiste Porcher (or Portier) and Thomas Bahu—nicknamed "La Rose"—accused of the theft of towels (or perhaps napkins) from the house of one de Baume. The sentence is typical of the heavy penalties of the day. "La Rose" was acquitted, but as for Porcher's sentence, let me quote from the record itself:

> We have condemned the accused . . . to be flogged during three days by a negro, and to serve the Company during three years as a convict in whatsoever place in the Colony to which he shall be sent, all of his effects acquired here to be confiscated to the King, or as shall be ordered, the sum of fifty *livres* fine to be previously deducted from them to the benefit of the said Lord the King.

That is all. Porcher disappears and is seen no more.

In 1728 we find the case of Jean Melun, charged with stabbing with a knife. The record gives a good idea of what took place.

Melun, who is said to be "an undesirable colonist," went, on the afternoon of May 4, 1728, "to the Coupart woman's house to steal a piece of bacon, and that having been caught in the act by one Dinant, who was in the woman's house, Melun struck him several times with a knife." He is jailed for this, and witnesses are summoned. Character witnesses, called by the Council, state that the accused has been leading "a bad life." Then follows the testimony of the physician, Pouyadon de la Tour, as to the injuries of the wounded man. There are two wounds, both slight. The physician's report is rather amusing, it is so explicit: "Having examined his whole body, I found two wounds, one situated on the left arm, on the exterior middle part of the bone called the radius, which penetrated the skin to the depth of *one twelfth of an inch on a length of six or seven twelfths of an inch.*" The other was a similar scratch on the abdomen. The doctor reports that the patient has neither fever nor inflammation, but states that he is "not able to answer for any accidents which might supervene."

Nothing is said in the record about the attempted theft of bacon—so whether this is merely an empty accusation or a true statement cannot be ascertained. But the sentence is severe:

> I require in the King's name that the said Jean Melun be declared guilty and convicted of acts of violence and of having wounded with a knife, in satisfaction of which he be sentenced to be whipped at the crossings of the city by the executor of justice [sheriff] and banished from this city forever, enjoining him not to break his ban under the penalties which will follow. The condemned is to bear the costs.

The document is signed by Fleuriau and is dated May 29, 1728.

However, there is another document in connection with this case, in which Melun's wife begs for his pardon. "Very humbly petitioning," Marie Fontain, wife of Jean Melun, states that her husband was "inflamed with drink and insanity" and continues: "Why—since the Coupart woman had money and wages due him—could she not leave him the meat and make him pay for it without striking him?" She declares that her husband did not come to the Colony of his own free will. (Was he, I wonder, one of those unfortunates sent to Louisiana in order that their families in France might be rid of them?) She goes on to say that two years ago she petitioned to the Council that if her husband did not return to France, "his insanity and despair from being retained in the Colony by force would cause him to commit some mad act:—the misfortune she dreaded has happened!"

The record becomes an impassioned plea: "She throws herself at your feet to beseech you to allow yourself to be moved to pity; let your justice give way to mercy, not in regard to her husband who is unworthy of it but for herself, who being obliged to work with her hands cannot find work to do. . . . She begs you to consider, to relent. . . . He was a lunatic. . . . He was the one attacked." She begs that he be allowed to go free and leave the Colony, to be returned to France at his own expense; that he be allowed to pay the physician for dressing the wounded man, and that he be allowed to pay for the wounded man's food while the man is unable to work. "This is what she hopes for, what, with crossed hands, she implores you to grant her; not being able to show her gratitude otherwise, she will never cease to offer prayers to the Lord for your preservation."

No record exists that her plea was heard. We cannot tell whether the husband and wife went happily home to France, or whether he was sent out into the wilderness to die alone. It is probable, however, that this story did not have a happy ending. But one conjecture is as good as another. You may have it your own way.

We have seen men punished for theft and for fighting, now let us look briefly upon a murder case tried in New Orleans in 1760. This is one of the most complete records that we have, and a note is appended telling the final phase of the affair.

Michel Degout is charged with the murder of one Crette at Natchitoches, in what is now northwest Louisiana. The village was more than two hundred miles from New Orleans. The first name of the murdered man is not given in the record. The initial hearing took place in Natchitoches before Mr. Pain, an acting judge. As usual in such cases the accused was not present when the witnesses were interrogated. He had been brought to the jail in New Orleans prior to the hearing. Each written deposition is preceded by the declaration of the witness under oath that he is neither a relative nor servant of either party, meaning the deceased and the accused. At the end of each deposition there is a formal statement that this paper has been read to the witness and that the witness "has persisted therein," also that each one took or refused the witness fee to which he was entitled by the court. Each deposition is signed by the witness, the judge and the clerk of court. These papers show that Judge Pain examined six witnesses whose occupations were those of: a blacksmith, "a trainer of parrakeets," a merchant, a planter, the planter's wife, and a negro slave woman belonging to them. Two witnesses are described as *voyageurs* "who could not be found." One of the witnesses, Madame Darbanne, is ordered to proceed to New Orleans in order that she may be confronted by the accused and to give further testimony before the Council there.

Now into the record comes, for the first time, a description of the prisoner himself. He is Michel Degout, "a master sculptor of Paris." He is forty-seven years old. He was apparently interrogated upon his past history and makes some damaging admissions. The principal one is that "twenty-two years ago he had been arrested at Leogane for having stolen three silver pieces from another man while drunk, for which he was whipped through the town, branded with a *fleur de lys* and banished." He admits the slaying, but contends that it was in self-defence.

In the first hearing we have the testimony of Pierre Darbanne, a planter of Natchitoches. He tells that Crette quarrelled with Degout about a flagon of wine. Crette had invited Degout to drink with him, but upon Degout's arrival there was no wine in Crette's house. Crette then asked Degout if he would go to a neighbor's and borrow a bottle. Degout did so but the neighbor, M. de Lemur, refused to send the wine unless Crette sent him a note promising to pay for it. This resulted in a quarrel between Crette and Degout. They fought. Crette knocked Degout down; others intervened and Degout in a fury returned to Darbanne's house, where he lodged. Crette followed him there and the murder ensued. Darbanne did not see the murder committed. He does not sign the statement as he cannot write.

The trainer of parrakeets testifies much in the same manner as Darbanne, but with less detail. He refuses the witness fee, and signs his name "Dudoit."

Now comes the testimony of an eye-witness, Marie Leclerc, wife of Pierre Darbanne. After declaring that she is not related to either the deceased or the accused, she tells that she and her negro slave woman, Jeanne, were folding linen, having finished ironing table-cloths and wearing apparel. Degout came in. He seemed very much upset and directly after entering he began searching for something in the room where she and the negress were working. She asked him what he was looking for, but he did not reply. She repeated the question several times, which exasperated him. He came up to her, and standing between her and the negress, looked out of the window. Some one came up outside, and the witness states that she heard Degout cry out: "Who is there? Is it you, Pierre Darbanne?"

From outside came the answer: "It is I, Crette!"

Degout leaned out of the window. "Well, here's for you!" he shouted. She did not see the weapon that Degout used, but she thinks it was a sculptor's chisel. Crette lay dead outside the window. This is all she knows. The statement is read to her and she "persists that it is the truth." She declares that she does not know how to read, nor how to sign.

Now comes the testimony of Jeanne, the negro slave woman. She states that she is not a relative of any of those implicated in the affair, that she is the slave of the Darbannes. She tells of folding the linen, of Degout's entrance, of Madame Darbanne's question, and of the cry from outside the window. After Degout struck the blow—which like her mistress she did not see, although he stood between the two women at that moment—Madame Darbanne cried out, "What have you done, wretch?" and fainted. Degout then opened another window and left without a word. Crette lay dead outside. That is all she knows. She signs with a cross, as she cannot write.

All these documents were written in Natchitoches. Madame Darbanne is then ordered to report before the Council in New Orleans in order that she may "confront" the accused who is in jail there.

Now we have Michel Degout's first testimony. He has been brought into court and his chains "have been struck off." The testimony of Madame Darbanne is read to him. He states that she has perjured herself in the first formal statement relative to her relationship with the dead man. She is his kinswoman, Degout claims, and that if she has not deliberately perjured herself, then she has made this statement unwittingly, through fright and unfamiliarity with the legal language. Degout then goes on to say that the remainder of her testimony is entirely false and that she has lied maliciously. He states that he had a sculptor's tool in his hand when he entered his lodgings at Darbanne's house, and he intended laying the tool aside when Crette followed him into the room. In the presence of the two women who were folding clothes, he declares, Crette attacked him and knocked him down. At that, he states, Madame Darbanne began screaming, "Stop, do not fight in my house!" and continued screaming during the duration of the struggle. He declares that both Madame Darbanne and the servant have lied, and that Pierre Darbanne is "a miscreant who forced them to take this course." He goes on to say that Darbanne upon coming in and finding Crette's body on the floor, cried out: "Why did you kill that man in my house? Why did you not kill him outside? You put me in trouble!"

Madame Darbanne is brought back into court. She sticks to her first statement, and declares that there is no truth in what Degout says about her. She is taken out of the room and Degout is brought back. Her second statement is read to him. He says that his own story is true and that he can add nothing to it.

Now we have the last official document in the case. It is the Council's sentence upon Degout. It states that Degout is guilty of "premeditated murder committed with a sculptor's chisel on the person of one Crette, in reparation of which the Council has condemned and condemns him to make honorable amends, barefooted and gowned, a rope around his neck, holding in his hand a flaming torch weighing two pounds, to be led to the main entrance of the parochial church of this city, where he will be brought by the public executioner in a tumbril, with a poster on it: 'Murderer and Assassin,' front and back; and there, bareheaded and on his knees to declare that he wickedly, with premeditation, murdered the said Crette, for which crime he is repentant and begs forgiveness of God, of the King and of Justice; after which, in the same cart, he is to be led by the same public executioner to the public square of this city, to have arms, legs, thighs, and back broken on a scaffold which, for this purpose, shall be erected on the said square, and he shall afterward be placed on a wheel, to expire there with his face turned to Heaven until death ensues, his body be then borne to and exposed on the public road."

His goods and property were ordered confiscated to His Majesty the King, or "to those to whom they belong."

And now comes the strangest part of Degout's story. There is a note affixed to the records which declares that, on second consideration, the Court has decided to show Degout mercy. "The said Degout will be strangled under the scaffold before receiving a blow."

There is also a marginal note which reads as follows: "On this day February 1, 1766, I, chief clerk of the Superior Council, do certify that the decree rendered on this day by the Council against one Degout was *executed in its entirety,* by the public executioner, and that the said Degout suffered it, as stated, at New Orleans on the above mentioned day and year."

The italics are mine. It is evident that Degout was driven about in a cart, carrying a flaming torch, was brought to the church door, then taken into the Place d'Armes where he was hanged or "strangled." Then the rest of the sentence was carried out. The arms, legs, thighs, and back of the corpse were broken. He was elevated on the wheel, and at last his mutilated body was exhibited at the city's gate.

It must not be supposed that all of the records in the Cabildo Archives are as terrifying as those spoken of here. For the most part they are dull and commonplace enough: wills are filed; suits for slander are fought out; property changes hands; successions are opened—all the usual cases in a growing colonial city are recorded here. But there is one case which suggests a story so fine that I must speak of it, briefly at least. As a story of devotion it has few rivals. It offers a theme for a great novel—provided one were sympathetic enough to see the human story behind the court records, and provided one were wise enough to write it down. But such a novel would require the skill of a writer and scholar who was also a poet, and there are few enough of these.

The papers concerning the case are brief. There are only three short documents pertaining to the emancipation of Marie Aram, a slave, set free by her husband's labor during seven years. But the story behind these crumbling, yellowed papers is one of devotion of which few men—white or black—are capable.

Sometime prior to 1737, François Tiocou, a negro, was married to Marie Aram, a negro slave. Marie Aram belonged to the Charity Hospital of New Orleans. On July 10, 1737, her husband, a free man, came to those in charge of the hospital and made a strange contract. He promised to work for seven years without remuneration of any kind

—to become a slave voluntarily—if, at the end of that time, his wife were set free. If, for any reason, he left before the seven years expired, he was to receive nothing at all.

The first document pertains to this agreement. The second document, signed by one Raguet and also by Father Charles, the Superior of the Capuchins, states that "Whereas the said Tiocou and Marie Aram, his wife, have worked and served the Hospital well and faithfully during the time laid down in the said engagement and that it is just to grant liberty and freedom to the said Marie Aram, the undersigned Directors and Administrators very humbly petition you, Gentlemen, to confirm and grant freedom to the said Marie Aram, negress, wife of François Tiocou, that in future she may be free as are all the subjects of His Majesty in France, the intention of the husband and wife being to serve the hospital and to remain there as long as they give satisfaction." This paper is dated March 6, 1744.

Four days later, March 10, we have the following document, signed by Governor Vaudreuil and three others:

"We, the Governor, and Commissary of the Marine, Intendent of the Province of Louisiana, considering the above petition of the Directors and Administrators of the Hospital of the Poor by which they ask that liberty be granted to one Marie Aram, negress slave, as a recompense of the good services rendered to the hospital, by virtue of the power given us by His Majesty, have granted and confirmed by these presents and do grant and confirm the freedom granted to the said Marie Aram, that she may enjoy the privileges of persons born free, in testimony of which we have signed this present and had it countersigned by our secretaries and affixed our arms as seal."

And that is all. What became of them afterward, or what happened to their descendants we cannot say. Perhaps it does not matter. But some day, when the great love stories of the world are collected, I hope that Francois and Marie will not be forgotten.

Chapter XII

A GHASTLY EXECUTION

LATELY the people of America have been stirred with descriptions of life in the French penal colonies. Many have shuddered at the tales of horror, and we have assured ourselves that nothing so terrible could be charged to America. Not now perhaps—but in the early history of this country there are incidents which rival any of the revelations of cruelty elsewhere.

During the governorship of Kelerec in New Orleans, a wholesale military execution took place. In order to tell of it, it is first necessary to explain the military situation in Louisiana at that time.

There was a dearth of money in the colony. The soldiers were paid so irregularly, and fed so inadequately, that there were frequent desertions. The deserters would make their way into English territory and find a place with the English army; and it is needless to say that these deserters were warmly welcomed—as there were not too many fighting men in Louisiana at that time.

Now Kelerec did his best for the colony—or so historians tell us—and enforced all of the strict regulations in
his colonial army. The men deserted in such numbers that
New Orleans was obliged to depend upon Swiss mercenary
troops for protection. There were large numbers of Swiss in
the colony, men who had been sent over—men to whom
great promises had been made.

Ship Island, lying in the Mexican Gulf not far from the
mouth of the Mississippi, was a place of unusual beauty—as
it is still beautiful to-day. There were beaches of gleaming
white sand, and there were many flowering trees. To visit
the island nowadays, to walk under those gigantic trees, to
stand looking out to see where white-capped waves come
sweeping in to break upon the beach, to feel the lazy lan-
guor in the air—to visit Ship Island to-day is to feel only a
sense of great peace. It is incredible to think that this tropical island was once the scene of suffering as terrible as any
horror story of any age.

For it was on Ship Island that the Swiss mercenaries had
their headquarters. They were commanded by a Frenchman
—one Duroux. I can find no description of the man himself,
but from what one can learn from the documents of the
time, it is almost certain that he was a man of unusual and
meaningless cruelty. Finding himself in complete charge of
a large group of men—far removed from any higher
authority—he made himself a veritable monarch. He
amassed a private fortune from the labor of these soldiers,
men who were supposed to be used to protect the colony
from invaders. He forced them to labor in his charcoal
kilns, he forced them to work in the field under the tropical
sun. He made frequent use of the lash, and there were

subtler punishments for those whom he considered lazy, or
disobedient.

Here is an extract from the plea of one man:

Because I was unable to do the work assigned to me, I was
brought to him [Duroux] for an explanation. I swore to him that I
had done my best, but that my strength was insufficient for the labor
imposed upon me. He set four men upon me. They threw me to the
ground, stripped me naked. Duroux himself applied the whip. He
struck me again and again until I lost consciousness. One eye was
put out by a blow from the butt of the whip.

He ordered the four men to take me far enough from his dwelling so that my cries would not disturb his rest at night. There I
was bound to a tree. In my nakedness I was a prey to the mosquitoes
which settled upon me in swarms. I remained there for two days and
two nights without food or water.

My brother, who had made some attempt to soften his heart, was
tied naked to a tree near-by. In this position, standing with his back
to the tree, and with his body exposed to the sun, he presented a piti-
ful sight. His body was covered with blood and was black with flies
and mosquitoes. He was released at the end of thirty-six hours, but
died the following day.

At times there have been as many as fourteen men, naked and tied
to stakes in the sun on the beach. Duroux walked up and down before them, prodding them in the softer parts of their bodies with his
sword, enough to draw blood.

Driven almost mad by these inhuman tortures, some of
the men managed to escape and made their way up the
Mississippi to New Orleans. They appeared before Governor Kelerec, exhibiting their scars and telling their story.

Now Kelerec was, as we have said, a military martinet.
He received them with stern face, listened for a brief time,
cut short their argument—and had them thrown into prison.

From his point of view, they were merely mutinous. Duroux must be upheld—for Duroux was an officer.

The only excuse that we can find for Kelerec is this: perhaps he was afraid to give aid to the men. For surely he had enough deserters to contend with, as matters stood in the colony. And there was much work to be done, for he was then engaged in building a stockade around the city of New Orleans, and he was having excavations made for a moat around the palisade.

At any event, whether this were the reason, or not, the Swiss were sent back to Ship Island, loaded down with chains. What became of them afterward, we have no way of knowing.

The men at Ship Island, up to this time, had believed that if the governor of the Province knew of their plight, he would remove Duroux from power; but when these wretched men were sent back in chains, they knew that there was no help for them.

Duroux, now freed from any fear he may have had of a reprimand from his superior officer, treated the Swiss more mercilessly than before. He invented new tortures—tortures of a more subtle nature for those who did not do enough work to please him. Men were burned and mutilated now for the least offence—or for no offence at all. The island became a veritable hell.

Duroux was surrounded by a body-guard—a group of men who carried out his orders, and assisted him in the torture of those soldiers who worked in the fields and at the kilns. Up to this time, the guard had done his bidding without question—knowing only too well what their own fate would be if they failed to do as he directed. But now it seems that Duroux overstepped himself. His own men turned against him.

It was his custom to go hunting on neighboring islands, and it was his whim to be received in state when he returned. One day he went away on an expedition. He returned at sunset, and as his boat approached the beach, the guard filed out as usual, with drums beating and with flags fluttering. But as soon as he had stepped ashore, the men opened fire in unison. Duroux fell dead.

His body was thrown into the Gulf of Mexico, and then the armed guard went over the island, liberating the prisoners. One of the prisoners—a sea captain—was forced to guide them toward the English forces, for the Swiss had determined to join forces with the English arms. However, as no one seemed sure of the exact route, the party separated. Half of them managed to escape and join the English, but the others were captured and brought to New Orleans.

A court-martial was held by the officers of the Swiss regiment stationed in New Orleans—officers under the command of Kelerec. The penalty meted out to deserters was fully described in their code: and the men were condemned to death. The man who had accompanied the deserters as guide was broken on the wheel. All of the others were nailed alive in coffins and sawed in two.

Chapter XIII

THE FLAG OF SPAIN

Now we have reached the point in our story where Louisiana history becomes world history. The Seven Years' War —as we all learned in our school histories—ended disastrously for France. Gayarré, the Louisiana historian, expresses it aptly when he says that the loss of Canada "caused a painful emotion in Louisiana, which was bound to it by so many ties, and which, for such a long time, had formed a dependency of Canada. A vague presentiment made the colonists fear a change of domination. Indeed, on November 13, 1762, the King of Spain accepted, by secret treaty, the gift which the King of France made to him of Louisiana."

The treaty of Fontainebleau was kept secret, and on February 10, 1763, the treaty of Paris was signed. Louis XV ceded to Great Britain the Mississippi River, the port of Mobile, and all possessions on the east bank of the Mississippi, with the exception of the city of New Orleans and "the island in which it is situated." Spain, in turn ceded to Great Britain, Florida—later called West Florida—with the fort of St. Augustine and the bay of Pensacola, and all the country to the east and southeast of the Mississippi.

Kelerec, the governor of Louisiana, was recalled to France, charged with mismanagement of the colony and thrown into the Bastille; d'Abbadie arrived in New Orleans with a new title—Director-General, and proceeded to take charge of the city. It was not until October, 1764, that d'Abbadie received the official communication from the Court of France, and made the announcement in New Orleans: Louisiana had passed from the hands of Louis XV into the hands of Charles III of Spain. "The news," says Alcée Fortier, the historian, "threw the colony into consternation and despair."

We may well believe it, for here was a French community abandoned to an unknown ruler. The country near New Orleans had been given away. The eternal enemy, England, was now in possession of the Mississippi, just above New Orleans—and the French town of Baton Rouge had passed into English hands. On the west bank of the Mississippi, north of New Orleans, the land now belonged to Spain.

New Orleans was cut off completely from the French world to which it belonged. The city felt itself thrown away, and lost indeed. But it must be remembered that, in a sense, New Orleans *was* Louisiana—an island in the wilderness, except for the scattered archipelago of its plantations and hamlets—an archipelago as French as the city itself. So remote was New Orleans from other communities of the United States, that it might have been on another continent.

It is true that an ever increasing trade was coming down the Mississippi, but it came from far away, and the upstream trip was so arduous that few were brave enough to attempt it.

A meeting was held in New Orleans, and from every village and plantation came delegates. Lafreniere, the attorney-general, suggested a plan—it seems absurd enough to us now—but the Creoles believed in it then. It was naïve, to say the least. A representative from New Orleans was to go to the Court of Louis XV to ask him to reconsider his decision, and to take Louisiana back again. Jean Milhet, the richest merchant of the colony, was chosen for the mission.

Historians tell of Milhet finding Bienville—now eighty years of age, a tottering old man with "wild white hair," and Milhet and Bienville went together to try to soften the heart of the French king and to tell him of the love that Louisianians bore for France. Louis XV refused to see them. The two men were put off with excuses. They never succeeded in obtaining their interview. And the months dragged by.

In New Orleans, d'Abbadie had died and Aubry succeeded him as director-general. Milhet did not return; there was no news from him. Nearly a year passed. The Spanish king did not send any one to Louisiana to take charge of the colony, and in New Orleans the hope grew that the Spaniards would never come.

It seems that revolutionary ideas were in the air. On the Atlantic seaboard the British colonies were becoming restive; the American Revolution was to take place not many years later. In New Orleans the idea of revolution

HOUSE AT ORLEANS AND DAUPHINE STREETS

COURTYARD OF 1015 CHARTRES STREET

was growing. France had given them away—Spain had not claimed them. Why not a Louisiana Republic?

While this idea was taking root in the Creole mind, a letter came to Aubry from Havana, announcing the arrival of Don Antonio de Ulloa, appointed by the Spanish crown to rule Louisiana. However, when Ulloa arrived, he brought with him only two companies of Spanish infantry —ninety men—and did not assume his official position, but waited for the arrival of more troops. Aubry received him, treated him with respect—but continued to govern the colony. In a short time Ulloa sailed away and anchored his vessel at Balize, at the mouth of the river—no one knew why.

There was general dissatisfaction with the state of affairs. Nothing was certain, and the revolutionary spirit was growing. The colonists did not understand Ulloa, nor did they make any attempt to understand him or his policies.

Ulloa returned from Balize, bringing with him a young bride. She was a great heiress from Peru, and he had waited seven months for her at the river's mouth. She came in magnificent style, with a retinue of servants, and a group of her friends.

The Creole women were curious enough about this mysterious Peruvian bride, and some of them went at once to call. The heiress refused to see them, and remained shut up with her own friends—and her suppers and balls were for her friends alone. It was the cut direct. Then—and this is a very characteristic touch—the Creole women grew greatly incensed, urged the men to get rid of Ulloa, giving as their reason that the dark-skinned Peruvian friends of Donna Ulloa were mulattoes!

Jean Milhet returned from France about this time and the tale of his failure to gain the ear of Louis XV added fuel to the flame of resentment. Word was sent out for a mass meeting.

From every plantation, from every near-by village, men flocked into New Orleans. Shouts of "Liberty" echoed in the streets. The leading Creoles took charge—Lafreniere, Villere, Marquis, Caresse, Noyan, Milhet, Doucet, Mazent, Petit, and de Boisblanc. Lafreniere addressed the assembly, and after his speech a petition was drawn up, asking that Ulloa be expelled by the Superior Council. There were 560 signatures attached to the petition—which seems a small number—but the Creoles seemed to think these sufficient.

Immediately the inhabitants took up arms. On December 14, 1768, the Superior Council acted, Ulloa was asked to leave the colony. Aubry protested against these acts of violence, but the "revolutionists" would not listen. Ulloa withdrew to his ship at anchor in the river. That night there was a wedding among the Creoles, and a group of revelers, returning home at dawn, conceived the idea of cutting the moorings which held the sailing vessel to the levee. They did so, and the current carried the ship downstream. . . . Ulloa was gone.

But this last insult proved too much. Ulloa's report to the King of Spain hurls such charges as "childish extravagances" at the Creoles. And a little later, the Creoles paid dearly enough.

There was talk of a republic.

There is no doubt [says Gayarré], but that the colonists would have eagerly adopted this form of government, had it been possible at the time, for it must be recollected that from the earliest existence of the colony, almost all its governors had uniformly complained of the republican spirit which they had observed in the inhabitants [like all revolutions which fail, the revolt of New Orleans came to be known as a rebellion]. But they nevertheless bequeathed to posterity the right of claiming for Louisiana the merit of having been the first European colony that entertained the design of proclaiming their independence.

When Ulloa's report reached Spain, the king despatched Don Alejandro O'Reilly to Louisiana at once. And O'Reilly took with him three thousand Spanish soldiers. He reached Balize on July 23, 1769. News of his impending arrival was brought to New Orleans, and was received with consternation. "Resistance," says Martin, "was spoken of." But there was no resistance. O'Reilly arrived, took charge, marched his troops into the Place d'Armes, and raised the Spanish flag where the French emblem had flown since 1718. Lafreniere, Marquis, and Milhet went at once to see him, to try to make a peace for the colonists. O'Reilly assured them, says Martin, "that all past transactions would be buried in oblivion, and all who had offended would be forgiven." The delegates reported this to the assembly in New Orleans and they were quieted. The men from the plantations and villages laid down their arms and went home again.

Aubry reported at once to O'Reilly and, so historians tell us, reported the matter of the "revolution" in full. Historians wax bitter here. Aubry and O'Reilly are condemned together. For the outcome of the matter was this: O'Reilly had the leaders of the revolution arrested. Villere—or so his contemporary historian Bossu tells us—was killed in resisting arrest and fell pierced with Spanish bayonets. Judge Martin gives a different account of his death. It is sufficient perhaps to say that he died. But the others were brought before O'Reilly for questioning. They denied the jurisdiction of O'Reilly's court and argued that they had committed no act of insubordination against Spain, as Ulloa had never exhibited his powers. The tribunal, however, condemned Petit to imprisonment for life, Mazent and Doucet to imprisonment for ten years, Boisblanc, Jean Milhet, and Poupet to imprisonment for six years. They were taken to Morro Castle, Havana. Lefreniere, Noyan, his son-in-law and nephew of Bienville, Caresse, Marquis, and Joseph Milhet were condemned to death and ordered hanged. As no one could be found to act as hangman, the five men were shot by Spanish soldiers on October 25, 1769.

Of all the events in the history of New Orleans, this one is perhaps the most difficult to recount fairly and impartially. Fortier and Judge Martin are so bitter in their denunciations of "bloody O'Reilly" that it is hard to regard the matter in a dispassionate manner. Gayarré, whose account is by far the most reasonable, has been accused by the Creoles of favoring Spain! And even Gayarré denounces O'Reilly rather severely. There is no doubt that the execution stirred New Orleans more than any other event in its history. But it would be interesting to learn O'Reilly's point of view, aside from the terse documents in connection with the case. For, as Anatole France has said: "After all, we have never heard the devil's side of the story: God wrote all the books."

At any event, O'Reilly abolished the Superior Council and substituted a Cabildo, composed of six perpetual regidors, two ordinary alcades, an attorney-general-syndic, and a clerk. The Cabildo was directed by the governor in person. The laws of France were put aside and the laws of Spain substituted, and a number of ordinances were issued concerning the province of Louisiana and the city of New Orleans. He remained in office only a year, then returned to Spain. Aubry, who left the colony at the same time approximately, perished by shipwreck.

Don Luis de Unzaga succeeded O'Reilly as governor, and his administration, says Fortier, "was mild and paternal." In fact, this might be said of every Spanish governor who came after him. For New Orleans was well governed by the Spaniards. It was not long before the Spanish officers had married into the Creole families—which, oddly enough, the French officers had not done to any great degree—and French and Spanish blended into a pleasing Creolism. Unzaga's administration is remembered principally for the great tropical hurricane which swept over the city causing heavy damage, and causing havoc on the seacoast. It was during his administration that the War of the American Revolution began, and Unzaga gave aid to the American colonists by conniving at the purchase in New Orleans of arms and ammunition for the American forces.

There are some amusing old letters still extant which show rather clearly the attitude of the Spanish toward the French in New Orleans. The letters to which I refer were written by one Father Cirilo to the bishop of Havana, and they had to do with the so-called outrageous behavior of Father Dagobert, probably the best-loved priest in the old New Orleans. Father Cirilo had come with other Spanish priests to Louisiana. From his letters one would judge him

to be a man of austerity, and conventional to the last degree. He was frankly upset by the lax behavior which he
found in the colony. One wonders what he expected. But
he found Father Dagobert and the other priests living in
comfort and even luxury. They were men of simple manners
and good sense who had adapted themselves to the ways of
the city.

Father Dagobert was the Superior of the French
Capuchins of Louisiana, and the vicar-general of the dio-
cese. There had been a great row in 1755 between the
Jesuits and the Capuchins, and the quarrel ended with the
expulsion of the Jesuits from New Orleans. There are a
good many things about Father Dagobert which endear him
to us even after all of these years, and the very vitupera-
tions of the Spanish monks make him seem the jolliest of
good fellows. He lived comfortably and he dressed well.
He was round and fat and he hated trouble even more, it is
said, than he hated the devil. Nevertheless, he would help
any one who called upon him. He was a great trencherman,
and he liked good wine. He drank and was gay at christen-
ings and weddings. Some of the jokes that Father Dagobert is said to have told are still repeated in New Orleans.
He was popular with men and women alike, and he was
pious and jovial, or as one historian says, "He mingled
water with wine." He was very democratic and he would
eat at any table where a good dinner was served. His good
sense saved him from entering into the scheme of the colonists to resist Spanish rule, and in consequence he was undisturbed by the arrival of the Spanish rulers. However,
the hostile Spanish monks proved rather a thorn in his
side, but Father Dagobert's popularity in New Orleans was

such that public opinion was in his favor and the Spanish monks could do little toward ousting him.

His fame, it is said, had spread to Havana where he was spoken of as a "holy and influential ecclesiastic." It was said in Havana that he lived like a hermit, with fasting and prayer. It was rumored that he wore sackcloth, sprinkled ashes over his head and that he flagellated himself with appalling severity. The Spanish monks had heard these stories before they came to New Orleans, and they were scandalized beyond belief when they found him so fat, so sleek and so happy. Instead of being secluded from the world and its temptations they saw that he lived in a fine building, well furnished with comforts, and waited upon—oh, scandalous! —by handsome quadroons and mulatto women.

It was then that Father Cirilo, who had led the Spanish Capuchins to the scene of such scandal, wrote a series of letters to the bishop of Havana, whose spiritual jurisdiction extended over the colony. The Spanish priest is so very much in earnest, so outraged, so scandalized, and so vituperative, that his letters are full of unintentional humor. There are many of these letters still extant. The first is long and cunningly worded, in which he speaks of Father Dagobert in rather complimentary terms, but manages to make several innuendoes as to his moral laxity. But the letters reach their climax in the following, which I will quote here uncolored with any comment of mine:

Illustrious Sir—The evils by which we are surrounded compel us to expose the wicked actions which these monsters, rather than Capuchins, perpetrate against our persons, against God and His holy things. It is not my intention, most excellent sir, to trouble you with trifles; and therefore, with regard to what concerns ourselves, I shall

merely say that the very Spanish name is an object of abomination
to these friars, because they cannot even bear the sight of the things
which are of God and which appertain to our divine religion, because
these friars or monsters think that we have come to repress the abuses
which they love, and to reform their evil ways. Therefore they hate
us. . . . When they have bags full of dollars, we are obliged to have
recourse to our friends to relieve our necessities. . . . What is most
deplorable is to see in the convent the concubine of the friars, for
such is the reputation she bears. She has three sons, although who
her husband is God only knows. They eat at our table, and off the
plate of Father Dagobert, who, without shame, or fear of the world
at least, if not of God, permits them to call him papa. She is one of
the mulatresses who are kept in the house. She is the absolute mistress
of the establishment, and the friars have for her so much attachment
that they strive who shall send to the cherished paramour the best
dish on the table before any one else is allowed to taste it. . . .
There are, however, greater evils which afflict our hearts, and which
are the sins they clearly commit against God and His holy sacra-
ments. Baptism is administered without any of the ceremonies pre-
scribed by the Romish ritual; and the consecrated oil itself is impure
and stale. . . . As to the Eucharist, that mystery which makes
angels tremble with awe, we found that the sacramental elements
were so full of insects which fed upon them, and presented so dis-
gusting an appearance that we were obliged to fling them away, as if
they had been the veriest filth. So great is the detestable negligence of
these friars that I think they must be the disciples either of Luther or
Calvin. . . . You must also be made to know, most excellent sir,
that the Viaticum is not administered to the blacks, to the mulattoes, nor to the culprits who are sentenced to death; and having
asked Father Dagobert for the cause of it, he answered that it was to
establish a distinction between the whites and the blacks. Did you
ever hear a more cruel answer? . . . These priests also demean themselves in the choir, where they are seen stuffing their noses with tobacco, crossing one leg over the other, staring in all directions, and
moving the very angels to wrath. . . . The perversity of these men
is such that they are not content with being wicked themselves, but

they also wish us to follow their example, and to abstain from fasting and observing the holy days. As an excuse for their doings they say they are not Spaniards. . . . I can assure your grace that they spare no pains to make me like one of them, and to induce me to wear a shirt and stockings and to become as lax in my morals and habits as they are.

However, it is amusing to note that this quarrel petered out and nothing was done about it. The bishop of Havana in his replies put his finger upon the source of the trouble. "If you insist upon fighting among yourselves, what can I do?" the venerable bishop wrote back with rare good sense.

Unfortunately for us, we have no means of knowing whether the Spanish priests adapted themselves to the good-natured mode of life of Father Dagobert, or not, but this much we do know, that Father Dagobert did not change but remained until the end of his life jolly, good-natured, and tremendously popular.

In February, 1777, Don Bernardo de Galvez became governor, and his heroism and dramatic gallantry made the Spanish domination popular. Galvez was only twenty-one years old when he came to Louisiana. His father was viceroy of Mexico and his uncle president of the Council of the Indies. Galvez gave aid openly to the American Revolutionists. Their agent, Oliver Pollock, received from Galvez seventy thousand dollars to buy arms and ammunition. Spain declared war against Great Britain on May 8, 1779, and Galvez decided to lead the Creole forces himself against the English near-by. He left New Orleans at the head of an expedition, with a small fleet composed of one schooner and three gunboats and an army of 1400 men—a strange army made up of veterans, militiamen, eighty "free men of color," and 160 Indians. On September 21, he forced the English commander of the fort at Baton Rouge to surrender to him and took possession for Spain. Then he marched to Natchez and captured Fort Panmure. After that Galvez made an expedition against Mobile, which he captured on March 14. Determined to capture Pensacola, he went to Havana to obtain reïnforcements. On February 28, 1781, he returned, says Martin, "with a man-of-war, two frigates, and several transports, on board of which were fourteen hundred and fifteen soldiers, a competent train of artillery and abundance of ammunition." The fleet was commanded by Don Joseph Cabro de Jrazabal. The English commander capitulated on May 9, and by this capitulation the province of West Florida was acquired by Spain.

In August, 1780, Louisiana suffered another hurricane. There were inundations by the Mississippi, and New Orleans was damaged badly. A new difficulty presented itself. English trade had been driven from the river and the colony suffered in consequence. Galvez, according to Gayarré, "had recommended that Louisiana be granted the privilege of free trade with all the ports of Europe and America. But neither the court of Madrid, nor the spirit of the age, was disposed to go so far."

Galvez—a Spaniard—is surely one of the most romantic figures in the history of New Orleans. He married a Creole girl, won a series of brilliant victories, and became the most popular man of his time in the colony. His conquests were so highly appreciated in Spain that he was made lieutenant-general, and in 1785 he was made captain-general of the island of Cuba, of the province of Louisiana, and of the two Floridas. Later in the same year he succeeded his father as viceroy of Mexico, where he died in 1794, at the age of thirty-eight.

Chapter XIV

A CHANGING WORLD

RESTLESSNESS was beginning to make itself felt throughout
the American Continent; old barriers were going down before the surging tide of men; old borders were disappearing
to be replaced by new ones farther on. Men were pressing
on and out and westward; an urge as strong and as inevitable as the current of the Mississippi was drawing men
southward toward the sea.

Men of many nations were drifting with the tide to
Louisiana. A group of Canary Islanders—or *Islenos* as they
were called—had followed Galvez to New Orleans. They
settled near-by, in the country adjoining the city. They were
fishermen, hunters, trappers. Their descendants remain to-
day in Saint Bernard Parish, adjacent to New Orleans, in a
country which is still the richest fur-trapping region in the
world.

In 1765 the first shiploads of Acadians, exiled from
their homes in Nova Scotia, arrived at the New Orleans
levee. These were simple farming people, of French origin.

They remained in New Orleans for a time, but soon moved on, going along the bayous toward the north and west. They brought their language and their customs with them; their simplicity of manner was in strong contrast with the complexity of the Creole. The Acadian was not a lover of cities, and he found the rich, fertile lands of southwest Louisiana more to his taste. Settlements were made along Bayou Teche and Bayou Lafourche, and in the Attakapas country west of New Orleans. In 1785 more Acadians joined them. They were a prolific people, and the families grew with astonishing rapidity. To-day their descendants number approximately one hundred thousand. The land along Bayou Teche is still known as "the Evangeline country" or "the Acadian country."

From the Atlantic seaboard, from Kentucky and other lands on the Mississippi and on the tributaries of the Mississippi, men were moving toward the south. More and more flatboats were drifting with the river's current, to find a final resting-place along the levee at New Orleans. The country was filling up.

In 1785 Don Estevan Miro succeeded Galvez as governor, civil and military, of Louisiana and West Florida. It was during Miro's administration that the growing power of the United States began to alarm the Creoles. Despite all efforts to stop the Americans, it was not many years before the entire Mississippi, from its source to its mouth, was an American stream. Behind its levees, Spanish New Orleans sat watching the American vessels sail southward to the Mexican Gulf.

On March 21, 1788, the city of New Orleans was destroyed by fire. Constructed almost entirely of wood, it burned like a flaming torch. Because it was Good Friday, the Capuchin priests refused to allow the church bells to ring a warning to the populace—consequently, before enough men gathered to offer real help, the fire was beyond all control. Square after square was razed.

Everything went before the blaze: the government houses, the jails, the residences, the business section, the church; and, with fine irony, the monastery of the Capuchins who had refused to sound the bells. Only a row of houses along the levee escaped. The Ursuline Convent was of brick and tile, set far back in its walled garden—and "by a miracle" (according to the convent records) it was spared.

The city that fell before the flames was a congested French community of wooden houses, badly arranged and irregular. A stately Spanish city rose in its stead. When the rebuilding began, Spanish architects and builders played their part in its construction. The city which rose from its ashes was of brick and plaster, with arches of heavy masonry and roofs of tile. There were barred windows and long, dark corridors. Large fan-shaped windows looked down into courtyards which held banana trees, oleanders, and parterres of flowers. Houses were built flush with the sidewalks, or *banquettes;* and balconies, railed with delicate wrought iron, overhung the streets. The Vieux Carré, or "French Quarter" of to-day, is that Spanish city which rose from the ashes of the French New Orleans.

A census taken the year of the fire shows that more than five thousand people had been living in the burned area. The population of the province is given at 42,611.

And now into the history of New Orleans comes the

ST. LOUIS CATHEDRAL FROM JACKSON SQUARE

SLAVE QUARTERS OF THE VIEUX CARRÉ

name of Don Andres Almonaster y Roxas, an Andalusian
of noble birth, and the richest man in the colony. Standing
amid the smouldering ruins of the city he pledged to build
a church for the colony, to rebuild the hospital, and to erect
a new Cabildo, and a monastery for the Capuchins. And so
these structures came into being—the same three buildings
which face Jackson Square to-day, their façades crumbling
under the touch of time. It is true that certain renovations
were made in 1850—mansard roofs were added to the flat-
topped buildings which flanked the Cathedral—and a cen-
tral spire was added to the church of St. Louis. But the
buildings that we see to-day are the same that Don Almonaster gazed upon so proudly in 1795, when they were completed and opened to the public. And even now, should you
care to go at twilight on Saturday afternoon, you may hear
one of the "perpetual masses" which the priests of the
church of St. Louis promised to offer each week "forever"
for the repose of his soul. Don Almonaster is buried near
the altar in the Cathedral.

The two red-brick structures which flank the Place
d'Armes on the north and south were built by Don Almonaster's daughter, the Baroness Pontalba, fifty years later.
At the time of their building they were the only apartment
houses in the United States.

But to return to the affairs of New Orleans in the year
of the fire. . . .

Charles III had died in Spain and Charles IV, a weak
and incompetent king, had succeeded him. Soon after his
accession, Father Antonio de Sedella was sent by his
spiritual superiors to Louisiana as a representative of the
Holy Roman Inquisition, with the purpose of introducing

the Tribunal. Our historians tell us that Governor Miro, however, had determined that the Inquisition should not be established in New Orleans; and at night caused his soldiers to arrest Father Antonio, put him aboard a vessel and ship him back to Spain. "Thus," says Fortier, "did Louisiana escape the horrors of Inquisition."

And yet. . . .

When the old Calaboose or jail which stands near the church was destroyed many years later, strange things came to light. There were found secret rooms, iron instruments of torture, and other indications that a private court had held meetings there. These things were never explained satisfactorily. In addition to this, old newspaper files tell of the discovery of an underground passage which led from the rear of the Cathedral, or from even beyond that point in the direction of the Capuchin monastery—a passage which ended somewhere under the Calaboose. These newspaper accounts are very strange. One day the paper tells of the discovery and promises further disclosures on the following day, when the tunnel has been explored. But it is evident that some pressure was brought to bear on the editor, for there is not a line in any of the later editions of the same paper regarding this discovery. One can only draw his own conclusions.

At any rate, there is no official record of an Inquisition in Louisiana.

In 1791 an insurrection of negroes broke at Santo Domingo, and many people of wealth and distinction became *émigrés* to New Orleans. This was a highly civilized, somewhat decadent, brilliant group of men and women; and they brought with them their civilization, their charm, their intelligence—and their vices. Some of them opened schools, some taught dancing or music; a troupe of comedians from Cape Françoise opened a theater in New Orleans. The city became gayer and more frivolous than before. Among this group were some famous men, and many of the *émigrés* were titled personages. They soon formed a sort of society of their own and exerted an influence in the social life of the city.

In the same year Miro returned to Spain and was replaced by the Baron de Carondelet.

The great events of the French Revolution were finding an echo in New Orleans. The Creoles became filled with the fire of patriotism, and there were cries of "Liberté!" in the theaters and other public places. When the news of the execution of Louis XVI reached New Orleans there were open manifestations of excitement. Governor Carondelet, in order to quell what he feared would become a dangerous uprising, had six ringleaders arrested and imprisoned for a year in Havana. Then, in order to guard against any insurrection or foreign attacks, Carondelet proceeded to fortify the city. A wall of masonry was built around the original parallelogram of the Vieux Carré, and a moat was dug outside the wall. Forts were erected at the corners, two facing the river and two facing the swamp back of the town. Congo Square and the cemetery were left outside of the fortifications, beyond the ramparts.

What Carondelet really feared was an American invasion, and in order to offset this he made various treaties with the Indians in the vicinity, including the Chickasaws, the Creeks, the Talapouches, the Cherokees, and the Alibamons. He estimated that he could marshal a force of twenty thousand Indians to fight with his Spanish troops against the Americans.

In 1794 the first newspaper was published in New Orleans—"Le Moniteur de la Louisiane." New ideas were penetrating into the colony. French Jacobins in Philadelphia circulated in Louisiana an address in which the colonists were urged to establish an independent government. At the same time the French minister to the United States, Genet, endeavored to prepare an expedition in the West, against Spanish possessions. George Washington, however, frustrated Genet's schemes, and Carondelet began again his intrigues to separate the West from the United States.

However, the year 1794 is remembered for another reason in Louisiana, for it was that year that marked the cultivation of sugar-cane by Etienne de Boré, whose plantation was at the spot where Audubon Park is to-day—then miles away from the city along the river road.

In one of the opening chapters of this book we have seen a quotation from Iberville's diary relative to his attempt to plant sugar-cane he had brought from Martinique, but it was not until 1751 that the Jesuits managed to produce a successful crop on their plantation, south of the city. Two planters, Mendez and Solis of Terre-aux-Bœufs, were the first to cultivate it on a large scale. They made a syrup from the juice and an alcoholic beverage called *taffia*. Now, in 1794, the indigo plant had been attacked by an insect pest, so the principal crop of the colonists failed. Etienne de Boré resolved to undertake to cultivate cane for the manufacture of sugar. His friends attempted to dissuade him from the enterprise, but he persevered, and in 1795 made a crop of sugar which brought twelve thousand dollars. After his success, sugar-cane was cultivated extensively and is still the staple crop of the state.

Carondelet was succeeded in 1797 by Don Manuel Gayoso de Lemos, who died two years later. It was in his time that New Orleans was becoming increasingly rich and increasingly gay. Stories of that Golden Age of Spanish society still persist, for it was in 1798 that the Duke of Orleans visited Louisiana. He was accompanied by his brother, the Duke of Montpensier, and the Count of Beaujolais. These princes were then in exile, and no one could have predicted that the Duke of Orleans, who was a fugitive from his country at that time, would become King Louis Philippe in 1830. In New Orleans these boys were entertained most extravagantly. They remained for some time with the Marigny family at their plantation just outside the city wall, where Elysian Fields Avenue ends at the levee and the Mississippi River. Fortunes were spent in lavish balls and dinners given in their honor. The visit is without historical significance, but it affords another view of the social life of the time.

Casa Calvo was governor of the province from 1799 to 1801 and Salcedo was governor from 1801 to 1803.

Chapter XV

PERHAPS IT WAS LIKE THIS

IT is pleasant to think of New Orleans on a Sunday morning in spring toward the end of the eighteenth century, for it was then like a part of old Spain.

At the convent near the river bank, black-robed nuns are counting their beads in the high-walled garden; others pass with quiet steps over the worn door sill, and climb the dim stairs. One hears the sleepy sound of children's voices droning pious verses in unison; the cooing of pigeons under the eaves, and the click of their red claws on the tiles. . . .

Outside the grilled gateway, negro slaves pass by in the narrow street on their way to market in the plaza, negroes black and half naked, bearing upon their heads baskets piled with purple figs. . . . Silk-clad gentlewomen, with downcast eyes, walk under the sycamores and across the sunburned grass of the Place d'Armes on their way to the church of San Luis. The twin spires are sharp in the clear air; and on the flat roof of the Cabildo next door, yucca is growing in many squat wine jars, the leaves dark and jagged against the sky.

From within the church comes the sound of a priest's voice chanting; and through the arched doorway one can see the sunlight pouring in at a Gothic window, turning the dull stone floor into strips of yellow, red, and blue. A thin priest with black eyes stands motionless, his porcellaneous Spanish hands stretched stiffly into a gesture which accompanies the Mass. The odor of incense is heavy in the air.

Afternoon. An old house, close-shuttered against prying eyes. Within the dim rooms are high-backed chairs covered in dark leather, standing against vermilion brocade and gilded panels. Beyond, in the sunlit court behind the house, an old man dressed in tabbied silk sits writing with a quill at a table in the shadow of an orange tree.

Twilight comes and lanterns are lit in the town. The twanging of guitars comes from the cabarets; a man's voice is heard singing a song of the *toros*.

Before long the *zoom-zoom* of the tom-toms is heard in Congo Square, as hour after hour the sweating negroes dance—a dance as old as Africa itself.

And later still, the sound of singing in the streets as revelers are returning home. Then quiet again, and the voice of the watchman crying out the hours, and calling the message that all is well.

Yes, they say it was like this. . . .

On week-days the clang of hammer on anvil comes from the smithies of the king, as slaves beat out the iron-work for a grill above the door of the Cabildo. The sound of mallet strokes is heard in Royal Street, where mansions are rising to replace the wooden houses destroyed by fire. Brick walls rise, with wooden scaffolding rising beside them; unbroken walls of houses, filling the squares from end to end. Within the courtyards there is the smell of damp plaster, and of cedar and cypress wood. Black hands move to and fro, guiding the clumsy plane; and clean-smelling shavings curl and fall to the ground.

Smoke is rising above the brick-yards, there by the levee. Men are astir.

But from the Calabozo come muffled screams of agony, as Temba the hunter is stretched upon the rack in order that he may be made to confess the murder of his master. Lean Spaniards, wearing brocade and velvet, sit in the Council Chamber waiting for the slave to tell what he knows. Pain will break his spirit before long. When he confesses, there will be more torture, and at last his head will be stuck up on a pole at the Tchoupitoulas gate.

Near-by in the Place d'Armes, Creole children crowd around a puppet show—a marvelous toy which has come from Spain for their amusement. The small figures move their arms and legs stiffly as they dance, and above them the puppet-master's fingers dance too, as a youth with limpid eyes plays a gavotte on a sweet-toned violin. A priest comes by, through the checkered shade, looks for a moment at the peep-show, and pauses to pat the little boys on their heads: "You like the marionettes, my chickens?"

He smiles, but his heart is heavy. He is on his way to tell a quadroon mother that her daughter cannot be buried from the church. She has committed suicide—a sin against the Holy Ghost—because her lover has taken a younger mistress. She was a pretty wench too, and nearly white.

What a fool! As if there were not many men in the world. She lies dead to-day in a room where candles burn, yet just last night she danced at the quadroon ball, her high, red heels clicking on the polished floor: "Dansez Calinda! Badoum! Badoum!"

The priest pats the children's heads as he goes by: "That is right, enjoy yourselves, my lambs!"

The marionettes dance, the violin squeals in ecstasy and the children clap their hands.

From the Calabozo the cries of Temba can be heard no longer.

Perhaps it was like this. . . .

Chapter XVI

THE AMERICANS COME

IT is not my intention to discuss the Louisiana Purchase here. Any history of the United States will give the whole story. It is sufficient to say that in 1800, by treaty of St. Ildephonso, Louisiana passed back into the hands of France, and that Napoleon promptly sold the province to the United States.

On November 30, 1803, Laussat received the keys of New Orleans from the Spanish commissioners, Salcedo and Casa Calvo, and was put in possession of the province. On December 20, 1803, Louisiana was formally transferred to the United States by General Wilkinson and W. C. C. Claiborne, the commissioners appointed by President Jefferson. The transfer took place on the balcony of the Cabildo, overlooking the Place d'Armes. New Orleans was now, officially at least, an American city.

Old style American histories have a way of conveying the idea that any province acquired by the United States must, necessarily, be overjoyed with such a consummation.

As a matter of fact the day of the transfer of Louisiana to the United States was a day of mourning in New Orleans. And it is easy enough to understand this.

New Orleans was a city which considered itself highly civilized. At the time of the transfer, it was nearly a century old and it was exclusively Spanish and French. The Creoles did not know what to expect of the Americans—and they expected the worst. It must be remembered that New Orleans had taken no part in the American Revolution—unless the exploits of Galvez might, by some stretch of the imagination, be classed as a struggle for freedom, which of course it was not, but a conquest of British territory for Spain. It must be remembered, too, that in New Orleans the word "American" was synonymous with "barbarian," and the only Americans with which the Creoles were familiar were the flatboatmen who came down the river with their cargoes. The majority of these flatboatmen were a rough lot, men who boasted that they were "half-alligator and half-horse"; men who, while in New Orleans, gave endless trouble to the police and to the public in general; men who fought with the city guards, got drunk in the cabarets, and forced themselves into places where they were not wanted; men who spoke an alien tongue and who with their rough and uncouth manner, seemed barbarous to the Creoles.

This was the general impression. Of course there had been American visitors whom the Creoles had met and liked; and some of the Creoles had visited American cities. But these were the exceptions. The general feeling was that New Orleans had been handed over to the vandals.

There was, for a time, great hostility between American and Creole. Luckily, the Americans came but slowly to the colony at first and did not mix with the Creoles to any great extent. American women were snubbed by the Creole women, and accordingly the Americans set up a society of their own. They even built themselves a city, eventually, beyond the boundaries of the Vieux Carré. There are traces of this early American city left in the "garden district" of New Orleans, the section some squares above Canal Street. At the time of the American occupation, this section came to be known as Faubourg Ste. Marie. The boundary line was the city moat—the great ditch which gave Canal Street its name.

From some of the letters and diaries which I have read, the first Americans found the Creoles somewhat like the definition of the French people in an old history that I was unfortunate enough to study when a child. "The French," my history told me, "are a gay people, fond of dancing and light wines." Even as a child I had a vague suspicion that there must be more than that to be said for the French people. And it may be that the first American families in New Orleans really thought better of the Creoles than that. But it is certain there was a marked hostility—at first, at least.

The thing that the Americans seemed to resent most was a certain pagan spirit in the Creoles, and lest I be misunderstood, let me say quickly that the Creoles are most devout, that they are all good Catholics and that they remain so to-day. By "pagan" I mean something else entirely; I mean that the people of New Orleans seemed to believe in the philosophy: "Eat, drink and be merry, for to-morrow you die." They were a people given to

THE PONTABLA BUILDINGS ON
JACKSON SQUARE

MADAME JOHN'S LEGACY, DUMAINE STREET

merrymaking and laughter; they liked feast days and
fêtes. Among themselves they joked continually. They
liked to eat, to drink, to dance. They lived luxuriously. And
they seemed careless of the morrow.

Now with the two contending forces—snobbishness on
the part of the Creole and intolerance on the part of the
puritanical Americans—there was immediate discord.

Ah, but wait! Another thing entered in—a thing that
took the American unawares. This was the semi-tropical
climate of New Orleans. Louisiana is a fertile land where
a living is easily made. It is warm nine months in the year.
And there seems to be a certain insidious chemical sub-
stance in the atmosphere which tends to destroy puritanism.

The fusion came slowly, but slowly differences were
adjusted. Business—a mutual desire to make money—
brought the American and the Creole together. The
American was shrewder, and usually won in the end; the
Creole was better at a bargain perhaps, but he could not
match wits with the cold calculation of the Yankee. And
gradually the Americans became richer, while the Creoles
became poorer.

Well, we all know what happens in that case, and
though the shoe pinches, it must be worn. It was not long
before the Creole mothers were anxious that their
daughters marry the rich Americans, and more than one
impoverished Creole lad exchanged his aristocratic name
for good American dollars.

There were other things which brought the Creole and
the American together, common enemies of both: inundations by the Mississippi, hurricanes, plagues of yellow
fever and cholera. And not twelve years after the Louisi-

ana Purchase we find the Creole and the American united on the plains of Chalmette under the leadership of General Andrew Jackson, with Great Britain as the common enemy.

And it was not only the Creoles and the English-speaking citizens of New Orleans who gathered there. With them were companies of lean Kentuckians, men who had come down the river aboard flatboats, each with his rifle in the crook of his arm—men who had come to help protect Creole New Orleans because Louisiana was now a part of their United States. From the streams and bayous of inland Louisiana came the bronzed Acadians, to take their places in the line. Down the levee from the German Coast trudged the descendants of those flaxen-haired pioneers who had come to America a hundred years before. Companies of negroes—"free men of color"—came bearing arms, and took their places quietly, ready to do their part. Surely a strange group of men these were, gathering there under the oaks at Chalmette. But it was a group no longer merely French or Spanish, or a mixture of the two. Here was America! And as Americans they fought, shoulder to shoulder. The British outnumbered the American forces two to one, but the British were defeated with terrible slaughter. It was the last battle of "The War of 1812."

Ironically enough, it was a needless battle, for England had capitulated to the United States before the battle was fought on January 8, 1815. Nevertheless, it served a purpose; afterward there was respect at least between American and Creole.

And now, in time of peace, an endless stream of men came swarming down the river, and overland to New

Orleans. The full force of the westward movement in the United States was sweeping across the continent. Steamboats appeared upon the Mississippi. The population of New Orleans tripled in ten years. Trade boomed. The gaudy days were beginning.

• PART III • GAUDY DAYS •

Chapter XVII

SETTING THE SCENE

BY 1825 New Orleans had reached its most picturesque period.

More than a hundred years before, at the time of the city's founding, John Law's followers had described it as a place of tropical luxury. Now, a century later, the same tales were being told again—but the tales were told to Americans now, to men living in New England and along the Atlantic seaboard. And now the stories were true.

For here was indeed a strange city, a city that had been first French, then Spanish, and which was now Creole, a blending of both. Here in an atmosphere of the Old World lived rich and cultured men and women; here was a community which was indeed luxurious, with its opera, its theater, music, balls, its gambling, its bull-fights, and its circus; a city of men who inherited the Latin traits of both nations—fiery men who loved pleasure, men who lived for excitement, men who enjoyed any game that stirred the senses.

Opposed to the Creoles were the Americans; for many English-speaking men had come to Louisiana since 1803. It was the marked contrast between them which makes New Orleans so picturesque at this time; for the American was as unlike the Creole as red is unlike green. It was many years before red and green blended into a more somber tone.

The streets there were not paved in the middle of the road, but had sidewalks, or *banquettes* as the Creoles say, of brick—narrow walks which clung close to the façades of the brick and plaster houses. In many places *banquettes* were protected from the rain and sun by overhanging balconies railed with wrought iron. Between sidewalk and road were deep ditches, lined with cypress wood. Water stood in these ditches at all times. Dirt, trash, sewage was dumped into the drains in front of the houses. These open gutters were cleaned every day by the prisoners from the jails—mostly runaway negro slaves—who did their work in gangs under the whip of the white guard, negroes who dragged heavy iron chains after them, and who frequently were further loaded with iron collars.

Although nearly every courtyard boasted of a well, the water was unfit to drink, and drinking water was brought from the river and sold in barrels from wagons in the streets. The water was then poured into large jars in the courtyards, and filtered or cleared with alum and charcoal. Many of the courts had long lines of jars, resembling those in which Ali Baba's Forty Thieves lay hidden. From these jars the slaves dipped the drinking water in buckets.

All of the buildings were constructed of brick covered with stucco; the roofs were covered with slate or tile. All houses were built without cellars as the dampness of the ground prohibited underground rooms. One Creole who admired the fine houses he had seen in Philadelphia had an excavation made for a cellar but was forced to fill it up again, as water seeped in and made his house damp.

A steam ferry-boat crossed and recrossed the river from the levee beside the French Market. On the opposite shore were shipbuilding yards.

The incorporated portion of the city now embraced the suburbs—St. Mary (the American section) above and Marigny below. A City Council had been formed and had passed many ordinances to preserve law and order. At night the city was guarded by fifty men. They patrolled in groups of twos and threes, with lanterns. One of the requirements, found in an old ordinance for 1825, was that these night watchmen be able to speak both French and English.

A visitor from Philadelphia, who came to New Orleans in 1822, wrote of the excellent system of lighting the streets. On every corner, he said, swung a large oil lamp, which was lighted before sunset, and which remained lighted through the night, "unless put out by heavy rain." In some of the old buildings in the Vieux Carré, one may still observe the heavy iron hooks driven in the angles of houses diagonally opposite. From these hooks, in 1822, hung the chains which supported these oil lamps. This municipal lighting was maintained by a special "chimney tax"—every property owner was taxed one dollar a year for each chimney on his house.

A cannon was fired at eight o'clock on winter nights and at nine o'clock in summer as a signal for all sailors, soldiers, and negroes to get off the streets, and all such persons found abroad after the cannon fire—unless bearing a "pass" from their employers or masters—were taken to the Calaboose or city prison. The cannon was a signal for groceries and taverns to be closed. Those who went about at night were usually accompanied by a slave, carrying a lantern.

More than 40,000 people were numbered in the census of the city for 1822, and during the winter months there was a large increase in population. The French theater was tremendously popular, the opera drew large crowds. Then, too, there were the great balls. So rich and luxurious had the city become that these balls were magnificent and elaborate. The Creoles, still scorning the Americans, were beginning to feel social competition, and their public entertainments were unusually lavish. Then, too, there were balls of another sort—those entertainments spoken of in a whisper, but entertainments which were as colorful as any ever held in New Orleans. So important they became and so much trouble they caused that I must devote a chapter to them. The entertainments to which I refer were the famous—or notorious—Quadroon balls in the old Orleans Theater and Ballroom.

Chapter XVIII

THE RIVER

AND always, just beyond the levee, the Mississippi flowing by on its eternal way.

Along the river front, for nearly two miles, moored to the heavy timbers embedded in the batture lay the shipping. There were blunt-bowed trading brigs from the ports of Europe, coasting craft from New England, New York, Baltimore, and Philadelphia; there were heavy Indiamen, smaller craft from the Antilles—fleets of flatboats from up the river, and already a dozen or more Mississippi river steamboats, the latest development in American navigation.

From Europe and New England to the New Orleans levee came cotton and woolen goods, furniture, farming implements, the crude machinery of a new age, iron billets for the foundries, liquors, coffee, and spices, bound for plantations and towns of Louisiana and Mississippi and all the ports up the great river. The whole waterfront was astir. Negroes sang as they toiled, rolling the hogsheads, carrying the bales. Downstream came hemp, tobacco, flour, hoop-poles, staves, sugar—and the first bales of cotton, the beginning of the great cotton industry which was to develop before many years had passed. Downstream from St. Louis came the important shipments of furs, destined for the markets of fashion-making Europe.

Along the levee swarmed the seamen of a dozen nations, and among them the American river men, sons of the pioneers of an earlier generation; men who manned the flatboats that handled for nearly half a century the traffic of the heart of the continent.

They were a hard-living, fearless, reckless tribe, tall and lean; men whose fathers had carried rifles over the Wilderness Trail, and whose forefathers had crossed the seas from the British Isles. Their home-loving kinsmen were tilling the farms of Ohio, Indiana, and Illinois, farms of parts of Kentucky and Tennessee.

Here and there among them were men of a different class, sons of the planters of Virginia, the Carolinas, and Maryland, who had come overland or by boat, with slaves and oxen and planting outfit, to enter the rich lands along the Southern rivers. These men, too, were of the Anglo-Saxon-Celtic strain.

The full tide of emigration from the older American states that had swept into the valley of the Ohio in the thirty years following the Revolution, pressed on and out, southward and northward from the mouth of the Ohio.

Plantations were being opened in the delta of the Yazoo-Mississippi. Trading posts were established up the Arkansas and the White rivers. Farms dotted the shores of the Red River and the Ouachita. Memphis was a village. Vicks' Plantation was a settlement at the mouth of the

Yazoo—later it was to develop into the city of Vicksburg. Natchez was a rich and thriving city, the capital of Mississippi not far away.

Baton Rouge and Bayou Sara were river ports of thrifty neighborhoods. And along the river, from Baton Rouge south to the Gulf, the country was dotted with vast plantations—plantations with great white-columned houses and wide fields, with negro cabins in a long line behind the large house of the planter. There were orange groves, and vast fields of sugar-cane; there were cotton fields and acres of billowing corn. Levees had been thrown up along the Mississippi south from the bluffs of Baton Rouge, and the stretch of country from New Orleans to Natchez was as rich and as productive as any in the world. Fortunes were in the making. Flush times were coming. The country was filling up.

Steamboats—crude enough as yet, the great floating palaces were to come later—plied from New Orleans to St. Louis, to Louisville, to Pittsburg. Rapidly they were taking the place of flatboats. But still great numbers of these gigantic rafts floated down the river, bringing their cargoes to the levee at New Orleans. The crews of these flatboats—the rough and tumble American male, red of shirt and bronzed of face—lingered on the levee to drink and to fight, to terrorize the negroes and to get gloriously drunk, there in New Orleans which they called "The City of Sin." And how they liked this sinful city! And how they scattered their hard-earned dollars in a debauch which lasted but a single night. Then, penniless perhaps, they would strike out again along the overland trail which took them through hundreds of miles of forest and home again.

There were some river men, of course, who were more
prudent, and who saved enough money to pay their passage
back aboard a steamboat, or returned by keelboat, slowly
and laboriously, up the river. Others took sailing vessels
and returned through the river's mouth, up the Atlantic
seaboard and to some eastern port.

Outside the old city of the Creoles was the American
section, with its shipping offices, the chandlery stores, the
warehouses, where the new business between the interior
and the overseas markets was transacted by these new-
coming Americans. The names above the doors of these
establishments were the names which were found on like
signs in the ports of the Atlantic coast, for the shipping
folk of New England and Baltimore had begun to think
of New Orleans as a gateway to the continent and were
quick to seize the opportunity for making a fortune.

A new city was growing up about, and outside, the old
walled city of *Nouvelle Orléans*—a bustling, thriving city.
And yet, down in those narrow streets of the Vieux Carré,
the old life went on as usual. Plantation owners, city
tradesmen, notaries, hotel-keepers, lawyers, and priests
went on their placid way. French was still spoken there,
almost exclusively.

Chapter XIX

THE QUADROON BALLS

IF one stands just back of the St. Louis Cathedral and looks along Orleans Street, he will see, not half a square away, a long gray building with faded green window blinds, a building with a portico which extends over the sidewalk before the doorway; an austere structure surmounted by a cross. This is the Convent of the Holy Family, an order of negro nuns. Here they conduct an orphanage and school for negro children. Rather, let us say, for mulatto children—for a black child among them is rare indeed.

This building is within a stone's throw of the Cathedral. I use the hackneyed phrase with intention; for it was not so long ago, one Sunday morning, that I saw red-robed acolytes outside the Cathedral door, amusing themselves by throwing pebbles along Orleans Street. And as I watched, with careless eye, a pebble struck one of those half-bowed green shutters of the convent, bounded off and fell into the street. There was, of course, nothing remarkable in that. But suddenly the phrase, "within a stone's throw," came into my mind, with all that the phrase implied. For in the old days, the convent was a wing of the Orleans Theater—the wing which held the ball-room in which the quadroon balls took place.

How incredible that seems to-day! In the old days, the priests who lived next to the Cathedral must have heard the scraping of the fiddles when a dance was in progress. "Dansez Calinda! Badoum! Badoum!"

And how typical this is of the old New Orleans! I mean the proximity of the two buildings: for in one, men knelt in order to pray forgiveness for sins, committed in the other. Surely the quadroon balls were the most extravagant outcropping of an exotic city.

Those days seem fabulous now. But it must be remembered that New Orleans was not an American city then. It was as truly a part of the Old World as though it had been on another continent. And it may be well to remember, also, that the end of the eighteenth and the first part of the nineteenth centuries were not famous for a "high moral tone." Morality came into fashion with Queen Victoria.

Before I describe these entertainments, let me try to tell a little of the social life of the time.

The ladies of New Orleans were for the greater part convent bred; that is, the daughters of the wealthier families were educated by the Ursuline nuns. These girls learned to read and sew, to "enter a room gracefully," and they attained many other pretty social accomplishments. Among other things, every young lady was "a finished musician." Just how far their musicianship went, it is difficult to say, but it is certain that they attempted to play

MISSISSIPPI STEAMBOATS LOAD ALONG
THE LEVEE

BEAUTIFUL OLD HOUSES BY
ST. ANTHONY'S GARDEN

pretentious things. There are many old bound volumes of music in the second-hand book-stores of New Orleans which attest that the girls labored over "Variations from The Operas" and "The Grand March of Napoleon." It was in the convent that these ladies learned all that was thought necessary for them to know about life—and their "innocence" was proverbial.

A little later we find the young gentlemen referring to them as "fair females" and "frail flowers of pure Southern womanhood" (whatever *that* may mean). These were the girls whom the young Creoles married—eventually. Usually the young ladies were placed, so to speak, upon pedestals and left there, while the young gentlemen amused themselves in other quarters. Now a pedestal is a safe place to keep a woman, for she gives very little trouble perched high in this graceful, if somewhat constrained position. Woman's only business was matrimony. And the whispers that these priceless jewels of innocence heard relative to the amusements of their *fiancés* and brothers must have seemed mysterious indeed.

Well, as we have said, these were the young ladies who went out in society, who were chaperoned within an inch of their lives, and who made good marriages when they could. We never hear of the "innocence of young Southern manhood." And from the stories repeated sometimes by old gentlemen, it is safe to say that our great grandfathers had a good time.

From the very beginning there had been "free people of color" in New Orleans. Their origin is explained in various ways. In those first far-off days when there were no white women in the colony, there were numerous mulatto children born to negro slave-women. In some instances their fathers protected these children from becoming slaves by setting the mother free. The children's fortunes were the mothers' fortunes. There were laws in the colony prohibiting white men marrying negro women, and also laws prohibiting white men from living with negro women. Well, we all know something of prohibitions. I shall not go into the matter except to say that a great many mulatto children were born. In addition, there came many "free people of color" from the West Indian islands. Very early we find these free mulattoes with a society of their own—a society neither white nor black, but between the two. In generations which followed, more white blood came into these mulatto families. Many gradations of color resulted; mulatto, quadroon, octaroon, *griffe*—each one a little lighter than the last. The free men of color are always in the background; to use the Southern phrase, "they knew their place." But the women were said to dress elegantly, and in the theaters—where they sat in the balcony and upper boxes—their toilettes sometimes put the costumes of the white ladies to shame. So great became the beauty and the luxury of these women, that in 1788 Governor Miro passed an ordinance which is one of the most extraordinary documents on file in Louisiana. The directory of that year shows fifteen hundred "unmarried women of color, all free, living in little houses near the ramparts," and Governor Miro's ordinance makes it "an evidence of misconduct" if one of these women walks abroad in silk, jewels, or "plumes," and by so doing the woman is "liable for punishment." The only head-covering which the ordinance allows them is the madras handkerchief or *tignon*.

Now it must not be assumed that these women were prostitutes—they were not. They were reared in chastity, and they were as well educated as the times would permit. These were for the greater part the illegitimate daughters of white men and their quadroon mistresses. They were "free women"—not slaves. Their chastity was their chief stock in trade, in addition to their beauty. Their mothers watched them as hawks watch chickens, accompanied them to the balls where only white men were admitted, and did not relinquish their chaperonage until the daughter found a suitable "protector." The protector was usually a young Creole gentleman with enough money to support the quadroon girl in fitting style. The "little houses along the ramparts" were not houses of ill-fame, but domiciles of these women and the white men who "protected" them. And the women were proverbially faithful, just as the young white girls of the colony were proverbially innocent. For the quadroon girl's future depended upon pleasing the man with whom she lived. Sometimes these liaisons lasted for years —occasionally for life. But more often than not they were broken off when the young man married.

Harriet Martineau, in her book, "Society in America," published in 1837, writes her impression of the situation in New Orleans:

The quadroon connections in New Orleans are all but universal, as I was assured on the spot by ladies who cannot be mistaken. The history of such connections is a melancholy one: but it ought to be made known while there are any who boast of the superior morals of New Orleans, on account of the decent quietness of the streets and theaters.

The quadroon girls of New Orleans are brought up by their

mothers to be what they have been; the mistresses of white gentlemen. The boys are some of them sent to France; some placed on land in the back of the State. . . . They marry women of a somewhat darker color than their own; the women of their own color objecting to them, *"ils sont si dégoûtants!"* The girls are highly educated, externally, and are, probably, as beautiful and accomplished a set of women as can be found. Every young man early selects one, and establishes her in one of those pretty and peculiar houses, whole rows of which may be seen in the Ramparts. The connection now and then lasts for life; usually for several years. In the latter case, when the time comes for the gentleman to take a white wife, the dreadful news reaches his quadroon partner, either by letter entitling her to call the house and furniture her own, or by the newspaper which announces the marriage. The quadroon women are rarely known to form a second connection. Many commit suicide; more died broken-hearted. Some men continue the connection after marriage. Every quadroon woman believes that her partner will prove an exception to the rule of desertion. Every white lady believes that her husband has been an exception to the rule of seduction.

What security for domestic purity and peace there can be where every man has had two connections, one of which must be concealed; and two families, whose existence must not be known to each other; where the conjugal relation begins in treachery, and must be carried on with a heavy secret in the husband's breast, no words are needed to explain. If this is the system which is boasted of as a purer than ordinary state of morals, what is to be thought of the ordinary state? It can only be hoped that the boast is an empty one.

The passage quoted here was printed in 1837, and the ethics of the matter seems to trouble the writer. It is likely, of course, that she talked with American women in New Orleans about these things. In that connection her phrase, "women who cannot be mistaken," offers food for thought. It is likely, too, that her judgment is somewhat harsh. For the quadroon girl—according to her own standards—lost nothing by having served as a mistress for a white man, and later this former connection did not hinder her from matrimony with a free man of her own color. Also, in later life, these women were renowned for their successful businesses; rooming-houses, accommodating white gentlemen. As late as 1884 we find them enthusiastically described in a guide to the Cotton Exposition in New Orleans in that year: "Their houses are the neatest and best cared for in the city," says the guide book; bachelors are urged to try them. They are described as "something characteristically of New Orleans."

The diaries of travelers who visited New Orleans in the early nineteenth century contain many references to the balls themselves. The young Duke of Saxe-Weimar-Eisenach, who traveled over America in 1825, writes enthusiastically of them. The first of these balls he attended was in St. Philip Street, but the Orleans ball-room was visited too, later on. First, in the passage I shall quote, he tells a little of New Orleans society in that day:

My first excursion in New Orleans was to visit Mr. Grymes, who here inhabits a large, massive, and splendidly furnished house. . . . In the evening we paid our visit to the governor of the State. . . . After this we went to several coffee-houses where the lower classes amuse themselves. . . . Mr. Grymes took me to a masked ball, which is held every evening during the carnival at the French theater. . . . The dress of the ladies I observed to be very elegant, but understood that most of those dancing did not belong to the better class of society. . . . At a dinner, which Mr. Grymes gave me with the greatest display of magnificence . . . we withdrew from the first table, and seated ourselves at a second, in the same order in which we had partaken of the first. As the variety of wines began to set the tongues of the guests at liberty, the ladies rose, retired to another apartment, and resorted to music. . . . Some of the gentlemen remained with the bottle, while others, among whom I was one, followed the ladies. . . . We had waltzing until ten o'clock, when we went to the masquerade in the theater in St. Philip Street. . . . The female company at the theater consisted of quadroons, who, however, were masked.

The young Duke waxes enthusiastic as to the charms of the quadroon girls. "Like many others," he says, "I find the quadroon balls more entertaining than those of a more decorous nature," and he tells of flitting back and forth between them, in company with "many other gentlemen."

So many of the young Creoles would leave the balls where the young white ladies were dancing, that there were many wallflowers, or, as Saxe-Weimar says, "young ladies left to make tapestry."

"The quadroon women," he writes, "addressed me and coquetted with me in the most subtle and amusing manner." He adds that these women were the "most beautiful in the world."

An English traveler, who visited New Orleans at the same time, speaks of these quadroons as resembling high-class Hindus. He tells of their "lovely countenances, lips of coral, teeth of pearl, full, dark, liquid eyes and their sylph-like figures." He can hardly restrain his poetic appreciation: "Their beautifully rounded limbs, exquisite gait, and ease of manner might furnish models for a Venus or Hebe."

But we can imagine the chagrin and fury of the white wives whose husbands slipped away from their sides in a ball-room, in order to visit the ball-room of the quadroons, a few squares away! Some amazing family quarrels must have resulted from such behavior. And many a Creole

mother must have dreaded having her son form a connection with one of these quadroon girls. One can only surmise
the tear-stained pillows and the screams of anguish smothered behind closed doors. . . .

The quadroon balls were an institution which lasted for
many years. Men of color were not admitted; only white
gentlemen were welcome. It was an accepted standard.

But like all "unmentionable" things, certain troubles resulted. There were hundreds of duels growing from these
balls, and many a young Creole, whose marble slab in the
Old St. Louis Cemetery, testifies that he "fell in a duel,"
lies there because of his attentions to a quadroon girl
whose official "protector" objected to his flirtation.

The quadroon balls are difficult to describe. Officially
they did not exist. Little was printed about them, except
those references which found their way into the diaries of
travelers. Historians are wary in mentioning them, although
Miss Grace King, in her excellent book, "New Orleans, The
Place and The People," writes of them frankly and well.

But they were the principal diversion for white gentlemen. Even the gambling-rooms, which were near every public ball-room in New Orleans, were not as attractive, it
seems, as the Orleans ball-room when a quadroon ball was
in progress.

The room is long and high. The floor, even to-day, is
like glass. Many windows look down into Orleans Street;
and upon the balcony the swarthy beauties would retire
sometimes, in order to enjoy the cool breeze which blew
from west to east, from Lake Pontchartrain toward the
Mississippi. From the balcony they could look down upon
the garden just back of the church of St. Louis, or across

the narrow street to the fashionable residence which stood there. Back of the ball-room were many smaller rooms where card tables stood, and where the men would sit and play for hours on end. One likes to think of them there, in their evening clothes—at ease, informal, lifting a wine glass. And outside in the corridors the beautiful, dark-eyed, dark-skinned women, trailing their billowing silks and smoothing their plumes. In the rear of the ball-room a stair-case descended to the courtyard where tables and chairs were set out in the shade of the tropical, flowering trees and shrubs. Here the beauties could sip wines or cordials, as they cooled their flushed faces after dancing.

How pleasant it would be, if we could but turn back the clock of the years and could see them there in the old Orleans ball-room, as they flaunted their silks and satins and flashed their gems, making the most of their beauty and their happiness, both of which lasted but for a season.

Nowadays the ball-room is used by the nuns of the Convent of the Holy Family, as an assembly room. Quad-roon nuns go on silent feet through the corridors where once the gayest and most voluptuous of women flaunted their brocades and silks, their jewels and plumes; the soft voices of the nuns are heard in the ball-room which once reëchoed with laughter of these daughters of joy. In the courtyard, a swarm of mulatto children play where once the quadroon women and their white lovers sipped wines in the moonlight.

Surely no structure in New Orleans has had a stranger history than the old Orleans ball-room. Once it was as gay as Mardi Gras itself; to-day it is as somber and sad as Ash Wednesday.

Chapter XX

THE DUELLING OAKS

VISITORS to New Orleans are taken, nearly always, to see
the live-oak trees in the municipal parks. These trees are
extraordinarily large and the outer branches hang down
like the sides of a green and leafy tent. A single live-oak,
growing alone in a field, assumes a dome-like appearance, so
symmetrical is the curving sweep of bough and twig and
leaf; but in groves the trees are less regular. Here they rise
high in the air, and the branches are gnarled and twisted.
To my eyes they have always seemed eternal fountains,
dripping with their long streamers of gray Spanish moss.

If you will go one day along Esplanade Avenue, far beyond the boundaries of the old city, out that avenue which is
lined with fine old houses now falling into decay, you will
come at last to an equestrian statue of General Beauregard
which guards the entrance to City Park. Cross the bridge
over Bayou St. John, and there before you stretches a cool
green sweep with avenues of palms. Not far from the entrance on your left as you enter from Esplanade Avenue,

you will see a grove of magnificent live-oak trees. They are beautiful enough in themselves, but there is an additional interest too, for these are the duelling oaks.

By the beginning of the year 1830 New Orleans had begun to assume its fabulous quality. It was growing fantastic, unbelievable. The French era had given way before the Spanish domination, and the city had been handed over —full grown—to the Americans. Louisiana was now a part of the United States, but New Orleans was not in any sense an American city. It was still essentially Creole. The blending of the French and the Spanish had been accomplished, but the further blending with the American population was just beginning.

There was tremendous luxury in the city. The young men were sent abroad to be educated—usually to Paris. There these young Creoles were well liked, for they were handsome young fellows and they were plentifully supplied with money, money gained by the sweat of the negro slaves on Papa's plantation back in Louisiana. In Paris the young men did as they pleased, gambled, studied if they liked, fought, and made love. It is not surprising that they were bored when they returned to the lesser delights of New Orleans.

They were a fiery, high-strung set of young men, and they had leisure and plenty of money. And promptly they began getting into all sorts of scrapes. In the thirties the scrape was usually the duel.

Now there were laws in New Orleans which prohibited the duel; but we all know the American reaction to prohibitions of any kind. And just as the prohibition of alcoholic beverages in the United States has made drunkenness fashionable (as it has been fashionable in other periods of the world's history), so, perhaps, did the law against duelling whet the Creole appetite.

There had been sword-play in New Orleans since the beginning of the colony, but it was not until the beginning of the second quarter of the nineteenth century that the duello reached such extremes in Louisiana.

The rich young Creoles of the city constituted a sort of aristocracy founded less on birth than on manners, breeding, education, and tradition. It was a period of mock-modesty and "courtly manners" and of studied grandeur which seems preposterous to-day. The word "honor" hung in the air like the refrain of a popular song.

A contemporary journalist, describing the male society of the time, remarks: "The least breach of etiquette, the most venial sin against politeness, the least suspicion thrown out of unfair dealing, even a bit of awkwardness, are causes sufficient for a cartel, which none dares refuse."

The challenge did not mean that the two gentlemen must meet upon the field necessarily. The seconds, two representing each side, would meet and discuss the quarrel, and sometimes "with the assistance of a mutual friend" they would arrive at a settlement both "amicable and honorable."

To strike a blow was strictly forbidden, and to do such a thing was sufficient to debar the striker from the "privilege of the duello." A gentleman who would so far forget himself as to strike another was "exposed to the ignominy of being refused a meeting." Not even an insult was allowed to go beyond a certain point of nicety of behavior. Experienced friends, well versed in the law and the precedents of the code, settled beforehand every nice point, so that the adversaries met under the oaks "in full equality both morally and socially."

Causes for challenges were absurdly simple things. Many duels resulted from a slight rebuff in the ball-room. For example, a gentleman would approach a young lady and ask for a dance, she might reply that she must ask permission from her escort. The escort for some reason, or for none, might refuse. *Presto!* The oaks! Coffee and pistols for two!

These oaks were then on the plantation of Louis Allard, and the Allard plantation was far enough beyond the city limits to ensure privacy and freedom from legal interference.

Duelling was so popular, so fashionable, so inevitable, that many fencing masters made fortunes in New Orleans. The most famous "fencing academies" were in Exchange Alley, a short and narrow thoroughfare which runs from Canal Street to Conti, between Royal and Bourbon streets. The old houses where these fencing masters lived are still standing and may be seen just south of the Court House in Conti Street. These *maîtres d'armes* formed a class of their own. Some of them appear to have been men of intelligence, but others had only their skill with the foils to their credit. They gave suppers for their pupils—stag parties we would call them now—where there was much drinking, roistering, and sword-play. Many of the duelling masters had acquired their fame by having killed this one or that on the field of honor. Most of them led fast lives. Our contemporary journalist says that they divided their time between the cafés and *salles d'escrime*. But they were

FENCING MASTERS' HOUSES, EXCHANGE ALLEY

THE HAUNTED HOUSE IN ROYAL STREET

notable figures in the life of New Orleans in their day. They were pointed out in the streets, and were the envy and admiration of all young boys. They were spoiled by the waiters in the cafés, and revered by the clumsy young men who aimed to imitate their grace and skill with the rapier. Some of the fencing masters affected the manners of dandies, adopted an effeminate manner, dressed extravagantly, carried their handkerchiefs in their sleeves, and attempted to get a foothold in society. Few of them succeeded in attaining any sort of social position, but more than one of them was successful in his love affairs, and owing to his skill with the swords managed to escape the wrath of irate husbands.

Among the most noted of the *maîtres d'armes* was Marcel Dauphin, who was killed by A. Nora in a duel with shot-guns! (His skill with the rapier did him no good there!) Another was Bonneval, who was killed by Reynard, likewise a fencing teacher—probably a case of professional jealousy, as Reynard, it is reported, took over all of Bonneval's pupils after the duel. L'Alouette, who killed Shubra, a rival professor, was Pepe Lulla's teacher and subsequently his associate. Pepe Lulla was one of the most noted swordsmen that New Orleans produced.

Among the beaux of the more extravagant type was M. Beaudoin, a Parisian, who came to Louisiana in order to open an academy for the young bloods; there was Emile Cazere, whose clientele boasted the most aristocratic names in the city, among the younger generation; there was Gilbert Rosiere, called "Titi" by his adoring pupils, who considered him a model of masculine grace and strength.

But perhaps the most picturesque figure among them

was Bastile Croquere, who although a mulatto, is said to
have been one of the handsomest men in New Orleans at
that time. He was a great dandy, and is described walking
through the city in a suit of green broadcloth, with spot-
less linen, and with the widest of black stocks around his
neck. He was famous for his collection of cameos, and
wore cameo rings, breast pin, and even a cameo bracelet.
His skill with the sword was phenomenal, and such an excellent teacher he proved to be that the best of the Creole
gentlemen came to him for lessons. Despite the prejudice
against "men of color" his *salle d'armes* was crowded. The
Creole gentry did not hesitate to cross swords with him in
private *assauts*. Croquere lived in an old house at the
corner of Exchange Alley and Conti Street, the corner
nearest the river. The house is still standing and may be
seen by any one who is interested enough to climb the long
winding stairs. It is just opposite the south door of the
New Orleans Court House.

In fact, the whole stretch of Exchange Alley was filled
with fencing masters, and in the afternoon or evening those
passing by in the street could hear the rasping of the
swords, and the cries of the spectators who watched these
contests with approving and critical eyes.

Exchange Alley must have been a gay place in those
days, with the young bloods climbing the dim stairs and
practising for hours in the upper rooms with their masters
—and always a group of lookers-on, to hiss or applaud as
the case might be, a group of dandies who lounged at
ease, sipping coffee and liqueurs.

And what a colorful group the fencing masters must
have made as they walked about the street, followed

after by small boys, pointed out by the waiters in the cafés who neglected more important customers in order to dance to the bidding of these popular idols. They occupied a unique place in the community—being admired and in a manner respected—but being apart from the feminine society of the city. It is true that the young men flocked to their rooms and lingered there afterward to sip wine or liqueur with them, but the young men did not invite these swordsmen to their homes to meet their mothers and sisters.

Gilbert Rosiere, mentioned earlier in the chapter, became perhaps the most famous of the *maîtres d'armes*. He was a native of Bordeaux, a university graduate and a lawyer, who had come to New Orleans to try his luck at the bar. He is described by his contemporaries as gay, witty, and charming "although somewhat irascible." As a young man he was of "a wild disposition" and fell in with a gay set in New Orleans. Soon he gave up the idea of practising law and dropped the Code of Napoleon for the Code of Honor. He became a ringleader in the most spectacular escapades of the young men of the city and ended by becoming a fencing master. During the Mexican War he made a fortune teaching fencing to the young officers—a fortune which he squandered as easily as he had earned it. He is described as being everybody's friend—which means, of course, that he threw his money about, and he sprang into great notoriety early in his career in Louisiana by fighting seven duels in a week. Oddly enough he is described as a man of such tenderness that he could not kill a fly—although he had killed several men in the duel—and frequently wept audibly at the opera or theater. He was very handsome and his fine head was always noted on première nights in the Opera House.

On one occasion when he burst into tears a gentleman near-by laughed. Rosiere noticed that he was causing amusement and said quickly:

"C'est vrai je pleure, mais je donne aussi des calottes."

By this time the man's face had been slapped and the next morning he met Rosiere under the oaks and was wounded in consequence, a wound that taught him that it is not always wise to laugh at emotional fencing masters.

Early in the spring of 1840, the "professionals" held a magnificent *assaut d'armes* among themselves. It was held in the old Salle St. Philippe. None but those masters who could show a diploma was entitled to enter. Pepe Lulli, famous for a large number of successful duels, was refused the privilege of entering because he had no papers.

It is probable that you have guessed the outcome of this story already. A real duel resulted.

Poulaga, an Italian professor of counterpoint, bid defiance to all masters of the broadsword. He was a man of tremendous vitality and strength and was a giant to boot. Captain Thimecourt, another fencing master, a former cavalry officer, opposed and defeated Poulaga. This blow was too much for the Italian's pride, and he slapped Thimecourt's face. Without further ado they drove to the Oaks, followed by all the spectators at the exhibition. It was one of the bloodiest duels in the history of New Orleans, and Captain Thimecourt hacked his adversary to pieces.

After the duel the spectators went back to finish the exhibition. There a fencing master, one Bernard, refused to cross swords with Pepe Lulla because Lulla had no papers.

Another challenge, and the gentleman who had no diploma wounded Bernard twice, under the oaks.

Twenty duels between young bloods grew out of that exhibition of skill among the fencing masters.

The old newspaper files of the period are replete with stories of death on the duelling ground. Unfortunately the affairs were seldom reported in detail—reporters had a bad habit of writing as though everybody knew all about the matter anyway, and accordingly furnished only a slight outline of the duel itself and then went on to praise the excellent qualities of the gentleman who had succumbed.

Fortunately for us, however, there are a few stories told by eye-witnesses. A certain Pedesclaux, with more than one duel to his account, had a quarrel with a retired French cavalry officer. The cartel was passed, and the Frenchman, having the choice of weapons, selected broadswords, on horseback. They did not fight under the oaks but upon "La Plaine Raquette," so called because of the games of racquetball that were played there. Says the eye-witness:

It was a handsome sight. The adversaries were mounted on spirited horses and stripped to the waist. As they rode up to each other, nerved for the combat, their respective muscular development and confidence in their bearing gave promise of an interesting fight. The Frenchman was heavy and somewhat ungainly, but his muscles looked like whipcord, and his broad, hairy chest gave evidence of remarkable strength and endurance. Pedesclaux, somewhat lighter in weight, was admirably proportioned and his youthful suppleness seemed to more than counterbalance his adversary's brawny but somewhat rigid manhood.

A clashing of steel, which drew sparks from the blades, and the two adversaries crossed and passed each other by unhurt. In a moment both horses had been vaulted to face each other by the expert riders, and the enemies met again. A terrible head blow from the Frenchman would now have cleft Pedesclaux to the shoulder-blade, if his quick sword had not warded off the death stroke. It was then that, with lightning rapidity, before his adversary could recover his guard which had been disturbed by the momentum of his blow, the Creole by a rapid half circle, regained his, and with a well-directed *coup de pointe à droite* (having taken care to keep his adversary to the right), plunged his blade through the body of the French officer, who reeled in his saddle, fell, and was picked up senseless and bleeding by his friends. He died soon afterwards.

And now we come down to a later period where there is more detail to be obtained. Let me tell of one more duel and I am done. From perhaps a hundred duels, I choose this one because it seems so typical of New Orleans. It has to do with the French Opera.

Now there is nothing remarkable about a duel growing out of the Opera, for, in fact, many challenges resulted from nearly every performance. The Creoles were tremendously interested in music and particularly in the Opera, which furnished pomp and pageantry and drama in addition to the singing. Music critics had a hard time in New Orleans in those days. An article was printed in which it was stated that Madame So-and-so was not at her best in "La Vestale" or whatever it happened to be, and quick as a wink, some admirer of the lady's voice (or of the lady herself) would challenge the writer. And alas for the poor fellow, if he were not a frequenter of one of those abodes of the fencing masters in Exchange Alley! For there was no escape. One must either accept a challenge or leave the city.

In 1857 under Boudousquie's administration of the French Opera, there flourished a fascinating singer called

Mlle. Bourgeois, a contralto. Mlle. Bourgeois had many admirers in New Orleans and a wide circle of friends in addition, for she went about socially to some extent. Now there was another singer, a Mme. Colson, who was "one of the wittiest and most fascinating of the light soprani," who also had a circle of friends and admirers in New Orleans that season. The two women were rivals.

The end of the season approached, and as was the custom of the time, benefit performances were given for the principal singers. Mlle. Bourgeois chose Victor Massé's opera of "Galatée" for her benefit night. It was the old story of Pygmalion and Galatea, the myth of the artist whose love for a statue brings it to life. In order to snub Mme. Colson, Mlle. Bourgeois went outside of the company and chose a certain Mme. Preti-Baille, formerly an opera singer but at that time a teacher of singing in the city, to sing the important rôle of the living statue. The logical choice would have been Mme. Colson, of course.

This announcement created a great furor among the Creoles, for Mme. Colson was much admired. Immediately the names of the two singers were on every lip. Men and women took sides. Some declared that Mme. Colson's insult should be avenged, and declared that they would attend the performance and hiss Mme. Preti-Baille if she dared appear. The friends of Mlle. Bourgeois, however, declared their loyalty to that singer, and stated that they would be present in the theater and that any interruption in the performance would be properly dealt with. The matter was discussed in all sections of the city, in private houses, at balls, in the men's clubs, and in the *salles d'armes*.

It was in one of these fencing schools that Emile

Bozonier and Gaston de Coppens were lounging, sipping cordials and watching the other young men fence. A large crowd of young Creoles was present, and the discussion turned upon the excitement which the rival opera singers had caused. The talk had been of hissing the singer whom some thought to be an intruder in the opera.

Coppens was a great admirer of Mme. Colson, and said that he believed that Mme. Preti-Baille should be hissed from the stage, if she were indiscreet enough to appear. Bozonier said nothing, but Coppens feeling that his silence meant disapproval, turned and said:

"What do you say to this, Bozonier?"

And Bozonier, looking full at him, said deliberately and in a resonant tone clearly audible to many around them: "I think that the man who goes to a theater for the purpose of hissing a woman is a blackguard and should have his face slapped."

"And do you know," cried Coppens in a fury, "that I am one of those who have declared to hiss that woman down?"

"No," said Bozonier, "I did not know it, but what I said stands, just the same."

The matter was dropped, and the practice with the foils went on. The young men continued to sip their wines and cordials.

The benefit night arrived. The Opera House on Orleans Street was crowded to the doors. The social world had come to Mlle. Bourgeois's benefit; her champions had come and, in addition, her enemies were there too. There was an air of suppressed excitement in the theater which made the audience restless in their chairs. At last the lights were lowered and the director rapped three times for quiet.

The opera began. The theater was astonishingly still. There was not a rustle, not a cough. Mlle. Bourgeois, who was singing the rôle of Pygmalion, appeared and was greeted with generous applause. She seemed confident and sang unusually well, enjoying her triumph. All went well until the curtain covering the statue was drawn aside and Galatea began to live and move.

Immediately there was bedlam in the theater. There were hisses and catcalls; there were shouts and cries. Others began to applaud wildly, hoping to drown out the yells of derision. The opera continued. Mme. Preti-Baille, looking as cold and as white as a statue—which she indeed represented—continued to sing; the orchestra continued to play, and the audience continued to shout, to hiss, and to applaud. The noise went on until the end of the act. Those in the audience could not hear a single note that was sung. The ladies rose en masse to leave the theater. Some were hysterical; some fainted.

In the crowd in the foyer Bozonier came face to face with Coppens, both men dressed in their best, both highly excited. Coppens had hissed, Bozonier had seen him, but in the foyer they were separated by a dense crowd. A few moments later they met on the *banquette* outside. Coppens called out: "Well, Bozonier, how about those slaps?"

The answer was a blow which sent Coppens sprawling in the street.

They met under the oaks. As neither was skilled with rapier or pistol, they chose cavalry sabers.

Bozonier was a trifle above the middle height, but remarkably active and muscular. Coppens was small in stature, but wiry and of feline activity. Both were "dandies in dress and lions in courage," the reporter wrote.

In a twinkling the coats were on the grass. The principals were placed in position, and the usual recommendations made by the seconds, comprising the instructions that the fight was to last till one of the adversaries should be completely disabled.

The first pass was terrible; Bozonier engaged Coppens in a tierce, made a feint, then taking advantage of the movement of his adversary to parry, rapidly passed over his sword and made a swinging stroke at him, which would inevitably have severed his head from his body, had not Coppens, by a timely movement, warded off partly the effect of the blow.

But there was a vigor to spare in the cut, for Coppens fell, the blood spurting like water from a terrible gash on the cheek and a severe cut in the chest.

It was lucky for him at that moment that Bozonier's generous soul prevented him following up his advantage, for he had his foe at his mercy. He paused till Coppens rose. This rise was the spring of a wounded tiger; a furious *coup de pointe* penetrated Bozonier's sword-arm above the elbow, cutting the muscles and disabling him. Then Coppens had it all his own way, though his plucky adversary did his best, handicapped as he was by his now almost useless arm, which could scarcely hold the weapon. The seconds did not see his terrible position in time, neither could his furious foe appreciate it, and before the former could interfere, Bozonier had received two deep cuts in the chest, a terrible slash in the left arm, and a fearful *coup de pointe* in the side. He was bleeding at every pore.

Bozonier, however, did not die. Careful nursing and medical attention saved his life, but his magnificent physique was ruined forever. Coppens became a colonel in the Louisiana Zouaves and lost his life during the Civil War.

The old newspaper files are full of these duels. The list seems endless. And on many of the tombs in the older cemeteries of New Orleans, you will find the inscriptions: "Died on the field of honor," or "He fell in a duel."

The days of sword-play are over now, but in City Park you will find the old oak trees—the scene of a thousand encounters.

Chapter XXI

"THE HAUNTED HOUSE"

OF all the tales of old New Orleans, the story of "The Haunted House" in Royal Street is most dramatic. The real story is interesting enough, but the credulous have added many a supernatural touch: blue lights at the windows, a skeleton hand at the door, hoarse screams in the night, and the sound of chains jangling as they drag down an empty staircase. . . .

I cannot vouch for the authenticity of the ghosts, but I can give you the facts in the case of Delphine Lalaurie, the woman who tortured her slaves—and of her flight from New Orleans with a mob at her heels. But let us first look upon the house itself as it stands in quiet dignity at the intersection of Royal and Hospital streets. Its number is 1140 Royal Street, but there is no chance of mistaking the house; it is the largest and finest in the neighborhood, rich and beautiful in detail, and the highest building for squares around. From the cupola on the roof one may look out over the Vieux Carré and see the Mississippi in its crescent before Jackson Square, or looking back over the city's roofs, one can see Congo Square, where the negroes held their voodoo dances. The view is worth climbing all these endless stairs between the sidewalk and the roof top.

It is evident that the house was built in Napoleon's time, for the Empire motif is noticeable everywhere—it can be traced in the iron grillwork which closes the entrance, and in the black and white marble flooring of the vestibule; it appears again on the richly carved front door, with Phœbus in his chariot, and with wreaths of flowers and depending garlands in bas-relief. Inside, the mahogany-railed staircase curves upward three full stories, and on the second floor we find three large drawing-rooms, opening one into the other by sliding doors—doors which, like the one below, are richly ornamented. Glancing through the windows in the back of the house, the old slave wing can be seen, stretching away. Below is the paved courtyard.

The decoration of ceiling and wall in the drawing-rooms is exceptionally ornate; large rosettes in plaster from which chandeliers hung in the old days; carved woodwork; black marble mantelpieces; fluted pilasters; and a frieze of winged figures with trumpets. Standing in these old rooms one can picture them filled with the rich furniture of the period; one can fancy the vermilion brocades, the crystal sconces, the carpets, the brass-inlaid furniture. So it must have been in Madame Lalaurie's day, and so it must have remained until that day when . . .

But first, let us look for a moment at the history of the house itself.

Names have a way of persisting in New Orleans. This property was known for many years as the Remairie place, for early in the colonial history of New Orleans, Jean and Henri Remairie lived there. Later another house was built on the site and the property passed into the hands of Barthelmy Lois de Maccarthy, the descendant of an Irish gentleman who had lived many years in France and had acquired a title there before coming to New Orleans. For all I know, his title may have gone back even farther than that, but it is quite certain that he was "de Maccarthy" when he reached Louisiana. The daughter of Barthelmy Lois de Maccarthy was called Delphine. She married three times. First she was Mme. Lopez, then Mme. Blanque; and her third husband was Dr. Louis Lalaurie.

The house belonged to her father, but in August, 1831, she acquired it. This was after her third marriage.

It is quite evident, from the stories that come down to us, that Mme. Lalaurie was a vivid personality. She quite obliterates her husband; one can learn little of him. But she is described as an extraordinary woman. She was said to be beautiful, but beautiful or not, it is quite certain that she was charming. Her fame as a hostess was proverbial. Her balls were glamorous, and her dinners were noted for the brilliancy of repartee. When Lafayette visited New Orleans in 1825, she is said to have entertained him at dinner. There is even a story that he was a guest in the house, and the room in which he slept is pointed out. This is hardly possible, for Lafayette was entertained in the Cabildo, which had been fitted out for his use; and as he remained in New Orleans but seven nights, it is not likely that he spent one of them with the Lalauries. For that matter, the phrase, "Lafayette spent a night in this house," is a subject for jokes in New Orleans—for even a Frenchman would have had difficulty in sleeping in as many beds as Lafayette is said to have occupied while in New Orleans. Added to this conjecture is the stubborn fact that Lafayette visited New Orleans before the Lalauries took possession of the house.

We have said that Mme. Delphine Lalaurie was an excellent hostess. Men would linger over the wine and walnuts at her table, while sleepy slaves moved about snuffing the guttering candles and placing new tapers in the sconces. Her wines and cordials were beyond reproach; and her conversation was noted for its cleverness. The thing that is remembered best is her kindness. It is easy to account for the fact that so many remembered that quality of Madame's; the events which developed later made the quality startling.

She had, in addition to her colorless husband, two daughters. One was a cripple, or suffered from some deformity and was seldom seen at the gatherings. It may be that she was too young; that I cannot tell you. But the absence of others did not matter as long as Mme. Delphine sat there between the candles, throwing out her humorous *bons mots*. That is the way one likes to think of her laughing, her head thrown back, her dark eyes alight. And always behind her chair there stood a sleek mulatto butler—a handsome fellow in livery, an excellent servant. He was a favorite of Madame's. Always she left a sip of her wine for him in her glass.

The other slaves who sometimes appeared were not so prepossessing. In fact, they were surprisingly thin and hollow-chested, and they moved over the carpets like shadows, never raising their eyes. But they were in the background. The sleek mulatto butler is the only servant that men remembered, before April 10, 1834.

It may be well to note that date, for it was then that our drama begins—and ends. But there are other things that must be told first.

Now strange rumors were afloat in New Orleans concerning the charming Mme. Lalaurie. It was said that she treated her slaves badly. And that those lovely white hands, flashing with their emerald rings, sometimes were used for harsher purposes than for lifting her crystal liqueur glass to her lips. . . .

Odd, how these stories got about! Nobody believed them, of course. Mme. Lalaurie punish her slaves? Impossible. Why, if one's slaves were disobedient, there was always the whipping-post in the Calaboose. For a trifling cost, one could send his slave and have as many stripes laid across his back as one liked. It was cheap enough, a mere nothing, and saved all unpleasantness in the house. It was good for another reason, too. Those slaves who had been whipped in that dark old building were so afraid of being sent back there, that their behavior was excellent afterward; and they proved an example to the others. Why, why, should Mme. Lalaurie desire to lash the slaves *herself?* The thing was absurd on face value. It was inconceivable that any one—especially the refined, the delicate, the beautiful Mme. Lalaurie—should *enjoy* punishing her negroes. . . . Of course nobody could believe such stories. And yet . . . just the same, one found one's self looking at the slaves when one went to dine there.

There could be no doubt that the sleek mulatto was treated well enough. He served as coachman as well as butler, and on summer afternoons he drove Mme. Lalaurie when her carriage joined the line of fashionable vehicles along old Bayou Road, which led between bayou and swamp, to the borders of Lake Pontchartrain, four miles away. As she drove along, she was greeted on all sides by smiles, and by raised hats. And on the box, the mulatto coachman was sleeker than ever in his plum-colored livery and high hat. But the other slaves, those hollow-chested women who moved about so softly, passing the guests with averted eyes. What of them? Thin? Well, yes, but then are not others lean? Hollow-chested? Perhaps, but what of your old Aunt Euphrosine? Isn't she hollow-chested too?

But there were others who were not so easily satisfied. There was M. Montreuil for instance, a neighbor. He complained to the authorities that unpleasant things were happening in that fine house, late at night. He made no definite accusations, but he told of screams, smothered behind closed doors. And he told of the sound of the lash upon bare flesh. M. Montreuil must have found something radically wrong in the house near his own—for it was quite legal to punish slaves with the whip, if one liked. All we can say now is that the gentleman complained to the authorities, and that the authorities did—nothing. Mme. Lalaurie continued to entertain as before, or to go out in the evening with her husband to ball and opera.

Once, however, Mme. Lalaurie was fined. There is a record of that fact. But the court record is vague. A child had died in her house—a little negro girl, a slave, of course. She had been killed by a fall from the roof into the paved courtyard. Clearly an accident. Except that there was the testimony of a woman, a next door neighbor. The woman had been watching from a window, and had seen the child run through the courtyard shrilly screaming with terror.

Mme. Lalaurie, the kind, good Madame Lalaurie, was in close pursuit, armed with a heavy whip. The watching woman heard the scampering of feet from floor to floor, as the child climbed the stairs, pursued by the furious woman. At last they appeared on the housetop. The child ran down the steeply pitched roof, poised for a moment at the edge—and disappeared. The woman at the window saw the distorted face of Mme. Lalaurie, looking down. And from below in the paved court, she heard the thud of the child's body as it struck the flagstones.

Some sort of an investigation followed. Mme. Lalaurie was fined, as we have said, and the incident was closed. Her friends heard her explanation, believed and sympathized. And daily she drove along the Bayou Road behind her spirited black horses.

This much of the story has been taken from those who have written before about Mme. Lalaurie: Harriet Martineau, in "Society in America"—a contemporary account, published only three years later; George W. Cable, in "Strange True Stories of Louisiana," Henry C. Castellanos, in "New Orleans, As It Was"; one old court record, and stories that have been told to me by old people who have heard them from their fathers—men and women then living.

But those in New Orleans who defend Mme. Lalaurie will assure you that there is no truth in any of these stories. "Cable invented the story," they say. Which would be a tribute to Mr. George W. Cable, if it were true; unfortunately this explanation does not hold good, for Miss Martineau had written of it more than fifty years before. Mr. Castellanos wrote of Mme. Lalaurie in 1905. Well, even if we suppose that perhaps all of these excellent writers were mistaken, there is another source of information not so easily thrown aside—the daily newspapers. There were several papers published in New Orleans in 1834, and in four of them, Mme. Lalaurie figures prominently in the news on April 10 of that year.

A fire had broken out in the house. Incendiary. The cook (who was found chained in the kitchen) admitted that she had fired the dwelling as she preferred to be burned alive rather than continue her life under the torture of Mme. Lalaurie. However, this statement was made later in the day. At the time of the fire, she said nothing; she let her chains speak for her.

The streets were filled with people. Flames were pouring from a window in a wing of the building, and the main part of the mansion was filled with smoke. The volunteer fire department was on hand, armed with buckets of water, to extinguish the flames. Many people crowded into the house to offer assistance.

Mme. Lalaurie was at her best. She was composed, calm. She directed workers who were carrying out the handsome paintings, the bronzes, the brocades, the lighter pieces of furniture. She stood at the head of the stairs, near the carved door which led into the main salon: "This way!" she cried, "this way, please! Yes, take that. . . . Oh, thank you!" And men went down the stairs, laden with beautiful things. Dr. Lalaurie was in the background. But he was there. That fact was testified by many who saw him, including Judge Canonge, who gave out an interesting statement the same day.

M. Montreuil, the same neighbor who had made a com-

plaint against Mme. Lalaurie before, was present. He asked
if the slaves were in danger from the fire. The Lalauries
answered that he would be better if he did not meddle in the
affairs of his neighbors. M. Montreuil then appealed to
Judge Canonge. A Mr. Fernandez joined them. They made
an attempt to reach the third story, but found locked doors
barring their way. As Dr. Lalaurie refused to open the
doors, these three men broke them down. Slaves were
found, mutilated, starved, bound down with chains. Now,
let me quote from the newspaper of that day, "L'Abeille"
(The Bee). The article is by Jerome Bayon, the editor:

We saw where the collar and manacles had cut their way into
their quivering flesh. For several months they had been confined in
those dismal dungeons, with no other nutriment than a handful of
gruel and an insufficient quantity of water, suffering the tortures of
the damned and longingly awaiting death as a relief from their sufferings. We saw Judge Canonge, Mr. Montreuil, and others, making
for some time fruitless efforts to rescue these poor unfortunates,
whom the infamous woman Lalaurie had doomed to certain death
and hoping that the devouring element might thus obliterate the last
traces of her nefarious deeds.

The search went on. Two negresses were brought out
with heavy, spiked iron collars and irons on their feet; they
could not walk, and were supported. An aged negress was
found, bound in a kneeling position. She had been in this
cramped posture for so long that she was hopelessly
crippled. Her head had been laid open by a blow from a
sharp instrument.

We saw [wrote the editor of the "Advertiser" the next day] one
of these miserable beings. The sight was so horrible that we could

scarce look upon it. The most savage heart could not have witnessed the spectacle unmoved. He had a large hole in his head; his body from head to foot was covered with scars and filled with worms. The sight inspired us with so much horror that even at the moment of writing this article we shudder from its effects. Those who have seen the others represent them to be in a similar condition.

There were seven in all. Other slaves were there, three of them, the women of the averted eyes—those that had been seen by guests. The cook, her chains jangling from the iron band around her waist, was led out. Behind in the hallway stood Mme. Lalaurie and the mulatto coachman. Dr. Lalaurie had disappeared.

As the mutilated slaves were taken from the house, the crowd followed them out into the open air. Only one or two friends were left with Mme. Lalaurie. The coachman was quick-witted. He slammed the heavy door which led to the street, and barred it fast. He hastened to the courtyard and locked the heavy wooden gates.

Some of the furniture had been carried back into the house; only a small portion of it had been removed. The crowd remained in the street outside, looking up at the closed windows. They waited to see arrests made. For hours they stood there. Nothing happened.

"At least two thousand people," says the New Orleans "Gazette," "flocked to the Calaboose to see the tortured slaves." A long wooden table in the jail yard was filled with the instruments of torture which had been brought from the house in Royal Street. There were instruments the purpose of which was so terrible that the newspapers only hint at their uses. Among the statements which were made that day, is one which is particularly graphic. One of the slave women testified that Mme. Lalaurie would come sometimes to inflict tortures upon them while music and dancing were going on below. She would come in her ball gown to this tight-barred attic and lash the naked negroes as they cowered on the floor. After only a few strokes she would appear satisfied, and would go, taking the taper with her and leaving them again in darkness. Sometimes the mulatto butler would accompany her. One of the women testified that Mme. Lalaurie once struck her own crippled daughter for bringing food to the starving slaves.

While the curious crowd gaped at the starving negroes as they gulped down the food given them, Judge Canonge was making a formal statement to the authorities. The document is available. Let me quote:

Deponent, J. F. Canonge, declares that on the 10th inst. a fire having broken out at the residence of Mrs. Lalaurie, he repaired thither, as a citizen, to afford assistance. When he reached the place, he was informed that a number of manacled slaves were in the building and liable to perish in the flames. At first he felt disinclined to speak to Mr. Lalaurie on the subject but contented himself with imparting the fact only to several friends of the family. But when he became aware that this act of barbarity was becoming a subject of comment he made up his mind to speak himself to Mr. and Mrs. Lalaurie, who flatly answered that the charge was a base calumny. Thereupon deponent asked the aid of the bystanders to make a thorough search and ascertain with certainty the truth or falsity of the rumor. As Messrs. Montreuil and Fernandez happened to be near him, he requested those gentlemen to climb the garret stairs and see for themselves, adding, that having attempted to do so himself, he had been almost blinded by smoke. These gentlemen returned after a while and reported that they had looked around diligently and had failed to discover anything. A few moments later, some one whom he thinks to be Mr. Felix Lefebvre, came to inform him that having broken a pane of glass in a window of one of the rooms, he had perceived some slaves and could show the place. Deponent hurried on, in company with several others. Having found the door locked, he caused it to be forced open and entered with the citizens who had followed him. He found two negro women, whom he ordered to be taken out of the room. Then some one cried out that there were others in the kitchen. He went there, but found no one. One of the negresses was wearing an iron collar, extremely wide and heavy, besides weighty chains attached to her feet. She walked only with the greatest difficulty; the other, he had no time to see, as she was standing behind Mr. Guillotte. This latter person told him he could point out a place where another one could be found. Together they went into another apartment, at the moment when some one was raising a mosquito bar. Stretched out on a bed, he perceived an old negro woman who had received a very deep wound on the head. She seemed too weak to be able to walk. Deponent begged the bystanders to lift her up with her mattress and to carry her in that position to the Mayor's office, whither the other women had been already conveyed. At the time that he asked Mr. Lalaurie if it were true that he had some slaves in his garret, the latter replied in an insolent manner that some people had better stay at home rather than come to others' houses to dictate laws and meddle with other people's business.

Messrs. Gottschalk and Fouché sign as witnesses to what Judge Canonge has seen.

In the meantime, the crowd waited in the street, outside of the house in Royal Street. They expected to see arrests made. But the police did not come. More and more men came as the hours passed. And hourly they grew more restless. Now the crowd was murmuring, threats were being hurled up at the close-shuttered windows.

Late in the afternoon, the doors of the high-walled courtyard swung open, and the crowd in the street saw a

carriage emerge. It came furiously forward, directly into
the mob. The black horses plunged, and the men fell back
before their hoofs. On the box was the mulatto coachman,
lashing the horses. His whip fell across the faces of the
men nearest him. And the horses plunged through and
were gone, with a clatter of hoofs, out Hospital Street,
toward Bayou Road.

It had happened so unexpectedly that the mob was
taken off guard. In fact, there was a cry that this was a
ruse, and that Mme. Lalaurie was escaping at that moment
through the iron-grilled door which led to Royal Street.
Some swore that she was not in the carriage at all, and
that the veiled figure that they saw crouching on the seat
was an effigy, placed there to deceive the mob. But they
were wrong. Mme. Lalaurie had driven out of the courtyard behind those rearing horses. Some made a half-
hearted chase. But in a moment she was gone, in a cloud
of dust. If Dr. Lalaurie was in the carriage with her, he
must have been crouching on the floor, for those who saw
the carriage go, saw only one figure in it.

The daughters, it was said afterward, had made their
escape over a balcony into the house next door. At any
rate, only Mme. Lalaurie was seen departing—with a
mob at her heels.

It is said that the carriage drove furiously along Bayou
Road, passing many fashionable vehicles on the way—and
that men and women stood up in their carriages to watch
the foam-flecked horses which ran by under the lash of the
mulatto coachman. But no one made an attempt to stay
the lady in her flight—or if such attempts were made, there
is no record of them. It is also said that a sailing vessel

SPANISH COURTYARD IN MADISON STREET

GEORGE HOUSE IN ROYAL STREET

awaited at the end of Bayou Road, and that the lady set sail at once for Mandeville. Another story persists that she remained in hiding in New Orleans for several days and only gave up the intention to remain when she found public opinion hopelessly against her. Which of these stories is true, I cannot say, but we do know that she was in Mandeville ten days later, for on that day, in the town of Mandeville, she signed power of attorney to an agent, so that her business affairs in New Orleans might be looked after.

Behind her, in Royal Street, the crowd seethed and simmered. The authorities had let her go—and she had escaped violence at the hands of those who waited outside. Her flight enraged the crowd in the street. "In a few minutes," said the "Courier" next morning, "the doors and windows were broken open, the crowd rushed in, and the work of destruction began." We read of the mob's fury turned upon destruction. Feather beds were ripped open and thrown into the street; curtains were dragged down from the windows; pictures torn from the walls. Men carried furniture to the windows and sent it crashing into the street below. "Elegant pictures, armoires, bedsteads, china, glass, silver," were thrown out. "Pianos," says the newspaper, "were smashed into a thousand pieces." Then the mob, still unsatisfied, began to tear down the house itself; the mahogany balustrades were torn away from the staircase, the wainscot was hacked, glass broken, window blinds torn from their hinges. The crowd was "in the very act of pulling down the walls" when the sheriff and a group of armed men came and restored order. The value of the goods destroyed, says the "Bee," was more than forty thousand dollars.

The house was restored, but it continued to bear its evil reputation. Tenants never occupied it for long periods. The notoriety which they achieved by living there was too great. And the magnificent house began its decline. For a time it was used as a school. Later, in Reconstruction times, it was a school for negro girls. And it remained empty for long periods. Finally it fell into the hands of gamblers who used the fine rooms on the second floor as a "gilded den of vice," in other words, an unusually fine gambling house. When I first saw the building—twenty-five years ago—when I made my first visit to New Orleans for Mardi Gras—there was a sign across the façade on the ground floor: "The Haunted Saloon." The name arrested my attention at the time, but it was years later that I heard the history of the house. Later, when I came to live in New Orleans and passed the house frequently, it was for a time a tenement, occupied by many families. Then it stood empty. At last it was opened as a home for homeless and unemployed men. Nowadays it is called Warrington House, in honor of the old gentleman who for many years has welcomed those penniless men released from jails and penitentiaries.

But as for the ultimate fate of Mme. Lalaurie, I cannot answer. There are stories of her recognition in New York city in a theater, and it is said that popular feeling was so strong against her that she was hissed, and forced to leave hurriedly. It is known that she went to France, and in New Orleans it is said that her later life was spent in pious devotions and many good works. In Harriet Martineau's book, the writer speaks of her "skulking in the provincial towns of France," three years after her flight.

The stories of her good works in later life may well be true, for in New Orleans, even during the period when she was torturing her own slaves, her generosity to the poor and afflicted was proverbial. And she was very devout in observance of her church duties. These strange contradictions in character have added to the mysterious quality which enters into any discussion of Mme. Lalaurie among the older writers. They deny emphatically that she was insane; sometimes they speak of her as a fiend incarnate; or else they say that it was impossible for such a charming lady to have been guilty of brutality toward her slaves.

Nowadays we know more of abnormal psychology. It seems to me from the evidence offered that Mme. Lalaurie must have suffered from some sex maladjustment which took the form of sadistic mania; otherwise she was sane enough. The case of Dr. Louis Lalaurie is more difficult to understand.

So much for "The Haunted House" in Royal Street.

Chapter XXII

THE YEAR OF THE PLAGUE

"It may be a mere fancy, but it has always struck me as a fact, that in Louisiana nature itself is, in many elements, less steady and uniform than in the higher latitudes of our country. Not unfrequently the alternations of health and sickness, joy and sorrow, commercial prosperity and misfortune, sweep over the Crescent City with the suddenness and fury of those autumnal hurricanes which occasionally visit it, by which in a few moments of time the strongest edifices are levelled with the dust, the majestic live-oaks and cypresses prostrated, and the vessels along the levee overwhelmed in the flood."

These are the opening lines in the "Autobiographical Sketches" of the Reverend Theodore Clapp, for thirty-five years a Presbyterian minister in New Orleans. His memoir, written in 1857, remains one of the most vivid pictures of the old New Orleans. He must have been a remarkable man, tolerant, broad-minded, clear-eyed. He came to New Orleans in 1821, and remained through the city's most

colorful period. Never was the community gayer than then
—with its balls, gambling, duelling, and mad extravagances,
as opposed to those calamities which reduced the population to horror and despair, for these were the days when
epidemic and plague entered the city, and for a time threatened its complete annihilation.

He came to New Orleans aboard a steamboat from
Louisville, to preach in the Presbyterian Church before a
handful of people, for at that time there were few Protest-
ants in New Orleans. Dr. Clapp admits in his memoir that
he was prejudiced against New Orleans before he saw it,
for he had heard the stories which pictured the city as the
new Sodom. In time he changed his mind, and after a few
years came to love New Orleans as he had never loved a
city before. All this he tells in his memoir. He is important
to historians because he gives a first-hand account of the
great plague of 1832. As the volume is very rare now, I
shall quote him at length:

The previous summer [he writes], in the month of August, a
frightful tornado had swept over and inundated New Orleans. The
Creoles said that this was the forerunner of some frightful pestilence.
I proposed to leave Mrs. Clapp and the children with her aunt in
Kentucky, till the overflowing scourge should pass through the land.
But she declined. . . .

We arrived at New Orleans, on our return home, about the first
of September. The weather was most sultry and oppressive. To most
of my friends our conduct appeared so unwise, that they hardly gave
us a cordial welcome back. . . . That very week, several cases of yellow fever occurred in the Charity Hospital and boarding houses along
the levee. It soon grew into an epidemic, and carried off hundreds
during this and the succeeding month.

On the morning of the 25th of October, 1832, as I was walking home from market, before sunrise, I saw two men lying on the levee in a dying condition. They had been landed from a steamboat which arrived the night before. Some of the watchmen had gone after a handbarrow or cart, on which they might be removed to the hospital. At first there was quite a crowd assembled on the spot. But an eminent physician rode up in his gig, and gazing a moment, exclaimed in a loud voice, "Those men have the Asiatic cholera." The crowd dispersed in a moment, and ran as if for their lives in every direction. I was left almost alone with the sufferers. They could speak, and were in full possession of their reason. They had what I afterwards found were the usual symptoms of cholera—cramps, convulsions, &c. The hands and feet were cold and blue; an icy perspiration flowed in streams; and they complained of a great pressure upon their chests. One of them said it seemed as if a bar of iron was lying across him. Their thirst was intense, which caused an insufferable agony in the mouth and throat. They entreated me to procure some water. I attempted to go on board the steamboat which had put them on shore. But the staging had been drawn in to prevent all intercourse with people on the levee. Thence I returned, intending to go to the nearest dwelling to get some relief for the unhappy men, whom all but God had apparently deserted.

At that instant the watchmen arrived with a dray. Happily (because, perhaps, they spoke only the French language), they had no suspicion that these strangers were suffering from the cholera. If I had pronounced that terrific word in their hearing, they too might have fled, and left the sick men to perish on the cold ground. I saw them placed on the vehicle, and subsequently learned that they were corpses before eleven o'clock A.M. the same day.

I walked home, attempting to be calm and resigned, determined to do my duty, and leave the consequences with God. I said nothing to my family about the sick men whom I had met, though they thought it strange that I had taken so much more time than usual in going to and from the market, and observed that I looked uncommonly thoughtful and serious. I felt that the hour of peril had come. . . .

The weather, this morning, was very peculiar. The heavens were covered with thick, heavy, damp, lowering clouds, that seemed like one black ceiling, spread over the whole horizon. To the eye, it almost touched the tops of the houses. Every one felt a strange difficulty of respiration. I never looked upon such a gloomy, appalling sky before or since. Not a breath of wind stirred. It was so dark, that in some of the banks, offices, and private houses, candles or lamps were lighted that day.

Immediately after breakfast I walked down to the post office. At every corner, and around the principal hotels, were groups of anxious faces. As soon as they saw me, the question was put by several persons at a time, "Is it a fact that the cholera is in the city?" I replied by describing what I had seen but two hours before. Observing that many of them appeared panic-struck, I remarked, "Gentlemen, do not be alarmed. These may prove merely what the doctors call sporadic cases. We do not yet know that it will prevail to an alarming extent. Let us trust in God, and wait patiently the developments of another morning."

That day as many persons left the city as could find the means of transmigration. On my way home from the post office, I walked along the levee, where the two cholera patients had been disembarked but three or four hours before. Several families in the neighborhood were making preparations to move, but in vain. They could not obtain the requisite vehicles. The same afternoon the pestilence entered their houses, and before dark spread through several squares opposite to the point where the steamer landed the first cases.

On the evening of the 27th of October, it had made its way through every part of the city. During the ten succeeding days, reckoning from October 27 to the 6th of November, all the physicians judged that, at the lowest computation, there were five thousand deaths—an average of five hundred every day. Many died of whom no account was rendered. A great number of bodies, with bricks and stones tied to the feet, were thrown into the river. Many were privately interred in gardens and enclosures, on the grounds where they expired, whose names were not recorded in the bills of mortality. Often I was kept in the burying ground for hours in succession, by the incessant, unintermitting arrival of corpses, over whom I was requested to perform a short service. One day, I did not leave the cemetery till nine o'clock at night; the last interments were made by candle light. Reaching my house faint, exhausted, horror-stricken, I found my family all sobbing and weeping, for they had concluded, from my long absence, that I was certainly dead. I never went abroad without kissing and blessing them all, with the conviction that we should never meet again on earth. After bathing and taking some refreshment, I started out to visit the sick. My door was thronged with servants, waiting to conduct me to the rooms of dying sufferers. In this kind of labor I spent most of the night. At three o'clock A.M., I returned home, threw myself down on a sofa, with directions not to be called till half past five. I was engaged to attend a funeral at six o'clock A.M., 28th October. . . .

The morning after, at six o'clock, I stepped into a carriage to accompany a funeral procession to the cemetery. On my arrival, I found at the graveyard a large pile of corpses without coffins, in horizontal layers, one above the other, like corded wood. I was told that there were more than one hundred bodies deposited there. They had been brought by unknown persons, at different hours since nine o'clock the evening previous. Large trenches were dug, into which these uncoffined corpses were thrown indiscriminately. The same day, a private hospital was found deserted; the physicians, nurses, and attendants were all dead, or had run away. Not a living person was in it. The wards were filled with putrid bodies, which, by order of the mayor, were piled in an adjacent yard, and burned, and their ashes scattered to the winds. Could a wiser disposition have been made of them?

Many persons, even of fortune and popularity, died in their beds without aid, unnoticed and unknown, and lay there for days unburied. In almost every house might be seen the sick, the dying, and the dead, in the same room. All the stores, banks, and places of business were closed. There were no means, no instruments for carrying on the ordinary affairs of business; for all the drays, carts, carriages, hand and common wheel-barrows, as well as hearses, were employed in the transportation of corpses, instead of cotton, sugar, and passengers. Words cannot describe my sensations when I first beheld the awful sight of carts driven to the graveyard, and there upturned, and their contents discharged as so many loads of lumber or offal, without a single mark of mourning or respect, because the exigency rendered it impossible.

The Sabbath came, and I ordered the sexton to ring the bell for church at eleven o'clock A.M., as usual. I did not expect to meet a half a dozen persons; but there was actually a congregation of two or three hundred, and all gentlemen. The ladies were engaged in taking care of the sick. There was no singing. I made a very short prayer, and preached a discourse not more than fifteen minutes in length. It made such an impression that several of the hearers met me at the door, and requested me to write it down for their perusal and meditation. I complied with the request. My text was the passage found in Isaiah, XXVI, 3: "Thou wilt keep him in perfect peace whose mind is stayed on thee, because he trusteth in thee."

For several days after this Sabbath, the plague raged with unabated violence. But the events, toils, trials, and gloom of one day, in this terrific visitation, were a *fac-simile* of those that characterized the whole scene. A fatal yellow fever had been spreading destruction in the city six weeks before the cholera commenced. Thousands had left it to escape this scourge. So that, at the time of the first cholera, it was estimated that the population of the city did not exceed thirty-five thousand inhabitants. During the entire epidemic, at least six thousand persons perished; showing the frightful loss of one sixth of the people in about twelve days. This is the most appalling instance of mortality known to have happened in any part of the world, ancient or modern. Yet, in all the accounts of the ravages of this enemy, in 1832, published in the northern cities and Europe, its desolations in New Orleans are not even noticed—a fact which requires no comment. The same ratio of mortality in Boston, the next twelve days, would call for more than twenty-three thousand victims. Who can realize this truth? The same epidemic broke out again the following summer, in June, 1833. In September of the same year, the yellow fever came back again. So, within the space of twelve months, we had two Asiatic choleras, and two epidemic yellow fevers, which carried off ten thousand persons that were known, and many more that were not reported.

Multitudes began the day in apparently good health, and were corpses before sunset. One morning, as I was going out, I spoke to a gentleman who resided in the very next house to mine. He was standing at his door, and remarked that he felt very well; "but I wonder," he added, "that you are alive." On my return, only two hours afterwards, he was a corpse. A baker died in his cart directly before my door. Near me there was a brick house going up; two of the workmen died on a carpenter's bench, but a short time after they had commenced their labors for the day. Often did it happen that a person engaged a coffin for some friend, who himself died before it could be finished. On a certain evening, about dark, a gentleman called on me to say a short service over the body of a particular friend, just deceased: the next morning I performed the same service for him. I went, one Wednesday night, to solemnize the contract of matrimony between a couple of very genteel appearance. The bride was young and possessed of the most extraordinary beauty. A few hours only had elapsed before I was summoned to perform the last offices over her coffin. She had on her bridal dress, and was very little changed in the appearance of her face.

Three unmarried gentlemen, belonging to my congregation, lived together and kept bachelor's hall, as it is termed with us. I was called to visit one of them at ten o'clock P.M. He lived but a few moments after I entered the room. Whilst I was conversing with the survivors, a second brother was taken with cramps. There was nobody in the house but the servants. They were especially dear to me because of their intrinsic character, and because they were regular attendants at church. We instantly applied the usual remedies, but without success. At one o'clock in the morning he breathed his last. The only surviving brother immediately fell beside the couch of the lifeless ones, and at daylight he died. We laid the three corpses side by side.

One family, of nine persons, supped together in perfect health; at the expiration of the next twenty-four hours, eight out of the nine were dead. A boarding house, that contained thirteen inmates, was absolutely emptied; not one was left to mourn.

Persons were found dead all along the streets, particularly early in the mornings. For myself, I expected that the city would be depopulated. I have no doubt, that if the truth could be ascertained, it would appear that those persons who died so suddenly were affected with what are called the premonitory symptoms hours, perhaps a day, or a night, before they considered themselves unwell. In this early stage, the disease is easily arrested; but when the cramps and collapse set in, death is, in most cases, inevitable. Indeed, that is death. *Then,* nothing was known of the cholera, and its antecedent stages were unnoticed and uncared for. Hence, in a great measure, the suddenness as well as the extent of the mortality.

Nature seemed to sympathize in the dreadful spectacle of human woe. A thick, dark atmosphere, as I said before, hung over us like a mighty funereal shroud. All was still. Neither sun, nor moon, nor stars shed their blessed light. Not a breath of air moved. A hunter, who lived on the Bayou St. John, assured me that during the cholera he killed no game. Not a bird was seen winging the sky. Artificial causes of terror were superadded to the gloom which covered the heavens. The burning of tar and pitch at every corner; the firing of cannon, by order of the city authorities, along all the streets; and the frequent conflagrations which actually occurred at that dreadful period—all these conspired to add a sublimity and horror to the tremendous scene. Our wise men hoped, by the combustion of tar and gunpowder, to purify the atmosphere. We have no doubt that hundreds perished from mere fright produced by artificial noise, the constant sight of funerals, darkness, and various other causes.

It was an awful spectacle to see night ushered in by the firing of artillery in different parts of the city, making as much noise as arises from the engagement of two powerful armies. The sight was one of the most tremendous which was ever presented to the eye, or even exhibited to the imagination, in description. Often, walking my nightly rounds, the flames from the burning tar so illuminated the city streets and river, that I could see everything almost as distinctly as in the daytime. And through many a window into which was flung the sickly flickering of these conflagrations, could be seen persons struggling in death, and rigid, blackened corpses, awaiting the arrival of some cart or hearse, as soon as dawn appeared, to transport them to their final resting place.

During these ineffable, inconceivable horrors, I was enabled to maintain my post for fourteen days, without a moment's serious illness. I often sank down upon the floor, sofa, or pavement, faint and exhausted from over-exertion, sleeplessness, and want of food; but a short nap would partially restore me, and send me out afresh to renew my perilous labors. For a whole fortnight, I did not attempt to undress except to bathe and put on clean apparel. I was like a soldier, who is not allowed, by the constant presence of an enemy, to throw off his armor, and lay down his weapons for a single moment. Morning, noon, and midnight, I was engaged in the sick room, and in performing services over the dead. The thought that I myself should be exempted from the scourge—how could it be cherished for a moment? I expected that every day would be my last. Yet, as I said before, I did not have the slightest symptom of the cholera. . . .

My escape was wonderful, considered in another respect. For fifteen days in succession, the atmosphere was loaded with the most deadly malaria, and every species of noxious impurity. I had to encounter not only the general insalubrity which always infects the air when cholera prevails, but to this were superadded the constant inhalations of the sick-bed effluvium which emanates from corpses in every stage of decomposition, in which life had been extinct for days, perhaps, and the offensive smells of the cemetery. Most of the bodies laid in the ground had a covering of earth but a few inches in depth, and through the porous dust there was an unimpeded emission of all the gases evolved from animal matter, when undergoing the process of putrefaction. The sick poor were often crowded together in low, narrow, damp, basement, unventilated rooms.

Many times, on entering these apartments, and putting my head under the mosquito bar, I became deadly sick in a moment, and was taken with vomiting, which, however, passed off without producing serious effects in a single instance. Let the reader imagine a close room, in which are lying half a dozen bodies in the process of decay, and he may form a faint conception of the physical horrors in which I lived, moved, and had my being continually for two entire weeks. My preservation has always seemed to me like a miracle. It is true, some constitutions are not susceptible of the cholera. Some can never take the yellow fever or small pox. It is not improbable that my safety ought to be ascribed to some peculiar idiosyncrasy, which enabled me to breathe the air of this plague with impunity.

In 1822, I knew an unacclimated gentleman who slept on the same bed with an intimate friend, whilst he was sick of the yellow fever: on the morning of his death, he himself, his clothes, and the sheets, were absolutely inundated by a copious discharge of the *vomito*. After the funeral, he continued to occupy the same room, and had the best health all that summer and autumn. During the next thirty years, he never left the city for a day, and was never sick. I have known numerous instances of the kind. . . .

The cholera had been raging with unabated fury for fourteen days. It seemed as if the city was destined to be emptied of its inhabitants. During this time, as before stated, a thick, dark, sultry atmosphere filled our city. Every one complained of a difficulty in breathing, which he never before experienced. The heavens were as stagnant as the mantled pool of death. There were no breezes. At the close of the fourteenth day, about eight o'clock in the evening, a smart storm, something like a tornado, came from the north-west, accompanied with heavy peals of thunder and terrific lightnings. The deadly air was displaced immediately, by that which was new, fresh, salubrious, and life-giving. The next morning shone forth all bright and beautiful. The plague was stayed. In the opinion of all the medical gentlemen who were on the spot, that change of weather terminated the epidemic. At any rate, it took its departure from us that very hour. No new cases occurred after that storm. It is certainly, then, in the power of God, not only by wind and electricity, but also by other means innumerable beyond our powers of discernment, to deliver a city from pestilence, in answer to the prayers of his children. Some one has said that "a little philosophy may make one an unbeliever, but that a great deal will make him a Christian.". . .

In the cholera of June, 1833, the disease first invaded our own family circle. Two daughters, the eldest four, and the youngest two years of age, died about the same time. I was so fortunate as to procure a carriage, in which their bodies were conveyed to a family vault, in the Girod cemetery, which had been constructed and presented to me, some years before, by the trustees of Christ Church, Canal Street—a church characterized for large, generous, and noble sympathies. I rode in the carriage alone with the two coffins. There was not a soul present but myself, to aid in performing the last sad offices. Most desolate and heavy was my heart. . . .

Dr. Clapp remained in New Orleans through several plagues and epidemics. In the latter portion of his memoir, he continues his description:

Let me attempt to suggest a general but very inadequate idea of my labors and sufferings in each of the campaigns above referred to. The term of a sickly season in New Orleans has never been less than six weeks. In a majority of cases it has extended from eight weeks to ten. In 1824 it began early in June, and did not entirely disappear till the November following. On an average, it is within bounds to say that the duration of each epidemic spoken of in these pages was at least eight weeks. Multiply eight by twenty, and the product is one hundred and sixty. Hence it follows that since my settlement in Louisiana I have spent over three entire years in battling, with all my might, against those invisible enemies, the cholera and yellow fever. In these three years I scarcely enjoyed a night of undisturbed repose. When I did sleep, it was upon my post, in the midst of the dead and wounded, with my armor on, and ready at the first summons to meet the deadly assault. . . .

Perhaps there is no acute disease actually less painful than yellow fever, although there is none more shocking and repulsive to the beholder. Often I have met and shook hands with some blooming, handsome young man to-day, and in a few hours afterwards, I have been called to see him with profuse hemorrhages from the mouth, nose, ears, eyes, and even the toes; the eyes prominent, glistening, yellow, and staring; the face discolored with orange color and dusky red.

The physiognomy of the yellow fever corpse is usually sad, sullen, and perturbed; the countenance dark, mottled, livid, swollen, and stained with blood and black vomit; the veins of the face and whole body become distended, and look as if they were going to burst; and though the heart has ceased to beat, the circulation of the blood sometimes continues for hours, quite as active as in life. Think reader, what it must be to have one's mind wholly occupied with such sights and scenes for weeks together, nay, more—for months, for years, for a whole lifetime even. Scarcely a night passes now, in which my dreams are not haunted more or less by the distorted faces, the shrieks, the convulsions, the groans, the struggles, and the horrors which I witnessed thirty-five years ago. They come up before my mind's eye like positive, absolute realities. I awake, rejoicing indeed to find that it is a dream; but there is no more sleep for me that night. No arithmetic could compute the diminution of my happiness, for the last forty years, from this single source. Setting aside another and better world to come, I would not make such a sacrifice as one epidemic demands, for all the fame, pleasures, and gold of earth. What, then, will you think of twenty?

A clergyman said to me not long since, "You have indeed had a terrible time in New Orleans. You will be rewarded for it some time or other, but not *here,* not *here.* A suitable remuneration awaits you in the kingdom of God, beyond the grave."

I shocked my friend exceedingly by saying, "I neither expect any such remuneration nor desire it. I have had my reward already. Virtue is its own reward. I am no more entitled to a seat in heaven for all I have done (supposing my motives to have been holy) than the veriest wretch that ever expiated his crimes on the gallows." I repeat it, every person who does his duty receives a perfect recompense this side of the grave. He can receive nothing afterwards, except upon the platform of mercy. For the good deeds done in the body, there is no heaven but upon earth. When will Christian ministers learn this fundamental truth of the gospel? . . .

The two most fatal yellow fevers which I have witnessed were those of 1837 and 1853. In the former year there were ten thousand cases of fever reported, and five thousand deaths. The epidemic broke out about the middle of August, and lasted eight weeks. This is the greatest mortality which was ever known in the United States, if we except that which occurred in the cholera of New Orleans, October,

1832. The year 1837 is memorable for the introduction of what is called the quinine practice. It is now, I am told by the physicians, generally abandoned. By some persons abroad, our doctors have been much blamed for thinking to overcome the yellow fever by the above-named medicine. For myself, I do not wonder that they made such an attempt. It had been recommended by the most celebrated practitioners in the West Indies, and in other tropical regions. New Orleans has always been blessed with the most learned, skilful, and competent physicians; but they are neither omniscient nor omnipotent. The cause of yellow fever is to this day a profound mystery. . . .

In writing of the epidemic of 1853, Dr. Clapp says:

On the day of my arrival, it rained incessantly from morning till night. In the space of twelve hours, the interments were over three hundred. The same day, I visited two unacclimated families belonging to my own church, who were all down with the plague. In these families were nine persons; but two of them survived. I knew a large boarding house for draymen, mechanics, and humble operatives, from which forty-five corpses were borne away in thirteen days. A poor lady of my acquaintance kept boarders for a livelihood. Her family consisted of eight unacclimated persons. Every one of them died in the space of three weeks.

Six unacclimated gentlemen, intelligent, refined, and strictly temperate, used to meet once a week, to enjoy music, cheering conversation, and innocent amusements. They had been told that it was a great safeguard, in a sickly summer, to keep up good spirits, and banish from their minds dark and melancholy thoughts. They passed a certain evening together in health and happiness. In precisely one week from that entertainment, five of them were gathered to the tomb. One of the most appalling features of the yellow fever is the rapidity with which it accomplishes its mission.

There is some difficulty in arriving at the true statistics touching the epidemic of 1853. It was supposed by the best informed physicians that there were fifty or sixty thousand unacclimated persons in New

OLD HOUSES AND SHOPS IN DECATUR STREET

GENERAL BEAUREGARD HOUSE IN CHARTRES
STREET

Orleans when the epidemic began, about the 1st of July. From that time to the 1st of November, the whole number of deaths reported were ten thousand and three hundred. Of these, eight thousand died of the yellow fever. The physicians estimated that thirty-two thousand of those attacked this year were cured. Of course, if this calculation be true, the whole number of cases in 1853 was forty thousand.

The horrors and desolations of this epidemic cannot be painted; neither can they be realized, except by those who have lived in New Orleans, and have witnessed and participated in similar scenes. Words can convey no adequate idea of them. In some cases, all the clerks and agents belonging to mercantile establishments were swept away, and the stores closed by the civil authorities. Several entire families were carried off—parents, children, servants, all. Others lost a quarter, or a third, or three fourths of their members, and their business, hopes, and happiness were blasted for life. The ravages of the destroyer were marked by more woeful and affecting varieties of calamity than were ever delineated on the pages of romance. Fifteen clergymen died that season—two Protestant ministers and thirteen Roman Catholic priests.

They were strangers to the climate, but could not be frightened from their posts of duty. The word *fear* was not in their vocabulary. Four Sisters of Charity were laid in their graves, and several others were brought to the point of death. It is painful to dwell on these melancholy details, but it may suggest profitable trains of thought. Set before your imaginations a picture of forty thousand persons engaged in a sanguinary battle, in which ten thousand men are killed outright. One thousand persons will fill a large church. Suppose ten congregations, of this number each, were to be assembled for worship in Boston, on the 1st day of July, 1858, and that on the first day of the following November, in the short space of four months, all should be numbered with the dead. This mortality would be no more awful than that which I have witnessed in the Crescent City.

It is interesting to note that Dr. Clapp pays the highest tribute to the Catholic priests of New Orleans for their work during the epidemics:

In the epidemic of 1832 I was the only Protestant clergyman that remained in the city, except the Reverend M. Hull, of the Episcopal church, who was confined to his house by a lingering consumption and unable to leave his room. This gentleman never left the city in sickly seasons, but fearlessly continued at his post, however great and alarming the mortality around him. So it was that in the first cholera I had no coadjutors but the Roman Catholic priests.

It is also interesting to note that Dr. Clapp speaks of his aversion for the Catholic religion at the time of his arrival in New Orleans. He soon changed his mind, for he found the priests to be cultured gentlemen some of whom were as broad as the good Presbyterian minister himself. It is interesting nowadays, in this time of religious hatreds, to read a memoir so intelligent, and so truly Christian in spirit as this one of Dr. Clapp's.

His name is still honored in New Orleans, by Catholic and Protestant alike.

His description of the yellow fever epidemics is particularly interesting in view of modern scientific knowledge. In the epidemics of his day, the fear of the unknown was added to the fear of the disease itself.

When it was discovered, in 1905, that the fever was caused by the sting of a mosquito, and by that alone, the city was able to protect itself. There have been no epidemics since that time.

Chapter XXIII

STRANGE SPORTS

THE advertisements in old newspapers prove that the people of New Orleans were always eager for novelty. In newspapers for 1820 we find notices of cock-fights on Sunday afternoon. A few years before bull-fights were advertised. One strange notice tells of a fight between a bull-dog and an alligator; admission, one dollar.

In Flugel's diary we find that on Sunday, April 11, 1817, the writer went for a walk.

I walked to the suburb of St. Mary [he writes]. Here I hoped to enjoy an hour of tranquillity, but scarcely had I gone two steps when I met a group of boxers with bloody faces. I proceeded a few steps further when I saw two Frenchmen busily engaged in a cock-fight. The poor animals were nearly exhausted, but they revived them by blowing garlic and whiskey into their bills. Low, brutish, savage-like, has been everything my eyes beheld to-day. Later I witnessed a negro dance. Their postures and movements somewhat resembled those of monkeys. One might, with a little imagination, take them for a group of baboons. Yet as these poor wretches are entirely ignorant of anything like civilization (for their masters with-

hold everything from them that in the least might add to the cultivation of their minds), one must not be surprised at their actions.
The recreation is at least natural and they are free in comparison with
those poor wretches, the slaves of their passions.

These negroes were the Voodoo dancers of Congo
Square, but Mr. Flugel was so opposed to the French and
Spanish Sunday of the New Orleans people, that he had
scant sympathy for what he saw that day. I quote this
fragment of his diary only to give an idea of Sunday recreation in those days.

Unfortunately there are few enough descriptions of the
strange sports which developed in New Orleans, and these
descriptions, like this one of Mr. Flugel's, are usually
written by one out of sympathy with the entertainment.
However, I have an excellent article—with a most amus-
ingly hypocritical foreword, which I will quote here in
order to give an idea of a popular diversion for Sunday
afternoon in 1853.

The New York "Illustrated News" for Saturday,
April 23, of that year reports a bull- and bear-fight in
detail:

A species of cruel Spanish amusement has been allowed to take
place recently in New Orleans, which has received the well-merited
reprobation of the intelligent press throughout the United States.
Were it not that our position as journalists, requires a portraiture of
all that is remarkable in our land, we should be loath to publish any
incident so calculated to blight the good name of our sister city.
But we regret to add that the fair name of our northern cities, and
of European cities, have not been less sullied, though in a different
manner. Prize-fighting, between reasonable men, has taken place
again and again near our northern cities, and has resulted in the

death and disfigurement of the participators. And who shall say that the cruelty of the former exceeds that of the latter—that the ten thousand citizens assembled to see a brutal prize-fight are not more degraded in their tastes than a Spanish population, delighting themselves over the cruelty of a bull- and bear-fight? This amusement is not confined to the Atlantic cities; it first commenced in California and attracted crowds of spectators, taking best among the mining population. There, as here, the intelligent portion of the press raised a strong voice against the inhuman practice, and of late it has there fallen into disrepute and has almost wholly ceased. Such we know must be the result here. We have too much confidence in the good sense of our citizens to suppose that such revolting scenes can be tolerated any length of time.

Our correspondent at New Orleans has not failed to supply us with a faithful sketch of the encounter, to which we append his own version of the affair. The excellence of the sketch almost causes forgetfulness of its subject.

In the arena was a cage about thirty feet square and twelve feet high, built of timber, grated, with bars of iron; in it stood a large powerful dark slate-colored bull, Napoleon Fourth—sole monarch of that establishment. By the side of this stood another cage, with a large and powerful grizzly bear, which would weigh about four or five cwt., and would stand from three and a half to four feet high, with a lank sort of India-rubber movement and action—about half devil. We had just time to notice the preparatory arrangements, when the crowd from the outside broke through. In rushed several thousand people; they flew like magic on to the top of the large, cage, which was covered with boards, so that the cage was soon surrounded and covered in every direction by sightseers. Those from the staging, and outsiders, who could not get a sight, commenced an assault on those on and about the cage, with stones, brickbats, clubs, boards, turf, and everything that came handy, to clear the way and give fair play. This having the desired effect, and all being ready, the slide door was hoisted and Bruin notified with a ten-foot pole that he was wanted in the other apartment. The bull was standing in the centre, ready to receive his guest. After the bear had made his entrance, the slide door was shut, so that both animals were secure in the large cage. The bull, considering the intrusion rather improper, for Sunday, commenced pawing and making a low bellow; the bear in the meantime, walking round by the bars of the cage, with a deep low howl.

After going quite around the cage, and finding it all secure, he stopped, and his eyes began to fire up. The bull by this time appeared to be up to the boiling pitch of rage, unable longer to bear the insolence of the bear. At him he plunged. The bear struck the bull's ear. This enraged the bull, who made another plunge at the bear—the bear, not counting exactly on the sport, got entangled in the bull's horns, buried his teeth in the upper side of the bull's head; the bull, however, whirled him off. After they had time to breathe awhile, they were stirred up with long poles. The bull made a desperate drive at the bear, knocked him on his back, jumped on him lengthways. There the two were, head to head. The bear, opening his paws quick as a flash of lightning, took the bull, clasped one paw each side of his head, grasped his nose with his tusks, and in this position held and hugged the bull—both bear and bull kicking with their hind feet, the bear still sticking to his embrace. After remaining some minutes in this position, during which time the blood flowed profusely, the bull, suspecting that the bear was sucking rather too much of his life, made a desperate effort and cleared himself. Another short respite, and the bull was again warmed up to the scratch. The bear missing hold, the bull caught him in the eye. The bear was perfectly savage. At it they went again; the bull threw the bear six or eight feet in the air, the bear fell and pretended to be dead. The bull, not being satisfied, with these pretensions, drove at him again—the bear grabbed him by the nose and another hug ensued. The bull extricated himself, and at the bear he went until Bruin sneaked into a corner, out of which he could neither be coaxed, flattered, nor driven. The bull set up a loud bellow, as he proudly walked about the cage, pawing. The excited multitude gave one long, loud yell for Napoleon Fourth, and departed.

Chapter XXIV

MARIE LAVEAU

THE first reference to black magic in official documents, or rather the first reference which I have been able to find, is in 1782 during the Spanish régime in New Orleans. Galvez was governor, and in a musty document on file at the Cabildo, a document which tells of imports and exports of the colony, one is startled to find a terse sentence prohibiting further importation of negro slaves from Martinique, "as these negroes are too much given to voodooism and make the lives of the citizens unsafe." There is subject for thought here, for Galvez was not a man given to superstition or fear. He was a soldier primarily and a daring one at that, and if he saw fit to bar negroes of Martinique from the city of New Orleans, it is probable that he had good reason.

It is likely that from the very beginning of the colony in 1718, African superstitions had given trouble to the colonists; for in the very beginning ship-loads of "brute negroes" were shipped to Louisiana for the purpose of clearing the ground, building houses, tilling the fields, and doing other manual labor. These negroes were in truth brutes, for the earliest shipments of slaves to the colonies consisted of captives taken in battle on the African coast. It was the custom of cannibal chiefs to sell their prisoners after a battle to the owners of slave ships. These savages, packed into the holds of the vessels, were brought to the coasts of the United States. Many of them died on the way; many committed suicide—and that is a strange thing, as one finds the suicide rate among negroes very low. But even discounting the death rate, hundreds and hundreds of these savages poured into the colony. Here they labored under the lash of their white masters.

In a swamp near New Orleans, there was a slave farm, a place of horror, where these negroes were herded and kept until they were tamed or killed. Here they were taught to use rough implements; they were taught to plow and to handle an ax. After a time they were brought to New Orleans and sold, sometimes by auction and sometimes directly to individuals.

Now these negroes, who knew no French and who conducted their dealings with the white men by means of gestures and the few words which they had learned, brought with them from Africa their old religions, superstitions, charms, and spells. And while very early in the history of New Orleans we find these slaves being baptized into the Roman Catholic church by their masters, it is only natural to believe that Catholicism was but a thin veneer over their own tribal beliefs.

It was soon after the introduction of negro slaves that we first hear tales of voodooism. According to the

Africans of the Arada nation, the god Voodoo signified an all-powerful, supernatural being from whom all events derived their origin. This being was a creature vast and terrible, not altogether unlike the God of the Old Testament. The Voodoo god was all-powerful, but at the same time frivolous and malicious. The symbol was a snake, and in this one finds a similarity to phallic worship found among many primitive nations.

To understand properly the workings of this black magic, one must understand something of the negro's characteristics. It must be remembered that he is intensely emotional, that he possesses a childlike credulity, that his imagination is easily inflamed, and that the powers of darkness are potent powers. Good may be, but evil is. The negro's folklore is full of ghosts and demons. Evil is all powerful. In a book recently published, "The African Saga," by Blaise Cendrars, a Frenchman, translated into English and published by Payson and Clarke, we find many stories which have a strong resemblance to Uncle Remus and other negro tales which have been handed down to us. The arresting thing in a consideration of these stories is their lack of what we call a moral tone. Goodness and virtue are seldom rewarded, but rather quickness of wit. It is better to be wise, we learn, than to be good, and better still to be crafty. It is well to bear this in mind when thinking of voodoo or snake worship, for it must be remembered that these negroes in New Orleans were slaves held in bondage by the lash, were cruelly treated, and in addition their gods had been taken away from them and an alien God substituted. They could do nothing but submit, and no doubt they enjoyed the symbolism of the Catholic church, with its incense and pageantry, but it is also certain that they kept their own beliefs. Persecution has a way of strengthening religions. It may be that Nero's persecution of early Christians helped spread Christianity more than anything else; for men have a way of glorying in their martyrdoms. And in a similar way, perhaps, the African slaves drew pleasure from the secrecy of their ceremonies, just as early Christians did.

In any event, voodooism was firmly implanted in early Colonial New Orleans, and it was not long before white men and women felt its power and learned to fear it. There is an old volume, "Souvenirs d'Amérique," in which there is a discussion of voodooism:

At some remote spot, usually near the borders of a dismal swamp, the members of the sect were wont to assemble, always in the dead of night, and after divesting themselves of their raiment, would gird their loins with a number of red handkerchiefs and encase their feet in sandals. These conclaves were shrouded in deepest secrecy. The manner of dress, however, varied at different times and places, with frequent modifications of the above-mentioned costume. The King and Queen, distinguished from the others by a blue cord fastened around the waist, would take their position at one end of the room, near an impromptu altar upon which rested the box containing the imprisoned serpent. After making sure that no intruders were within earshot, the adoration of the serpent would begin, the King and Queen exhorting their subjects to have entire confidence in their power, and to make known their individual desires. Thereupon, each according to his wants would step forward to implore the voodoo God; one for the gift of domination over his master's mind, another for success in love, a third for a speedy cure and long life, a fourth for fortune, and so on. The King would then seize the precious box, lay it on the floor, and place the Queen upon the lid. No sooner had her feet touched the sacred receptacle, than she became possessed, and like a new Pythoness, her frame quivering, entire body convulsed, the oracle would pronounce its edicts through her inspired lips. On some she bestowed flattery and promises of success, while at others she thundered forth bitter invectives. As soon as the oracle had answered every question, a circle was formed, and the serpent replaced upon the unholy fane. Then each would present his offering, which the King and Queen would promptly assure them was acceptable to their Divine protector.

An oath was administered which bound the members not only to secrecy, but to assist in carrying on the work agreed upon as well. Then the famous voodoo dance would begin. The initiation of a candidate usually inaugurated this ceremony. The King would trace with a piece of charcoal a large circle in the center of the room, placing within it the sable neophyte. He would next thrust into the latter's hand a small package of herbs, horsehair, broken bits of horn, and other equally stupid fragments. Then striking him lightly on the head with a wooden paddle, the King would launch forth into a weird African chant. This chant, taken up by the chorus, would increase in volume, the gyrating dancer becoming convulsed. He would then drink some stimulating liquor, be led to the altar to take the oath, and finally lapse into a hysteric fit. Upon the termination of this ceremony, the King would place his hands on the box containing the snake, make a distorted movement of the body, communicate this impulsion to the Queen, who in turn would convey it to every one in the circle. All would now show signs of convulsions in the upper part of the body, the Queen being particularly affected, and going to the voodoo serpent to gather a fresh supply of magnetic influence. Copious draughts of spiritous liquors are offered around, the hideous shouts grow louder, and general pandemonium is let loose. Fainting and choking spells succeeded one another, and a nervous tremor seemed to possess the entire audience. The dancers would spin round with incredible velocity, at times tearing their vestments and even lacerating their flesh. The tumultuous orgy would continue, until the savage participants, entirely deprived of reason, fell to the ground from sheer lassitude, and were carried, panting and gyrating, to the open air. . . .

By the end of the eighteenth century, voodooism was firmly entrenched. This secret society extended through the entire slave population and among the free negroes as well. A message could be conveyed from one end of the city to another in a single day without one white person's being aware of it. It is said that a negro cook in a kitchen would sing some Creole song while she rattled her pots and pans, a song which sounded innocuous enough to any white listener, but at the end of the verse she would sing a few words intended as a message. Another negro working near-by would listen intently and at the end of the second verse would hear the message repeated. This second servant would then go outside to attend to her duties. She would sing the same song and her voice would be heard by servants in the house next door. In this way, by means of a song, news of a meeting of a voodoo society would be carried from one end of the city to another and upon the appointed night negro men and women would slip from their beds before midnight and would assemble for their ceremonies.

So strong a fear was inspired by the voodoo rulers that members of the sect could be induced to commit almost any crime. Whether the Voodoos possessed supernatural power or not is not for me to say, but it is quite sure that they possessed a knowledge of subtle drugs and poisons, and it is easily seen that their white masters were powerless before them. It is known that many masters were poisoned by their slaves, and in a great many instances no motive could be proved.

In any discussion of voodoo, the name of Marie Laveau must be mentioned. She was the Queen of the

Voodoos, and a subject for hundreds of tales of terror and wonder in New Orleans. According to records in the archives of the St. Louis Cathedral under the signature of the famous Père Antoine, there is registered the marriage of Jacques Paris and Marie Laveau on August 4, 1819. Both were free mulattoes. Jacques Paris died in 1826, and shortly after his widow formed a liaison with Christophe Glapion, another mulatto. Several children were born to them, among them Marie, who being a natural daughter, took her mother's maiden name, Laveau. She was born on the second day of February, 1827. We know nothing of her childhood, but as a very young woman we find her known to the police as a worker of black magic. She became known officially as the Voodoo Queen and even to-day her name is used to frighten children. "Marie Laveau will get you," the Creole mothers say to their naughty children.

Henri Castellanos in his book, "New Orleans As It Was," has this to say of Marie Laveau:

In her youth she was a woman of fine physique. Introducing herself into families as a hair-dresser, she would assist in the clandestine correspondence of sweethearts, and aid youthful lovers. She was an essentially bad woman. Though Queen of the "voudous," she exercised the ritual of the original creed so as to make it conform to the worship of the Virgin and of other saints. To idolatry she added blasphemy. She was the first to popularize "voudouism" in New Orleans, inviting members of the press, of the sporting fraternity, and others to the yearly festivals held on St. John's eve (June 24) at some spot not far from the bayou which bears that name. She also dealt in charms against malefices, and pretended to cure ailments produced by "gris-gris" (little red bags containing powdered brick, yellow ochre, and cayenne pepper, which were supposed to cause untold injury to the recipient) and other criminal devices.

There are many other stories told of her. In an article
by G. William Nott, which appeared in the New Orleans
"Times-Picayune," we find the following:

It will not be amiss to relate the story of an octogenarian mammy,
who says that Marie Laveau was not a wicked woman, but much
maligned by her enemies, and that what powers she had were used for
the good of others, as the following tale will prove. A certain wealthy
young man in New Orleans, many years ago, had been arrested in
connection with a crime, and though his companions were in reality
the guilty ones, the blame was laid upon his shoulders. The grief-
stricken father immediately sought Marie Laveau, explained to her the
circumstances of the case, and offered her a handsome reward if she
would obtain his son's release. When the day set for the trial came
round, the wily "voodoo," after placing three Guinea peppers in
her mouth, entered the St. Louis Cathedral, knelt at the altar rail,
and was seen to remain in this posture for some time. Leaving the
church, she gained admittance to the Cabildo, where the trial was
to be held, and depositing three of the peppers under the judge's
bench, lingered to await developments. After a lengthy deliberation,
though the evidence seemed unfavorable to the prisoner, the jury
finally made its report, and the judge was heard to pronounce the
words, "Not guilty." The joy of the anxious father may well be
imagined. His first act was to find Marie Laveau, and as a recompense for her miraculous intervention he gave her the deed to a small
cottage. The latter, situated on St. Anne between Rampart and
Burgundy, remained her home to the time of her death. As a further
proof of her charity, an incident is related, which though exhibiting
the above named virtue, shows traces of cunning as well. A young
man came to her door on one occasion, ragged and destitute, begging
for alms. As she herself was short of funds, she could give him nothing, but summoning her nimble wits, she evolved a scheme that
promptly bore fruit. Laying the man on a couch in her front room,
and covering him with a sheet, she proceeded to light candles which
she placed at his head and feet. This done, she stationed herself on
the door steps, tin cup in hand, begging the money with which to

CONGO SQUARE FROM ORLEANS STREET

OLD BANK BUILDINGS AT ROYAL STREET
AND CONTI

defray the poor deceased man's funeral. The success of the plan was almost instantaneous (she well knew the negro's love for "wakes"), and, cup overflowing with coins, she returned indoors to share the profits with the speedily resurrected "corpse."

Another quaint occurrence in the same house is recounted by an eye-witness.

One of Marie Laveau's protégés had passed away, this time in reality, and the interment was to take place from her "front parlor." Came the hour for the funeral. As soon as the coffin had been borne away, followed by the Queen and a motley assemblage, three negresses, one with broom, the others with buckets, and a negro man, rushed out of the house, the former like some ancient Furies, and scoured with savage energy the brick *banquette,* removing every trace of the mourners' foot-prints.

And then, a little later in the same article, Mr. Nott has this to say:

Again a narrative of Marie Laveau's strange career. In 1884 a violent hurricane passed over the city. She was then living in a shanty on Lake Pontchartrain. The force of the wind was so great that her cabin was wrenched from its foundations and hurled into the angry waters. Obliged to seek shelter on the roof, there she remained for several hours, discouraging the attempts of her would-be rescuers and telling them, "Mo oulé mourri dan lac lá" (I want to die in that lake). However, she was finally prevailed upon to accept the assistance offered, and none too soon, for the cabin she was so loath to leave, was completely shattered by the waves a few moments later. To this day, the superstitious darkies will tell you that not until Marie was safe ashore did the fury of the storm abate.

It was previously mentioned that the black priestess dealt in "gris-gris." To the casual reader this word will mean little or nothing, but to an impressionable negro, it is one to be conjured with. If by chance a dusky house-keeper, upon opening her front blinds, found a "gris-gris" deposited on the door sill, loud were her vociferations. Immediately would she repair to Marie Laveau, wailing in the

streets, "appé voudou moin, appé voudou moin" (I have been vou-
doued). Terror-stricken and almost speechless, she would inform the
black Queen of the dire calamity that had befallen her, and implore
her assistance. This, Marie would immediately promise. Searching
some little chest or drawer, she would find a counter "gris-gris,"
guaranteed to destroy the evil effects of the original, which for the
modest sum of one or two dollars she would place in the hands of the
grateful suppliant. Of course, there could be no doubt as to the
efficacy of the second package, for had she not manufactured the contents of the first as well? This latter fact, however, she deemed wise
to keep to herself.

An old gentleman who remembers Marie Laveau from his childhood days, will tell how she was held in dread by many of the residents below Canal Street, white as well as colored. He describes her
as having a "Voltairian look," penetrating and taking in everything at
a glance; an attribute quite disconcerting to the children of the neighborhood, who would listen with terror when their black nurses
threatened to "give them to Marie" if they failed to obey.

Whether or not the famous Marie Laveau possessed supernatural
powers, has long been a subject of discussion among the ignorant.
More enlightened people have dismissed her as a crass imposter,
though not denying for an instant the prestige she held among her
own race. However, with her death, "voudouism" all but disappeared
from New Orleans. The little that is practised to-day assumes a
harmless form; a few chicken bones placed on a door step, a black
cross mark on a front board, a bright red powder sprinkled on the
banquette; these are the last vestiges of the once dreaded "gris-gris."

In the Old St. Louis Cemetery on Basin Street is a neat brick
tomb, with the following inscription:

Famille Vve. Paris,

née Laveau.

This is all that remains to recall the former greatness of the all
powerful Voudou Queen.

Chapter XXV

THE END OF THE GOLDEN AGE

THE thirty-year period from 1830 to 1860 marked the Golden Age in Louisiana. Those were "the good old times." With the coming of the steamboat, the wealth of the continent was carried down the Mississippi and spread out on the levee at New Orleans. In rural Louisiana the plantation system was at the peak of its success, and the planter, with hundreds of slaves to do his labor, reaped a rich harvest. Commerce on the river, and prosperity on the plantation caused the flood of gold that New Orleans came to know.

The city was extravagantly gay. Royal Street was lined with gambling houses, where in candle-lighted rooms Creole planters matched their skill against the professional gambler, or against the American who had come down the river. There were balls every night. The Mardi Gras festivities had begun, and were growing more lavish every year. The Americans had learned something of the Creoles' art of good living. Old differences between Creole and

American were being eliminated. The city was spreading; villages which had been miles beyond the town limits a few years before were now incorporated within the city itself. The American section above Canal Street was filled with magnificent mansions. Theater and opera flourished.

It is true that plagues swept the city and a fearful number of inhabitants died—but this was an era of transition and quick recovery. The year following the plague found the Mardi Gras festivities gayer than before. . . . It would seem that there was a volatile, mercurial quality in the very air. Pestilence, gaiety, love, and death.

Nobody looked into the future. Every one, it seems, made the most of the present. In New Orleans, in the "flush fifties," no one foresaw the disaster and despair that was to come so soon.

The prosperity of New Orleans was based upon an economic system which Louisianians believed to be sound: river commerce and slave labor. The river commerce seemed a wholly natural development, for did not the current of the river carry the produce of the nation to the city at the river's mouth? It seemed incredible that any artificial transportation—such as canals offered—could compete with the natural carrier. And railroads were a dim dream. The plantation system was based upon the work of slaves; for without cheap labor these immense tracts of land were almost worthless. The South knew nothing about production except on a large scale. Gaily and blindly, it went onward to its doom.

Who could have foreseen the Civil War, or realized that the whole economic system would collapse like a house of cards?

Let us look at river commerce for a moment:

The introduction of the steamboat as a means of transportation on the river brought a radical change in trade lines and gave an immense impetus to business in New Orleans. Trade is larger in the aggregate to-day, but not relatively and proportionately, and there is not as much profit in it.

During the early days of steamboating, in spite of plagues and epidemics, New Orleans rose to be the wealthiest city in the Union, the third in population, and disputed with New York the rank of first port in America. No other American city ever occupied the metropolitan position that New Orleans filled for half the century during its "flush days."

The first blow to New Orleans trade came as early as 1832 when the waters of the upper Ohio were connected with Lake Erie by canal, and the latter with the Hudson River by the Erie Canal. Over the route the State of Ohio shipped to New York 86,000 barrels of flour, 98,000 bushels of wheat, and 2,500,000 staves in 1835. But at that time so much produce was coming down the Mississippi that no attention was paid to this slight diversion of traffic. But a greater enemy was to come—the railroad.

Railroad building began in 1830, but it was many years before river traffic had anything to fear. For a long time railroads were considered as expedients for getting goods to the river, where they could be shipped to their destination. In 1849 the receipts from commerce, in spite of canals and railroads, reached the magnificent total of $81,989,692. This was at the time when New Orleans was entering its career as the cotton city of the world. But by

1845 it was estimated that half the produce of the Mississippi Valley shipped to seaboard found its way to the market via the canals, railroads, and other routes, and half by way of the river to New Orleans. In 1846 the receipts of flour and wheat at Buffalo exceeded those of New Orleans. This created a sensation. The New Orleans press expressed the belief that the diversion "was only temporary"! The newspapers predicted that the trade would return. It never did.

Nevertheless, the season just before the Civil War— that is, the year 1859-1860—saw the largest receipts of produce at New Orleans, and the heaviest and most profitable trade the city had ever done. It was the summit of commercial prosperity. The total river trade that year was valued at $289,565,000.

The Civil War, the backwardness of the lower Mississippi Valley people in seeing the advantages of railroads, and numerous other causes have been set down for the decline of river traffic. Probably all of these factors influenced. But in those golden days, no one suspected that the prosperity was doomed to end so soon.

In those days the levee was the show-place of the city. The description of the levee in ante-bellum days reads like a fairy-tale. The New Orleans levee was the storehouse for the whole Mississippi Valley.

"All along the wharves lay steamboats, two or three deep, for the wharfage was not sufficient to accommodate all the vessels loading in port," writes Norman Walker in the "Standard History of New Orleans."

"All was action; the very water was covered with life. It was beyond all question the most active commercial center of the world, with which not even the docks of Liverpool and London could merit comparison; and whenever anyone expressed fear that the railroads would sap the commerce of New Orleans, he was taken to the levee and asked if that looked like commercial decay."

The Civil War killed prosperity on the river. True, there was a sort of second-blooming in the few years that followed, but by 1865 the shipments of western produce through the port of New Orleans had declined between 75 and 90 per cent!

Again the history of New Orleans becomes a part of the history of the United States. I shall not go into causes of the Civil War, nor shall I attempt to tell the history of New Orleans during wartime. This is a story which has been written again and again. Suffice to say that New Orleans fell—it was an unfortified city—on April 24, 1862. The men, both Creole and American, were with the Confederate army, fighting, many states away. Farragut's fleet managed to pass the blockade at the river's mouth, managed to pass the two inadequate forts below New Orleans, and took the city without further struggle.

The invasion by the Federal army marks the end of the Golden Age in New Orleans. When the news reached the city that the Federal fleet had passed the forts, the popular frenzy was unrestrainable and the wildest confusion followed.

In order to burn all the cotton and prevent it from falling into the hands of the enemy, ten or twelve thousand bales were rolled from the cotton warehouses into the streets, or carted to the levee and set on fire. This was done by common consent. It was mob-madness. The cotton was too valuable, the people thought, to let it fall into Federal hands. A vast lot of other property was burned. Some over-zealous patriot set fire to the tobacco and sugar ware-houses. Next the ships at the wharves, already loaded with cotton, were burned to the water's edge. As some of them were burning, they were set adrift and floated down the river. Next the steamboats were set on fire. Soon the whole surface of the Mississippi was aflame.

Lawlessness was at its height. The warehouses were broken open and the goods scattered. Men and women broke open the doors and took what they could; hams, meat, sugar, molasses. What they could not take, they spilled on the ground. Gutters flowed molasses; sugar lay like drifted snow along the sidewalks. New Orleans was sacked by its own people. And that day marked the begin-ning of years of poverty and misery.

· PART IV · THESE TIMES ·

Chapter XXVI

TRANSITION

THE history of the old New Orleans ends with the Civil War. Again, I must say that this history is known too well for me to write of it here. The period of Reconstruction in Louisiana is the most tragic part of its story. New Orleans had been one of the richest—if not the richest—city in the country. It became one of the poorest. Not only were men stripped of all they had, but the basis of their commercial life had been destroyed. The slave system was gone, and the commercial usefulness of the river had been destroyed by the railroads.

The history of the city that we know to-day was built upon the ruins of the old system. The building has not been easy; nor has it been spectacular. But in the sixty-three years intervening, a new community has come into being. To-day New Orleans is an American city—no longer can it be called Creole—with a population of 425,000 people. It has crept back slowly into a position of power in the world of commerce. To-day it is the second port in the

United States, only New York ranking above. It is the financial power of the far South.

It is probable that the city has faced greater odds than any other American city-in-the-making. And the problems were peculiar to New Orleans itself. The greatest friend and the greatest enemy of New Orleans has always been the Mississippi River. As a friend, it has brought commercial prosperity; as an enemy, it has threatened destruction time after time by its floodwaters. Yearly the levees have been built stronger and higher, yet in 1927 there was still grave danger.

Now—as I write this—government engineers are surveying the ground for the Bonnet Carre spillway, a vast opening in the levee system near New Orleans which will divert much of the water from the river to Lake Pontchartrain. Flood levels at the New Orleans water-front will be lowered so that danger will be averted. At last, after many years, Congressional legislation has made this possible. Now it seems that the greatest enemy of New Orleans will be rendered impotent.

The other enemy has been made powerless before now. That second enemy was the eternal danger of epidemic. In 1905, the cause of yellow fever was discovered—the *stegomyia faciata*, the yellow-fever mosquito. Once known, the matter of protection became comparatively simple. Up to that time, New Orleans had depended upon cisterns for drinking water. These cisterns were the breeding places for this particular type of house-mosquito, the yellow fever carrier. Accordingly, a water-purification plant was installed and the city was furnished with drinking water by the municipal government. The cisterns were destroyed.

A NEW CITY TOWERS ABOVE THE
VIEUX CARRÉ

MELON BOATS FROM THE GULF

The houses were screened. Since that time yellow fever has been unknown.

Another fear has been that of bubonic plague. It was discovered that this was a rat disease and spread by a certain type of flea which escaped to humans when the rat died. Now New Orleans was rat-ridden. The old section especially was infested, also the warehouses and the docks. To rid the city of rats was a monumental undertaking. First the houses were made rat-proof. . . . How easy that sounds! But I was living in New Orleans at the time of the rat-proofing and I saw what a monumental undertaking it was. It cost a vast sum of money. The exact figure will never be known, probably, for each property owner paid for his own. The rat-proofing ordinance was more strictly enforced than any other ordinance that I have observed in effect. Inspectors invaded every house; the ground floor of each one was gone over thoroughly, foot by foot. In the old section, every ground floor was cemented; wooden floors were destroyed. In other sections, the houses were, for the greater part, raised on pillars. But so costly was this rat-proofing of the city that many owners of property were unable to pay for it, and accordingly the city did the work, offered the bill, and if the money was not forthcoming the property was sold at public auction. It was like a tax. While this proved a great hardship for some, the result was for a much greater good in the community at large.

When the work was finished, the rat-catching began. Hundreds of men were employed, and armed with rat-traps. They went over the entire city. This work went on for a year. More than two million rats were caught. It was as though the Pied Piper of Hamelin himself had passed by.

These things can be done, but they are difficult prob lems and they are problems peculiarly of New Orleans. I cite these instances to show something of the struggle that has taken place since the Civil War; a constant warfare against influences which tended to undermine the city's health.

Another thing—one of many—peculiar to New Orleans is the difficulty presented by the matter of drainage. In the old days, water was found a foot underground. That was the reason for burying corpses in vaults, as a hole dug for a grave filled with water in an hour or so. The soaked condition of the soil made city drainage very difficult. Very little of the rainwater which fell into the city of New Orleans had ever drained into the river. When levees were built no water could drain there. The city level is higher on the river bank than further inland—which is true all along the Mississippi in the Lower Valley. In New Orleans, then, the water drained back of the city into Lake Pontchartrain. Until forty years ago the sewers were open ditches, flushed with water—obviously a condition breeding disease and filth. The problem has been solved by a mammoth municipal pumping system. Nowadays the sewerage system in New Orleans is identical with that in other American cities outwardly; but all of the sewage—and the drainage, including rainfall—goes into culverts, far underground, and is pumped out. These pumps run night and day—always. For without them, the city would fill up with water from a heavy rain. The floor of the city is like the bottom of a cup, the levees are the sides of the cup; obviously, it is necessary to pump out rainwater that falls within the limits of the town.

These are a few of the problems that the growing city has had to meet. These are problems which the average American city has never had to solve. The visitor to New Orleans sees a city, with the usual American trimmings— high office buildings, paved streets, street-car system, hotels, chain stores, all the usual things; but the visitor rarely realizes the problems which the city has had to surmount before it could develop into the type of community that it is to-day.

I wish it were in my power as a writer to make the reader realize the importance of the things which I have touched upon so briefly here. If I could make him see that they were important, he would see, automatically, that they were interesting in themselves. There is something so excessively American in this determination to get ahead, and to continue in the face of all odds. It does not seem a picturesque struggle, for it is too near us, too much of our own times. But it is this curious quality of *indestructibility* which is most characteristic of New Orleans to-day.

Chapter XXVII

THE NEW NEW ORLEANS

THE new New Orleans, the city of to-day, has grown and spread until the old quarter, or Vieux Carré, is but a small division of the city's map. Many visitors have come to New Orleans, looked at the principal residence streets, the business section, the banana wharf, and the race-tracks, and have departed without knowing or caring to know that there is an old New Orleans tucked away north of Canal Street.

As far as I am concerned, the old section must always remain the most interesting, for it was the cradle of the city's history. To me the modern city is—a modern city. There are the cañons of office buildings, the department stores, the chain stores of standardized variety: the United Cigars, the "five-and-ten," the cafeterias, newspaper offices —all the rest of it. In this respect, New Orleans is like other American cities of its size. Nevertheless, some odd things are seen even in the business section: quaint shops selling only imported articles; shops selling nothing but pralines—the favorite pecan candy of Louisiana; little French book-stores and perfume shops; and shops selling religious goods abound. Also, the food in the restaurants is exceptionally good. Dining in the cafés of New Orleans quite spoils one for other cities where the food is prepared as a necessity rather than as a rite. Yea, verily, the people of New Orleans like good eating.

In the pre-war days the alcoholic beverages were of unsurpassed excellence. The Ramos gin-fizz, of sainted memory, the Sazarac cocktail, may it rest in peace! The absinthe frappé and the absinthe-anisette. One may tell of the charm of these dear, forbidden beverages, perhaps, without being accused of being a city "booster." Inasmuch as they are gone from us now, I mean. For they are really gone. It is true that some sort of substitutes are dispensed illegally occasionally; but the days when fizz was prepared almost as a religious ceremony are over. Perhaps it is for the greater good, I cannot say; but New Orleans misses the stimulation, just the same.

Canal Street, the main shopping thoroughfare, is exceptionally wide, and the buildings are of irregular height. Some are old and are still wearing their balconies with wrought-iron railings; others are new. The street has a definite character. Just south of Canal Street is the financial section, with its higher buildings, its many banks, its noise and bustle. But even here one can detect little differences. Visitors never fail to comment upon the coffee-houses tucked away in corners. For French drip-coffee is the favorite legal beverage of the men of New Orleans. And it is no unusual thing for a business man to say casually: "Well, let's go and get a cup of coffee," as a visitor in his office is making ready to depart. It is a little thing perhaps, this drinking of coffee at odd times, but it is very characteristic of the city itself. Men in New Orleans give more thought to the business of living than men in other American cities, I believe. . . . There is a certain leisureliness, a certain willingness to amuse one's self by the way, which is, to me, very delightful. I have heard Northern business men complain bitterly about these little interruptions for coffee or what-not; but it is strange how soon they adapt themselves to the habits of the city. In time they seem to grow to like it.

The Mississippi River curves around New Orleans. Once the city was in the river's crescent—hence "The Crescent City"—but that was long ago. To-day the river is rather like a large *S,* for the city has spread beyond its old boundaries in every direction, north, south, east, and west—although in order to go to the eastward it crossed the river. The small city opposite New Orleans is called Algiers, although it is incorporated as part of the city itself.

As one goes south from Canal Street, away from the old section, he passes through a thinning retail business neighborhood, the wholesale district, the section devoted to automobile showrooms, and emerges after twelve squares or so, in another residential section. Following St. Charles Street, for example, after ten squares or thereabouts, the street widens and becomes an avenue, with greenery in the middle and a double roadway. This street is several miles long, gently curving, and follows the curve of the river. It is lined with fine residences, most of them set in gardens. One is very conscious of the semi-tropical climate, for there are endless palm-trees and flowering shrubs. In the spring there are blossoming magnolia trees along the avenue. At approximately twenty-five squares south of Canal Street, as one continues "uptown," the Garden District is found. This is a part of the city which is particularly charming; old houses built by American families in what was then known as Faubourg St. Mary. Magnificent houses these are, many with high white columns, and all with wide verandas. They are set deep in gardens and are covered with vines. Many visitors find the Garden District more to their liking than the Vieux Carré. Here one finds high brick walls with wicket gates, and in some instances one can only guess at the garden that lies behind. Over these walls hang banana trees, flowering oleanders, and other tropical trees. Fountains trickle. The air is sweet with the breath of flowers. It is pleasant to walk here in the afternoon.

The Garden District is quite large, and comprises perhaps sixty squares, bounded by St. Charles Avenue, Jackson Avenue, Louisiana Avenue, and Camp Street. To a visitor it is well worth while.

Continuing up St. Charles Avenue one encounters modern dwellings, each with its carefully kept garden; some with magnificent live-oak trees. Here and there a large apartment-house has crept in. Others will be erected soon. The street is changing its character. Some of the finest houses are in the cross streets leading away from St. Charles Avenue—those beginning, let us say, in the neighborhood of the fiftieth square, and continuing beyond the seventieth square above Canal Street.

To the left, as you ascend the avenue, lies the Mississippi, many squares away. Its length within the town limits is lined with shipping. The banana wharf has definite pictorial value. New Orleans—as the Association of Commerce will tell you—is the biggest banana port in the world. But quite aside from that fact, this is one of the most picturesque spots in the city.

An hour before the boat arrives a small army of men invades the wharf; they are a cosmopolitan and polyglot crowd made up of American laborers, sailors from tramp schooners putting in an idle day's work, Greeks, Italians, and negroes. The Italians and negroes predominate.

Machines hoist the bananas from the hold of the ship, and the banana carriers grasp them as they are brought up. A man shoulders a bunch and is gone. Some of the negroes especially have acquired such skill at "toting" bananas that they are able to handle a bunch weighing eighty or ninety pounds with the grace of a belle in a ball-room handling a bouquet. All day long the men trudge from ship to box-car.

The green bunches of fruit give a vivid touch of color to the wharf; out in the river the sunlight streams down on the white ship and the green fruit, but under the sheds it is cool and shady. When twilight comes and lights flash on, with their garish brightness, the fruit seems even more green; there are long swaying shadows. Among the moving men come old negro women with white cloths tied about their heads; these are the vendors of sandwiches and home-made candies. They do a thriving business.

Hour after hour the work of unloading goes on. It is something to see! The Port offers a hundred sights almost as interesting.

The Orleanian likes his river. He likes to walk upon the docks to look at the Mississippi. In the evenings one

will find many families there. It is an old custom, this
"going down to the levee." For the river is fascinating
almost always. Even when it is at flood stage and the big
vessels ride high over the town, there is a certain fascin-
ation in walking up the slope of the levee and finding the
ships high above one's head. A strange feeling, as though
the world is awry.

To continue along St. Charles Avenue—after this stop
at the banana wharf: far up the avenue, one reaches Audubon Park, with its golf course, its zoo, its tree-bordered
drives, and its swimming pools. New Orleans is a city that
lives outdoors, and in Audubon Park one is brought face to
face with this fact. For the swimming pools are unbelievably large. And in summer these pools are filled to capacity.
The climate makes swimming in the open one of the most
desirable summer sports. There are bathing beaches in
Lake Pontchartrain; the Mississippi Gulf Coast is within
an hour's travel on a train; and every club of importance
in New Orleans has a pool. In addition there are pools in
the parks and in several public squares. Summer comes in
with a splash!

Opposite Audubon Park—this some three miles from
Canal Street, but still on St. Charles Avenue—are the
colleges: Tulane, for men, is one of the most important
universities in the South; allied to it is the Sophie New-
comb Memorial College for women; adjoining the Tulane
Campus is another group of college buildings in a pleasing
quadrangle: this is Loyola College, a Catholic institution.
The juxtaposition of the three is symbolic of New Orleans,
for the city's population is divided almost exactly into
Roman Catholic and Protestant denominations. It is likely

that there are a few more Catholics in New Orleans than the combined Protestant church membership. This is easy to understand when one considers that until the Louisiana Purchase in 1803, the city was entirely Catholic; no other church was tolerated in French and Spanish Louisiana. Formerly the Catholic vote was predominant in the State, but a recent survey shows that in the last year the Protestant vote, for the State at large, was slightly higher.

But this is aside from a trip through "uptown" New Orleans. If one continues along St. Charles Avenue, he will arrive, many squares further on, at its termination. It ends at the levee—for the curve of the Mississippi is sharp here. Carrollton Avenue begins here, extending at a right angle. Unlike St. Charles, it is straight. By continuing along this residential thoroughfare for more than a mile, one reaches Tulane Avenue, and by following Tulane Avenue, one reaches Canal Street again, almost where one left it—without realizing exactly how the trip has been accomplished. A glance at a map of New Orleans solves the mystery. Tulane and Carrollton avenues are at right angles one to the other; St. Charles Avenue curves in a vast semi-circle. The map looks like a design for a folding fan, with St. Charles Avenue as the curved edge, the other two thoroughfares comprising the end sticks. And to carry the resemblance further, there are many streets following the lines of the folding sticks of the fan. They radiate wheel-like, with curving streets crossing them. This is one of the most puzzling features which tourists find in "uptown" New Orleans. Even natives are sometimes heard exclaiming that they have discovered "short cuts" in driving that they did not know existed.

The residential section is pleasing; even the humblest homes boast of a small garden plot. The city has an enormous area. It spreads and spreads. One thinks he has reached the end—lo and behold! another town stretches out before him. Beyond the limits of the city are found country villas, country clubs—several of them—taverns, and road-houses.

One cannot end a description of the city without mentioning the race-tracks which lie near-by. For New Orleans has always liked horse racing. Nowadays the season begins at Thanksgiving and lasts until Easter. And in addition there are dog races which are popular.

For those seeking excitement, there are gambling houses beyond the city limits. Although prohibited by law, the demand for gambling houses is such that there are always many to be found. Any taxi driver will tell you about them, should your taste lie in that direction. Just ask.

It is impossible, of course, for this chapter to drag itself out into a guide to the present day New Orleans. It may be that the reader is tired already. Now let us go back to the French Quarter for an afternoon walk.

Chapter XXVIII

AN AFTERNOON WALK

WOULD you like to visit the old section of New Orleans un-
chaperoned by the usual guide? Do you care to wander at
will along the quaint old streets of the Vieux Carré? If you
do, you may get your hat and come along with me. We will
start in the late afternoon, because at that time the soft
colors of evening will fall across the battered façades of the
old houses and will treat them kindly. They are like
wrinkled faces, these old houses, and one must look upon
them with the deference that youth should show to age.
Some of the houses have outlived their usefulness, like so
many of the old, and while you may look upon them as
much as you please, you must look with friendly eyes. If
you do not, you may come away with only the idea of dirt
and squalor—and you may miss altogether that lingering
charm which clings to these old mansions even in the last
stages of their decay.

How shall we make this trip? Walk, of course. The
Quarter is small, only ten squares from end to end and less

than that distance from the river to Rampart Street. Why do they call it Vieux Carré? It means literally "old square," that is all, the old square which constituted the walled city of *Nouvelle Orléans,* when Americans such as you and I did not profane the streets. Are you ready? Very well, then we will start at once.

We will leave Canal Street at Royal, and turn from our present-day world into the past. Royal Street is the same as St. Charles, but the name changes when you have crossed Canal Street. Notice how narrow the street is. Notice how the balconies overhang the sidewalk. And by the way, we call the sidewalks *banquettes*—that's a Creole word. No, not French, just plain Creole. No, you won't find it in the French dictionary. It is a word that is particularly our own.

Modern needs are pushing the Quarter further and further from Canal Street. We will walk hastily along the street until we have passed the Monteleone Hotel, this large and gleaming hostelry on our right at the first corner. Oh, wait! Don't forget to look at the old Union Bank at Iberville and Royal streets. That is one of the oldest buildings here. If you will look up at the cornice, you can still see the raised lettering with the bank's name, but the lower portion of the structure has been changed beyond recognition. I remember the old columns which supported the roof. Only a few years ago they were taken away. There is a legend in New Orleans, and perhaps it is true, that the word "Dixie" came from this very spot. Before that building was occupied by the Union Bank it was occupied by an institution known as the Citizens Bank, which still exists to-day. There was a Louisiana bank-note, a "dix," issued by the old Citizens Bank. Money was plentiful in New Orleans then. Ten-dol-

lar bills were easier to obtain than they are now. Strangers
in New Orleans referred to the city as the "land of dixies."
That was the American way of saying that money was plentiful in New Orleans. I have heard other explanations
offered, but this one seems logical to me.

Well, let's be going. You can stop if you will and look
into the windows of the antique shops. There are many
beautiful things to be found here. It has always seemed to
me that these shops are the most interesting and the most
tragic things in the city. How tragic? Well, they contain
the wreckage of old families—people who once had everything that their hearts desired. Where are these old families
now? Lord, I don't know. Here are their most cherished
possessions; you can buy them if you like. Can't you be satisfied with that?

What does "Creole" mean? No, of course not. I don't
know why tourists always say that. The Creole is not of
colored blood. Locally, the word means of French or Spanish descent, or of a mixed descent, French and Spanish.
The Creole was the child of European parents born in a
French or Spanish colony. The New Orleans Creole is our
finest product. The women are lovely, and the men are
brave. They have charming manners. They are exclusive;
they are clannish; they keep to themselves. Can any one
blame them? They have their own language, their own society, and their own customs. What language do they
speak? They spoke, and they still speak, a pure French. The
reason the word "Creole" has been so often misunderstood
is because their slaves spoke a Creole dialect bearing about
the same relation to pure French as our Southern negro talk
bears to English purely spoken. Then, of course, there was

PAUL MORPHY HOUSE IN ROYAL STREET

OLD COURTYARD AT 823 ROYAL STREET

the Acadian French—or the "Cajan" French—which is the language spoken in the outlying districts of Louisiana. Then, too, there is the "gumbo" French—that means simply French incorrectly spoken—a sort of patois.

Well, here we are at Royal and Conti streets, three squares from Canal. Let us stop here for a moment in front of the Court House and I will point out the interesting houses from here. The Court House is new, of course, it was built in 1910 when a whole square of delightful old houses was destroyed in order to make room for it. But on the corner of Royal and Conti, the corner toward the river, is the old Hall of Mortgages. It was the Bank of Louisiana, built in 1812. Notice how interesting it is architecturally. Do you see its irregularities? The pilasters which support the cornice are not the same distance apart, and the pedestals at the top of the cornice are not placed above the pilasters, and even the urns on the pedestals are not placed in the center of the pedestals. Odd? Of course. But following the law of symmetry nevertheless. That's what gives these old houses their intense personality. Do you see what I mean? Look closely.

Now notice the iron scrollwork on the balconies of that antique shop on the opposite corner, the southwest corner. All hand-hammered wrought iron. It is very beautiful. They tell us it was all made in the workshops here, the old forges, hammered out by negro slaves. It is priceless to-day, and to duplicate it is a process so expensive that few are willing to undertake it.

Now look at the old mansion opposite on the southwest corner. It is always called "The Dome" on account of the vaulted ceiling inside. This was another bank building.

Notice the monogram in the ironwork upon the balcony. The building is peculiarly typical of the residences of its day. Did "first families" live above shops? Yes, they did; some of them still do. The rooms upstairs are tremendous. They have most magnificent marble mantlepieces and crystal chandeliers. In the old days it was the custom for the banker's family to live above the bank, just as the lawyer's family lived above his law offices. There was a reason for this, of course. The city was so congested, so small, that space was at a premium. Of course, this was not always true. There were many houses which were only residences. But on the principal streets of the Vieux Carré you will find throughout this combination of business and dwelling houses.

From where we are standing we can see the Paul Morphy house at 417 Royal Street. Notice the round windows on the third floor. The Creole was fond of window decoration. This building was also a bank once and the banker's family lived above. Later the Morphy family lived there. They were prominent Creoles. Paul Morphy was the world's greatest chess player, he died in that house. They tell us that he used to play chess in the courtyard. And behind one of those round windows under the roof is a tiny room reached by a secret staircase. It was his study. Of course, it is not secret any longer; everybody knows about it now. Yes, you can go into the courtyard if you like. The court is one of the loveliest in the city. Look, do you see the magnolia trees growing there? In the spring they are filled with large white flowers heavy with perfume. One can lean from the balcony and pick them. A lovely place. Now it is known as the "Patio Royal." You may lunch there if you like.

Come, let's be going. We must continue down Royal Street. Just beyond the court house at the corner of Royal and St. Louis streets on this empty stretch of ground there once stood the old St. Louis Hotel, sometimes called the Hotel Royal. In its day it was the most fashionable hotel in the South. It was torn down in 1917, and a great pity it was, too. It should have been preserved, for it was a beautiful building. I remember so well how a group of us tried to save it from destruction and how we were laughed at for our pains. It was a fascinating old building with its winding stair, its magnificent dome, its frescoes; it was all so ornate, and such a complete outgrowth of its period. It was to the old St. Louis Hotel that the rich planters came when they shipped their cotton to New Orleans in the fall. It was here that magnificent balls were given, and in the great hall downstairs, that hall paved with black and white marble, stood the slave block where the negroes were sold at auction. It was the center of society once, but in time it was outmoded. The hotel lost money. For years it stood deserted. When John Galsworthy, the English writer, was in New Orleans, he wandered through the old building and met a white horse ambling through one of its corridors. This surprised him so that he wrote an essay about it. It is called "That Old Time Place."

At the corner of Chartres and St. Louis streets, just opposite the site of the St. Louis Hotel, stands the Napoleon house. It has a cupola. This was once the residence of Governor Girod. They tell us that the house was built for Napoleon, built and furnished for him. It is interesting to think what it might have meant to New Orleans had Napoleon been rescued from St. Helena and had come to spend his declining years here. The plot to rescue Napoleon was fostered by the young Creole bloods of the old New Orleans. They planned to send a light sailing vessel for him as he languished on St. Helena. Dominique You, one of Lafitte the Pirate's lieutenants, had been engaged to head the expedition, but on the eve of the sailing of the vessel, the news reached New Orleans that Napoleon was dead. It is a pretty story. One wonders how much truth there is in it. Governor Girod afterward occupied the house. All in all, it has had a peculiar history. It has been sold over and over again. For many years it was a tenement, filled with Italians and negroes. When Lord Dunsany visited New Orleans a few years ago, he stood looking up at the façade of the Napoleon house, watching the negro children who played in and out of the old doors, looking upon the lines of drying clothes which stretched from the windows, and he said to the man who was walking with him, "What a strange, wonderful doom." The whole French Quarter, he said, was as fantastic as though he had invented it himself.

As we continue down Royal Street, we find just next door to the site of the St. Louis Hotel a very beautiful old house. It is now known as "The Arts and Crafts Club," and its courtyard is as charming as any in New Orleans. You may go in if you like, the courtyard gate is always open. If you are interested in exhibitions of paintings, there will be something for you to see in the studio beyond the court. Once this was the house of Brulatour, the richest wine merchant in New Orleans. His shop was on the ground floor. His family lived at the top of the house, and in the *entresol,* that half story between the main floors of the house, he kept his casks of wine. On damp days, if you climb to the *entresol* you can still smell the faint vinegary odor left behind. You will notice that this house is more Spanish than French. It was built by Spanish architects shortly after the fire of 1788. Notice the large slave quarters at the rear of the building. And notice on the south side the open terrace of the roof. There is much charming detail in the old Brulatour house. The winding wooden staircase ascending under archways of masonry, the overhanging balconies, the batten shutters, all this is very typical of the houses of the old régime.

As you proceed down Royal Street, you will find that you have reached the heart of the Vieux Carré. Here you find overhanging balconies across the second floors of the houses and small individual balconies before the windows on the third floor. It is quite easy to imagine the Creole beauties leaning out looking down, waving a scarf to a suitor, perhaps. The old house at the southwest corner of Royal and Toulouse streets is particularly interesting. It has an Egyptian design on the pilasters supporting the roof. That was the influence of Napoleon's visit to Egypt. Egyptian fashions were popular in all of Europe then. It seems odd, doesn't it, that because Napoleon went to Egypt there should be Egyptian designs in the French Quarter of New Orleans? That is the reason, nevertheless. The entrance to this old mansion is on Toulouse Street, just around the corner. Two stone lions guard the gateway. It is a rooming-house now, and a second-hand furniture shop occupies the ground floor, but once this was the very center of fashion in the old New Orleans.

Toulouse Street was the street of banks and cotton brokers. It was the Wall Street of the old New Orleans. At

628 Toulouse, in the square between Royal and Chartres, is the house occupied by Claiborne, the first American governor. It is filled with artists' studios now.

The house at 612 Royal Street, sometimes called the Court of the Palm, is typical of the fine old residences. The courtyard is particularly lovely, with a gigantic palm-tree rising in the center, a palm-tree which shades the entire court with its wide leaves. Opposite, at 613 Royal Street, is one of the most famous courtyards. Yes, this is the one you see on post-cards. It is quite typical. Once there was a formal garden here with an old iron fountain and conventional flower beds. If you will go far back into the court and look at the house you will notice its beautiful irregularities. Heavy fan-shaped windows which swing some in and some out, a large slave wing, once said to house thirty-seven servants. This is called the "Court of the Two Sisters." The house has no particular history, but it was on this spot that de Vaudreuil's house stood—he was the Grand Marquis of the early settlers. The house that he occupied was destroyed in the fire of 1788. This house dates from about 1800.

Some of the old New Orleans families still live in the square of Royal Street between Toulouse and St. Peter streets. One family has occupied the same house for more than ninety years. The fine old residence at 624 Royal Street was built by Dr. Isidore Labatut in 1831. His descendants still live there. The lower floor was formerly occupied by the office of Justice Bermudez, a distinguished jurist, and it was here that Edward Douglas White received his early law training.

Just opposite the quaint two-story dwelling at 629

Royal Street was the home of Adelina Patti, the opera
singer, on the year of her memorable début at the French
Opera. The young Creoles of that day used to promenade
before her window to try to catch a glimpse of her or to
hear her practise for her nightly performance.

At the end of the next square you will find a small
garden just back of the Cathedral. This is called St. Anthony's Close, where duels were fought in the old days.
Orleans Street begins here, and standing at the corner of
Royal and Orleans Street you can see the old Orleans
Theater and Ball Room, the scene of the notorious quadroon balls. It is a convent of negro nuns now, called the
Convent of the Holy Family. You may go in if you like.
The colored nuns will show you through if they are not too
busy and if you will leave a small offering for the negro
children. Be sure and notice the old houses which flank
St. Anthony's Garden. They are most interesting. Walk
through the alley beside the Cathedral and you will emerge
at Jackson Square, the Place d'Armes. This is the very
center of social life in old New Orleans. From the center of
the square you can see the Cabildo, the Cathedral, the Presbytery, and the two Pontalba buildings.

The Cabildo now is the state museum, and it is open
to the public. If you are interested in the old New Orleans,
take an hour and wander through. In there are enough relics
to enable you to reconstruct the whole life of the Creoles.
The paintings of the types existing in wartimes and before
are particularly interesting. Notice the beauty of the
women; notice the poetic expression of the young men.
You do not see faces like these nowadays; our commercial
spirit has killed the poetry in young men's faces. There are

many other things to be seen here. Relics of the Indian days, old furniture, old jewelry, glass, and even the death mask of Napoleon. The Cabildo was erected in 1795 and was the scene of the transfer of Louisiana from France to the United States in 1803. Later it was the city hall. Here Lafayette was housed when he visited New Orleans in 1825.

The St. Louis Cathedral stands where the first church of New Orleans stood. The present building was erected by Don Almonaster y Roxas and presented to his fellow Catholics in 1794. The building flanking the Cathedral on the other side is the Presbytery. It is almost identically like the Cabildo. Once a Capuchin monastery, later the Civil District Court, it is now a museum.

Now a word about the Square itself. This is the Place d'Armes laid out by Bienville, founder of New Orleans, in 1718. The French and the Spanish flag flew here, and the American flag was unfurled in 1803 to mark the possession of the United States after the transfer of Louisiana from France. It was in this square that the executions took place in the old days. It was here that the celebrations were held. It was here that General Jackson was acclaimed after his victory at the Battle of New Orleans. A statue of General Jackson, designed by Clark Mills, stands in the center of the square—General Jackson on his rearing horse, his hat raised in salute.

To the north and south of the square you will see the Pontalba buildings which occupy the entire block on St. Peter and St. Ann streets. They were built by Micaela, the daughter of Don Almonaster. Micaela was the Baroness Pontalba. You can see the Almonaster-Pontalba monogram in hundreds of places, interwoven in the ironwork. At one time these houses were filled with the most aristocratic families of the old city. Many famous guests have been entertained here. Jenny Lind, the Swedish Nightingale, and her manager, P. T. Barnum; Adelina Patti, the opera singer, Fannie Kemble, the dancer, and Lola Montez, "The Uncrowned Queen of Bavaria," who flashed like a comet through Creole New Orleans, leaving a string of duels in her wake.

The old New Orleans is a city of intense personality. Time and decay have not killed its pristine charm. The old houses to-day are as full of beauty as they were in their prime. Architecturally they are tremendously interesting. My advice to you is to stay for a while in the old section of the city, sit for a time in Jackson Square and let the old world charm you. Give the atmosphere a chance to lull you. Take your time and wander slowly; look twice at the old houses, they are worth it. Talk to the beggars in the street; talk to any one you chance to meet. The natives of the Quarter are pleasant people and they will gladly tell you anything they happen to know. Those who live in the Quarter live there because they like it. They are proud of the old houses; they like your admiration and your interest. Go where you will; do what you please, you will not be molested nor will you be annoyed. Take your time and wander through, and then if you have a heart in you, you will want to return, for in the Vieux Carré of New Orleans, and in the Vieux Carré alone, you will find that lingering charm of the Old World, that remnant of a bygone culture which is unique in America.

Chapter XXIX

THE FRENCH OPERA HOUSE

ON Thursday morning, December 4, 1919, the French Opera House at Bourbon and Toulouse Street burned to the ground. The "Times-Picayune" carried the following account of the fire and its tragic meaning to the people of New Orleans:

The French Opera House burned early Thursday morning. Only the toppling walls remain, surrounding a heap of ruins. Gone is all the glory which marked the building for more than half a century—gone in a blaze of burning gauze and tinsel, a blaze more splendid and more terrible than Walpurgis Night, that long-famous brocken of the opera "Faust."

And into the hearts of the people of New Orleans there has come a great sorrow, a great mourning. For there are few women here who have not tender memories of their vanished youth, their débutante days, loves, heartburnings, joy—all intimately linked with the French Opera. There are few men who have loved or been loved, who have not recollections of the nights when they sat in the dreamy darkness of the old building, listening to the voices of the great singers blending with the orchestra, and thrilling at the touch of a bit of gauze, as it brushed their cheeks.

Children, taken to the opera with their mothers, learned their first lessons in art and music, while watching the singers upon the brilliantly lighted stage. Later, the girls as débutantes received homage as they sat in the horseshoe, surrounded by flowers, admiring and admired, loving and beloved. Still later, as matrons, they joined gay parties, listening to the same old operas, the same dear, cherished operas, sung by different voices, never losing their charm; here they watched their daughters and sons growing to love light and color and music as they had done, in the old Opera House.

Then, last of all, as old ladies they have come to see and hear, while their grandchildren have wandered about the foyer and the promenade, chattering, laughing. The old are not so merry in their pleasures at the opera, but they return to it as to an old friend, to listen, to look and to enjoy. It seems like returning home. The opera is hallowed in their hearts; it belongs to them by right of years of possession. For in New Orleans, and in New Orleans alone, is the opera so personal, so completely ours.

Gone, all gone. The curtain has fallen for the last time upon "Les Huguenots," long a favorite with the New Orleans public. The opera house has gone in a blaze of horror and of glory. There is a pall over the city; eyes are filled with tears and hearts are heavy. Old memories, tucked away in the dusty cobwebs of forgotten years, have come out like ghosts to dance in the last ghastly Walpurgis ballet of flame.

The heart of the old French Quarter has stopped beating.

And all this—as florid as it may sound ten years later —is literally true. New Orleans went into mourning for the French Opera.

The building was erected in 1859 from designs made by James Gallier, the younger. The old city was full of fine buildings designed by the Galliers, father and son, who were among the most renowned of many distinguished architects who made New Orleans their home during the past century.

In 1859 Boudousquie, the manager who had been con-

ducting opera at the old Orleans Theater, formed a French
Opera Association, with a capital of $100,000, and the site
was purchased and the building erected. It was formally
opened in December, with "Guillaume Tell," and it is remembered that opera alternated with drama for several
years. As time went on, many of the most noted singers of
the world were heard in the French Opera House; and
among these was Patti, who made her début there. During
the Civil War the house was closed, but in 1866 it reopened.
On that year, as the new director was on his way from
France with a large company of artists, on board the
Evening Star, the ship was lost, and the entire troupe perished. Among those who went down were James Gallier, the
architect who had designed the Opera House, and his wife.

L. Placide Canonge, Max Strakosch, and de Beauplan
were among the succeeding directors; and there were many
years of most successful opera, through which New Orleans
became known as a music-loving city.

The French Opera season has always been the gala time
from a social standpoint; and nowhere was there a more
alluring scene than the glittering horseshoe of boxes, filled
with wealth and fashion. It must be said, however, that very
many of the most devoted music-lovers were in the upper
galleries, where they struggled for seats and drank in the
music with tears and wild applause, such as would not be
considered "proper" in the more fashionable seats below.

It is to be noted that visitors to the city have always
considered New Orleans music mad, even from the times
when opera was given in the old Orleans Theater. There
was no cutting of the great operas then; and people went to
the performance at six in the evening, and left the opera to

THE NAPOLEON HOUSE. CHARTRES STREET

SLAVE GALLERIES OF BYGONE DAYS

attend midnight mass at the Cathedral. It is doubtful if any one can be found who loves music to that extent now; but at any rate, one will hear the boys in the streets and the negroes on the levee whistling bars from some tuneful opera without slurring one liquid note.

The outbreak of the World War prevented the coming of French troupes and the Opera House was running to neglect when it was purchased by an anonymous benefactor and presented to Tulane University in order that it might be preserved and not fall into less worthy uses. With the gift went an important sum of money to put the old structure into repair.

The university carried only fifty-seven thousand dollars' worth of insurance on the building and when it was destroyed by fire, architects estimated that the rebuilding would cost at least a million dollars. It has never been rebuilt. New Orleans has no longer an opera company of its own.

As this is written the question of a municipal opera house and auditorium for New Orleans is under discussion. There are funds available for such a structure, and a site has been chosen just beyond the borders of the Vieux Carré —a plot of ground fronting on old Congo Square.

Chapter XXX

HISTORY IN STREET NAMES

THE street names in New Orleans offer an interesting field for speculation—for in them the history of the city is written, and something of the character of the changing times is mirrored. In an earlier chapter we have considered the names in the Vieux Carré. These names told of the spirit of the founders; and as the city grew, and new streets were opened up, new history was written. Let us consider the names beyond the rectangle of the old walled city.

In naming the streets of the city as it grew beyond its original boundaries, a dozen different systems were pursued. The gallantry of the French Creoles is commemorated upon old city maps by a number of streets christened with feminine names. Some of these were christened after the favorite children of rich parents, but again not a few were named after favorite concubines. The old maps of New Orleans were covered with such names as Suzette, Celeste, Estelle, Angélie, Annette, and others; some of these have died away into later titles, but many still survive.

The religious tendency of the population showed itself in giving religious names to many of the streets. There are several hundred saints so honored, and scarcely one in the calendar has escaped a namesake. There are besides these, such streets as Conception, Religious, Nuns, Assumption, Ascension, and so on.

At the time of the French Revolution there was an outbreak in France of Roman and Greek fashions. The French tried to imitate the ancient classics by assuming the Roman dress and Roman names. The Creoles who, although dominated by the Spaniards, were red republicans in those days, followed that fashion and all the names of antiquity were introduced into Louisiana and survive there to this day. Achille (Achilles), Alcibiade (Alcibiades), Numa, Démosthène (Demosthenes), came into fashion. The streets found a similar fate and the new Faubourg Ste. Marie was liberally christened from pagan mythology. The nine muses, three graces, the twelve greater gods and the twelve lesser ones, and the demi-gods, all stood godparents for streets. The city fathers went beyond this, and there was a Nayades and a Dryades street, a Water Work, a Euphrosiné street, and so on without end.

Then came the Napoleonic wars, and with them, intense enthusiasm over the victories of the Corsican. A general of Napoleon's army who settled in Louisiana after the St. Helena captivity named the whole upper portion of the city in honor of the little Emperor. Napoleon Avenue, Jena Street and Austerlitz Street are samples which survive to this day.

In addition to these came the names and titles of the early Louisiana planters, such as Montegut, Clouet,

Marigny, Delord, the early governors of Louisiana, mayors of New Orleans, and distinguished citizens.

These, however, failed to supply the 500 miles of streets that New Orleans boasts of, with a sufficiency of names.

In the naming of streets the French are not quite so matter of fact as the Anglo-Saxons, and they have shown this in some titles they have left behind. In New Orleans no Anglo-Saxon, for instance, would ever think of naming a street Goodchildren Street, *rue des Bons Enfants,* or Love Street, *rue de l'Amour,* Madman's Street, Mystery Street, or Piety Street. Old Bernard Marigny christened two thoroughfares in the Faubourg Marigny which he laid out, "Craps" and "Bagatelle" in honor of the two games of chance at which he lost a fortune. A curious mistake was that of the first American directory-maker who insisted upon translating Bagatelle into English and described it as Trifle Street.

But even when a person is acquainted with the names of the New Orleans streets, the next thing is to know how to pronounce and spell them. This is very important, for they are seldom pronounced as they would seem to be. Tchoupitoulas—pronounced Chopitoulas—and Carondelet are the Shibboleth by which foreigners are detected. No man is ever recognized as a true Orleanian until he can spell and pronounce these names correctly; and the serious charge made against an auditor of the State, that he spelled Carondelet, Kerionderlet, aroused the utmost indignation of the population, who could never forgive this mistake.

The classical scholar who visits New Orleans and hears the names of the muses so frightfully distorted may regard

it as unfortunate that Greek mythology had been chosen.
The explanation of the mispronunciation, however, will relieve the people of New Orleans of any charge of ignorance.
The Greek names are simply pronounced in the French
style. Thus the street that the scholar would call Melpo-
mene, of four syllables and with the last "e" sounded, would
be in French Melpomène, and is translated by the people
of New Orleans into Melpomeen. So Calliopé is Callioap;
Terpsichore, Terpsikor; Euterpe, Euterp; and others in the
same way. Coliseum is accented like the French Colisée, on
the second instead of the third syllable; and even Felicity
Street—it is named, by the by, after a woman (Félicité),
not happiness—is actually called by many intelligent persons
Filly-city. The influence of the old French days is seen in
the spelling of Dryades, instead of Dryads, as the word is
pronounced, and in a number of other apparent violations of
orthoëpy or orthography, the truth being that the old
French pronunciation and spelling are preserved and have
become current among the English-speaking portion of the
population.

The constant annexation to New Orleans of suburban
villages and towns, with streets of the same name, produces
considerable inconvenience to strangers and even to natives
of the city. There is a duplicate to many names, and sometimes four or five streets bearing the same title.

Thus there is a North Peter's and a South Peter's miles
apart, one in the First, the other in the Second District;
then there is a simple Peter's in the Sixth District, and a
Peter's Avenue in the same division, while in the Fifth District there is a Peter Street, and in the Third a Petre, pronounced Peter. A fine chance this to get confused.

Some of the street names which are somewhat unusual are: Coliseum, Benefit, Cotton Press (now merely Press Street), Desire—which is next to Nun Street—Exchange Passage, Frenchmen, Genius, Grand Route St. John, Humanity, Industry, Independence, Lower Line and Upper Line; Mystery, Magazine, Tchoupitoulas, Perdido (because once upon a time it lost itself in a cypress swamp); Piety, Pleasure, Mandolin, Rabbit, Poet, Plum, Religious, Ptolemy, Socrates, Solomon, and Shakespeare; Varieties Place, Virtue Street. Then too, street crossings make amusing combinations sometimes—Conti and Tonti, for example. The list of absurd combinations is almost endless, and some of them are startling enough. Some of the names give an interesting picture of the times—such as Julia Street, which the old guide-books assure us was named "for a free woman of color." After the Americans came it was, for a time, the most fashionable residence street in their section. Later it became a street of boarding-houses; now it is in the wholesale district. But it is still Julia Street—although who Julia was, I cannot tell you.

Chapter XXXI

ST. ROCH'S CHAPEL

ONE of the most interesting shrines in New Orleans is St.
Roch's Chapel in the Campo Santo. The chapel was erected
in 1871 by Father Thevis with his own hands, in fulfilment
of a vow that if none of his parishioners died during the epidemic of 1866-1867 he would build, stone by stone, a chapel
in thanksgiving to God. None of his congregation died, and
the chapel was built accordingly. The cemetery was called
Campo Santo, or Holy Field.

Soon after, the shrine became a favorite place for pil-
grimages for the pious, and all about the altar were hung
the "ex votos" of believers. The shrine is surmounted by a
statue of St. Roch, and by his side is the figure of a dog, in
commemoration of the animal which fed him when he lay
afflicted with the plague and abandoned in the forest.

The chapel itself is rather striking in appearance. Its
area is small but it is of great height. The chapel seats but
twenty-four worshippers. The walls are tombs, and in kneeling to pray, one is not more than a foot or two from the

mouldering bodies behind the marble slabs. The chapel is impressive, but rather gruesome, for piled behind the communion rail is a fantastic collection of offerings from those who have been cured by this miracle-working shrine. There are hundreds of crutches, a few wooden legs, plaster casts of arms, legs, and even torsos. . . . One of the outstanding offerings is a lifelike cast head of a child. The walls are covered with small marble plaques presented by the pious, each bearing only one word, "Merci," or "Thanks," and occasionally the phrase, "Thanks to St. Roch."

It is very quiet and peaceful in the chapel and in the cemetery surrounding it. The cemetery, in which German names predominate, has a curious air of age which is hard to explain, for the whole is little more than fifty years old.

On Good Friday, St. Roch's Chapel becomes the center of attraction for the young girls of the city, Protestant as well as Catholic. There is a legend that if a young girl will visit nine churches and say a prayer and make an offering in each one of them, and then visit St. Roch's and make the "Way of the Cross," closing by buying a candle and lighting it before the altar, she will be sure to marry happily before the year is out. We have no record of how many happy marriages have resulted from these expeditions, but no doubt those who have made this pilgrimage have found their hearts' desire and have passed the information on to other young girls, for as sure as Good Friday comes around you will find St. Roch's Chapel crowded—and hundreds of candles guttering out.

Chapter XXXII

GALLATIN STREET

THERE was a time when the very name would make a man shudder, but that has been a long time ago. It lies far down in the French Quarter, a street so hidden that one might pass it a dozen times and never notice it. It is the first thoroughfare parallel with the river, between the docks and Decatur Street. It stretches its length for two scant squares, from Ursuline to Barracks streets, from the French Market to the Mint.

Nowadays it is deserted, forgotten, given over to warehouses and storage rooms of produce merchants. It is permeated with the smells from the fish market, and with the odors of decaying garbage. Its narrow width is littered with trash and dirt—old shoes, broken barrels, rotting fruit. And yet, before the dark doors of one or two old houses, battered signs sway, signs proclaiming that "rooms" are for rent.

Even in daylight there is a sinister atmosphere in Gallatin Street, and at night—but we will speak of that later.

Now let us try to turn back the hand of time, to the street as it used to be.

It was some time in the early eighties that Henry Parmalee disappeared. Vanished. It was a strange case, and men remembered it and talked of it long afterward. There were many theories, many surmises, but only one woman knew the truth, and fear kept her silent.

Briefly, it was like this: Parmalee was the son of a wealthy planter who lived "up the river." He was twenty-two years old and a handsome chap, well over six feet, and broad proportionately. He was blonde and sinewy, and he was very strong. Women liked him, and he liked them. He was engaged to marry the daughter of a prominent Creole attorney.

A week before the wedding a bachelor supper was given for the boy. The guests met in a small but fashionable restaurant in the French Quarter. There was champagne. Two of the guests dropped out of the party, and three young men walked over to the market "for coffee" some time after midnight. A policeman on duty in Decatur Street obligingly climbed a lamp-post and lighted a paper quill over the gas flame, in order that the men might light their cigars. Young Parmalee, the policeman said afterward, was gay but a little unsteady on his feet. When the officer saw them for the last time, they were entering a dance hall in Gallatin Street, arm in arm. The hall, a resort for sailors, was half-way along the lane of narrow, dark, tall houses.

And Parmalee was never seen again.

There was an investigation, of course, but it took place many days later. There was a hue and cry. But nothing happened. His friends told the same story; they had lost sight of him for a moment in the hall in the jostling crowd. When they failed to find him, they thought he had gone back into the street again. They called, they wandered about, but he was not found. So they thought that he had gone back to his hotel. The next day, when inquiries failed to find him there, they supposed that he had gone back to the plantation. It was not until several days later that the police were notified.

Gallatin Street was searched from end to end. Sailors' rooming-houses were visited, doors were opened, closets searched. But there was no trace of Parmalee. A year later a signet ring, identified as his property, was found in a Royal Street pawnshop. And the story was revived. But the man was never seen again.

So much for old records, so much for old gossip. Now, let us see what occurred that evening, so many years ago.

Three young men, wearing immaculate evening clothes, and swaying slightly as they walked, crossed the cobbled roadway beyond the French Market. Before them stretched the dark cañon of a narrow street, its dark buildings cutting the sky with a fantastic pattern. So narrow was the street, so high the buildings with their overhanging balconies, that it seemed that they leaned together in mid-air, like old hags, whispering together in the darkness.

It was a foggy night, clammy, damp, and it was cold, as weather is counted in New Orleans. Gas lamps flared dimly in the fog, and the street between was dark, save for those streaks of light which came out through the glass doors of the sailors' dance hall. From within there came the sound of ribald music, and the stamping of feet. Only one or two of the houses were lighted, and the others seemed deserted —but the dark figures that lurked in the shadows knew better; they knew that there were dark alleys which led in to darker courtyards, where curving stairs led upward. Above were the rooms where the "ladies" lived, those harpies who preyed upon sailors, cheap women, companions for a night.

And an ugly crowd it was, too. Tough girls and older women, women of foreign tongue, Slav, Dutch, Danish; girls who could cry *skoal!* to the Scandinavian sailors as they held up their glasses of beer and cheap whisky—girls and women from God knows where—the flotsam and jetsam, the riffraff of the world, drifted from near and far, to the shabby rooms stuck above the bar-rooms of Gallatin Street.

One dance hall was kept by a man we shall call "Tony," although that was not his name; for even across the bridge of the years he is still remembered in that street of shadows. And for Tony worked many girls. There was Thelma and there was Hulda, Norwegians; there was Christine from Sweden—and there was Anna, who said she was English, and looked it. And there were others. But it is of English Anna that we wish to speak.

Anna was a "softy," according to the jargon of the other girls. She was always falling in love with some sailor, and getting beaten in consequence. One of her front teeth was missing. Tony had struck her in the mouth with his fist once, because she had tried to hold back part of her earnings, in order to give it to "Big Hans" of the *Eberhard,* a vessel which lay at anchor in the harbor. But drunken sail-

ST. ROCH'S CHAPEL, THE MIRACULOUS SHRINE

GATE OF THE TWO LIONS, TOULOUSE STREET

ors can overlook a missing tooth, and Anna was none the less popular because of it.

And it was Anna who saw young Parmalee that night when bad luck brought him to Tony's dance hall. Anna had just come downstairs, after a quarrel with Hans, and she was leaning against the bar, telling the bartender that she was "feelin' bad." She turned to find a handsome young gentleman at her elbow, a big fellow in immaculate evening clothes, and with an overcoat over his arm. He was obviously drunk. The woman smiled at him, and he bought her a drink—whisky at ten cents a glass. Anna asked him to dance with her, but he refused, and was turning away when she caught him by the arm.

If he wouldn't dance, she suggested, perhaps he would like to have another drink. She knew of a quiet place where they could sit and talk, and she wished to ask him something.

Now liquor plays strange pranks. In his sober moments Parmalee would have paid no attention to Anna, but drunk and jovial, he followed her through a swinging door which led into a hall at one side of the bar. Even the bartender did not notice their departure.

Anna would have taken him to her room, but Big Hans was lying across her bed. So she took him into Thelma's room instead, up another flight of stairs; and it was there that a negro waiter brought them drinks. The girl was sitting upon his knee, her arm around his neck, and she kept up a steady stream of chatter in her cockney English. Drunken men are easily amused. At intervals she explored his pockets with her free arm, and succeeded in getting his wallet and even some loose silver. As she sat there, she listened to a conversation which came through the thin partition of boards which separated Thelma's room from Tony's "office" at the back of the house. Tony sat talking business with the master of the *Eberhard*, and Anna gathered that Tony was promising to get four sailors before daylight. She knew what that meant. Four poor fellows, sodden with drink, or drugged, were to be carried aboard the vessel before daylight. Shanghaied.

"Poor devils," thought Anna, thinking of her Hans who lay across the bed upstairs, and wondering if he would be called into service in securing the men.

And Anna sighed a little, forgetting the business in hand, as she mechanically stroked the hair of the blonde young man who was almost helpless now from liquor consumed. She heard Tony's door open and steps go down the hall. From below she could hear the beat of the music and the shouts of the sailors. Then other footfalls resounded on the stairs, and the door behind her was burst open.

A hand gripped her shoulder. Hans was standing there, towering above her, his great red face redder than usual. He snarled at her, brutal through jealousy.

"Honest, I wasn't doin' nothin'—honest, Hans!" cried Anna, springing up.

Young Parmalee tottered to his feet. But a blow from the fist of the sailor caught him squarely on the chin, and he fell backward, across a broken chair, rolled over and lay still upon the floor.

Hans stood over Anna, his fists clenched. "Give it to me!" he said, indicating the wallet that the girl held in her hand.

What happened in that room remained impressed upon Anna's mind long afterward—for Hans did a strange thing. Slowly, methodically, he began stripping the clothing from the boy's body. First the overcoat, then the coat, the trousers, the underclothing, until Parmalee lay naked upon the floor, his body white against the grimy carpet.

Within a few moments the boy was dressed in a pair of tattered trousers and a seaman's jacket. A cap was pulled down over his eyes, a cap which turned red with the blood which was running from a wound in his forehead.

Catching the body up, the sailor threw it across his shoulders, as he might have shouldered a sack of meal. With a curt word to Anna, he was gone. Cautiously, Hans carried Parmalee down a rear stairway, through an alley, across the dock, and aboard the *Eberhard*. For Parmalee was a strong and husky man—and the captain would pay ten dollars for an able-bodied sailor.

Hans and Anna parted that night, after a drunken debauch, and she never saw him again. For the *Eberhard* and all on board went down in some fiord of Norway, months later. And by the time that the news had filtered back to Tony's dance hall in Gallatin Street, Anna did not care; she had forgotten Hans for a dark-eyed Spaniard, who wore gold earrings in his ears, and who kissed and beat her, just as Hans had done.

And she never told Tony what had happened in Thelma's room that night. She was afraid of his fists. So Anna was unsuspected. Tony was righteously indignant when the police searched his house for the body of young Parmalee. And fear held Anna silent.

But the thing worried her; she found that she would

dream of the young fellow as he lay naked upon the floor, with the blood running down from the wound in his fore-head. Anna had been guilty of things worse than her share in this—but this was the thing which worried her most. And she kept the signet ring which she had slipped from his finger, and which Hans had overlooked, hidden away in a hole in the chimney. It was a year later that she pawned it, after Tony had turned her out, and with the money real-ized she bought food. And she gave a fictitious name to the pawnbroker. Anna never knew that the discovery of the ring in the pawnshop had caused the city to revive the old story again—for Anna lay dying not many days later, dying of a loathsome disease which destroyed her usefulness to Tony's dance hall, and which made it bad business to keep her in his employ.

When Anna was dying she told her story to an old woman who had befriended her. And the woman told her husband. The story must have been true, the old woman thought, because Anna told it so vividly that the old woman remembered every word of it, and often repeated it to her husband.

And it was the old man who told it to me, just as I have told it to you, here.

But when I searched police records for the Parmalee case, I could find nothing of it. But there were other trage-dies. There was the murder of one Lee, a drum major in the Federal army, who met his death in Gallatin Street during the Reconstruction period in New Orleans. There was the killing of a policeman in that shadowy street in 1887, and there was the murder of John Hurley by Frankie

Lyons, years afterward. Old files of yellow newspapers tell more of the horrors. For life was held cheaply under the flickering lamps of Gallatin Street.

"Yes, strange things have happened down there," an old policeman said, his dark eyes flashing at the recollection. "And what they tell you of the house of shanghaied sailors is true enough. I heard about the place time and again when I was a young man. And I know the name of the man who ran it, the one you call Tony. But even now it cannot be told, except in a whisper, because with the money he made in Gallatin Street, keeping that house of his, he went into politics, made more money and became a popular politician.

"But he's dead now, and gone to a place where perhaps he'll meet some of those poor devils he sent to the bottom of the sea in rotten ships. Yes, he's gone, and so is the street. There's nothing left there now, only empty old houses."

But there are more than memories in that sinister street. If you do not believe it walk there late some foggy night, just before the cracked bell in the Cathedral tolls twelve. Walk slowly the length of that shadowy street, then turn and retrace your steps. Try it, I say, if you do not believe in ghosts.

Darkness, sagging buildings which tower crazily over your head, almost blotting out the sky. Dim archways, blacker shadows, all softened in a fine film of fog. Nothing moving in the whole stretch of the street; an arc light at the corner seems to intensify the gloom.

Suddenly from almost under your feet, a cat leaps and slides into a shadow, a streak of sleek blackness. You pause, startled. And you listen.

From the river comes the sound of the whistles, the lapping of the water against the piling of the wharf. From the French Market there is a muffled sound of voices, the rattle of wagons unloading produce. But you find yourself listening for other sounds from behind the tight-shut doors of the deserted houses.

What is it that you expect to hear? The sound of muffled music and the tread of feet? Or the hoarse scream of some woman, hidden behind those closed windows, which gaze down on you like sightless eyes?

No. There is nothing. Gone is young Parmalee, gone are his swaying companions. Anna is no longer here. Big Hans lies in the sea, half a world away.

There are only ghosts in Gallatin Street.

Chapter XXXIII

SAINTS IN THE CLASSIFIED COLUMN

To know a city, or so it seems to me, it is necessary to know something of the daily life of the people. The newspapers offer the easiest avenue of approach. There are certain peculiarities in the New Orleans papers which make them unlike newspapers in other cities.

Not the news alone, but from the advertisements as well, you may be able to deduce something of the people themselves.

The classified advertisements in the New Orleans papers have interested me for years. On Sunday I find myself reading the columns through. And in the "Personal" column I have encountered some unusual things. Let me give an example, clipped from the "Times-Picayune" during the month of March, 1928.

"Mr. and Mrs. Mairo Adelfio, 2427 Frenchmen Street, will have a St. Joseph Altar."

The Orleanian will understand this immediately. It means that Mr. and Mrs. Mairo Adelfio will, on St. Joseph's Day, erect an altar in their house. There will be a statue of the saint decorated with flowers and illuminated with lighted candles. Near the altar there will be a large table loaded with food; loaves of bread, cake, fruit, meats —enough to feed hundreds of people. Early in the morning, a group of poor people are fed—for the poor represent angels who may come unawares. All day long, crowds of people will throng the Adelfio house, paying homage to St. Joseph, praying and sometimes partaking of the food. No hungry person will be turned away.

As St. Joseph's Day approaches you will find scores of similar advertisements. If you question those men and women who build these altars you will find that they have "promised" these altars to the saint. And although the gift of such an extravagant amount of food may reduce the family to comparative poverty, this vow must be fulfilled, let come what may.

I remember that I spoke to a woman once who had erected a splendid altar in her humble little house. I estimated that the food alone must have cost not less than two hundred dollars. I asked:

"Why did you do this?"

"Ah," she said, "my husband was nearly dead—three, four months ago—I had done everything. The doctor had done everything. Still it seemed that he would die. Finally I prayed to Saint Joseph to save him. I promised Saint Joseph that I would give him an altar costing not less than three hundred dollars on his birthday. My husband began to get better that very hour. Saint Joseph kept his word. I must keep mine. But I tell you, it is not easy."

This custom may be observed in other cities, but I

know of no city where so many altars like this are erected. On St. Joseph's Day, you may visit ten, fifty, three hundred similar celebrations if you wish. Every one is welcome. And the stranger is treated with scrupulous politeness.

So much for one advertisement in the classified column.

The custom of thanking the saints, through the medium of the classified advertisement, is sometimes considered odd by the visitor to New Orleans. Especially so, if the advertisement is accompanied by the phrase "publication promised." In order to illustrate what I mean, I shall quote the "Personal" advertisements published in the "Times-Picayune" for one day in April, 1928. It was a day taken at random, but the reader may glean something from these items:

THANKS to Sacred Heart of Jesus for favor granted. Mrs. T. O'Neil.

THANKS to St. Jude for favor granted. Holy masses and publication promised. A. Client.

THANKS to the Sacred Heart of Jesus, His Immaculate Mother, St. Joseph, and St. Anthony for favors granted. Mrs. C.

THANKS to St. Rita and Little Flower of Jesus for special favor granted. Mrs. Charles H. Frantz, 920 Jena.

THANKS to the Blessed Mother and the following saints, 10 saints and Blessed Mother for Perpetual Help. J. T. W.

THANKS to Little Theresa, Flower of Jesus and St. Jude. N. N. M.

THANKS to Jesus, Mary and Joseph for favor granted. M.

THANKS to St. Rita, St. Theresa for favors granted. Mrs. J. S.

THANKS to St. Anthony, the Little Flower, St. Jude, St. Rita, Blessed Mother, Sacred Heart and the Poor Souls in Purgatory. Eliska Schurb.

MANY thanks to Our Lady of Victory for disposing of my property. Mrs. E. Golson.

THANKS TO
ST. JUDE

THANKS TO
SACRED HEART

THANKS to our Lord, Blessed Mother, St. Anthony for favor granted. Mrs. G. B.

THANKS to St. Rita for favors granted. Mrs. A. G.

MANY, many thanks to Our Mother of Perpetual Help, St. Anthony and St. Theresa for special favors granted. Publication promised. Mrs. Robert Aguilera.

THANKS to Sacred Heart of Jesus, Blessed Virgin, St. Theresa, St. Rita, St. Joseph, St. Anthony for favor granted. Mrs. R. Rihner.

THANKS to Sacred Heart of Jesus and Mary and St. Jude favor granted. E. E. H.

THANKS to St. Rita, Blessed Mother, Sacred Heart and Little Theresa and all saints. C. H.

THANKS to Lady of Lourdes, Miracle medal, St. Joseph and Sacred Heart. A. F.

THANKS to St. Expedite and all the saints I prayed for favors granted. Mrs. X. G. Brien.

THANKS to St. Michael the archangel, Our Lady of Prompt Succor, My Guardian Angel, my two little angels in heaven, Willie and Regina, also to Father Pro, the Mexican martyred priest for extraordinary favors granted me. W. T. L.

THANKS to St. Anthony, Jesus, Mary and Joseph for favor granted to Francis Fathers, the Church of Guardian Angel. Mrs. S. S.

THANKS to Our Blessed Virgin Mary, St. Rita, Little Flower of Jesus and St. Anthony for special favor granted. Publication promised. Theresa A. Johnson.

AM applying for a pardon or commutation of sentence. JOHN LIGHTFOOT.

THANKS to St. Anthony, St. Rita, Blessed Mother and St. Peter. E. R. C.

NOT responsible for debts contracted by my wife, George G. Moll.

THANKS to God for favor granted. Publication promised. E. R. C.

THANKS to the Blessed Mother and St. Rita. Mrs. E. L. S.

THANKS to St. Jude and Little Saint Theresa for great favor. Mrs. G. F. S.

THANKS to St. Anthony for finding silver. Promised publication. M. B. V.

PROMISED PUBLICATION
Thanks to Our Lady of Prompt Succor for saving city from flood last May. M. B. V.

THANKS to the Sacred Heart for favor granted. J. M.

THANKS to Sacred Heart, Lady of Lourdes, Little Flower and Infant Jesus for favors granted. A. E. Muller.

THANKS TO BLESSED VIRGIN AND SACRED HEART FOR RECOVERY FROM ILLNESS. MRS. M. L. FALCON.

THANKS to Our Lady of Lourdes for babies' recovery Mrs. J. Pedelahore.

ED—Am trying to make Tuesday as usual. Clara.

I AM NOT responsible for any debts contracted by my wife. STEVE CESKA.

THANKS to St. Joseph for favors received. H. H. M.

THANKS to St. Theresa, Little Flower of Jesus for favor granted. C. S.

THANKS to Sacred Heart, Blessed Mother, Little Flower, all the saints for favors granted. Mrs. E. A. S.

ANY member of Col. Dreure's Orleans Guards during Civil war remembering Charles L. F. Platz, please phone his widow. Uptown 2176-W.

THANKS to Infant Jesus, Our Mother of Perpetual Help, St. Jude, St. Peter, St. Lucy, St. Theresa of the Child of Jesus, and other saints for several favors obtained. CATHERINE ARCENEAUX.

THANKS to St. Janaarius and Companions for favor. Mrs. L. H.

THANKS to Little Flower of Jesus for special favor granted. Mrs. L. H.

THANKS for favors Our Lady Perpetual Help, St. Raymond, St. Expedite, Mrs. J. E. A.

NOT responsible for the debts contracted by my wife, Dinna Moran Durnin. Richard M. Durnin.

THANKS to St. Theresa, Little Flower of Jesus, for safe return of my dog. Mrs. F. F. P.

When first I began reading these messages of thanks in the classified column, I noticed that Saint Raymond was the most popular saint. Later Saint Rita grew popular very suddenly. She is called "The Saint of the Impossible." Now, Saint Theresa, Little Flower of Jesus, is the saint most frequently thanked.

In connection with the popularity of Saint Rita, I remember the reaction of an old woman who kept a store retailing religious articles and artificial hair. There are several such shops in New Orleans, but as I have never been able to understand the connection between the two commodities sold, I shall not try to offer an explanation, but shall merely say that such shops exist. At any rate, it was into one of these little stores I went one day in quest of candles. The old woman behind the counter gave me what I wanted, and as she was wrapping up my purchase, I asked her if she sold many statues of Saint Rita.

"Many? Many?" She cried out so shrilly that I was startled. "There's not a day passes that I don't have calls for statues of Saint Rita. It makes me sick and tired!"

Puzzled, and somewhat amused, I asked why she did not like these orders.

"Oh, I'm glad enough to sell statues," she said. "She's a good saint. But it's the fickle people that make me mad. A year ago it was Saint Raymond . . . always Saint Raymond. I couldn't get enough statues of that saint. And then what? Well, all of a sudden they stopped buying him. It was Saint Rita they wanted. And now . . . well, come here and I'll show you."

I followed her into a back room, where there were shelves filled with identical small statues; they were all covered with dust; and they were all Saint Raymond.

The old woman shrugged her shoulders and made a gesture toward them.

"I'm stuck with fifty statues of Saint Raymond," she said. "People don't pray to him any more."

She continued talking of her troubles as we went back into the outer room, and an old negro woman who had been waiting patiently to purchase something, made a suggestion:

"Ef it wus me," she said, "Ah'd pray tuh Saint Rita tuh help yo' sell 'em."

Whether the shopkeeper took her advice or not, I never found out.

It is not my intention to make the faith of any one appear ridiculous. To me there is something very fine in a belief in miracles and a firm conviction that good shall triumph and evil shall fail. In New Orleans one is confronted, every day, with a faith so childlike and so complete that one stands in amazement before it.

Chapter XXXIV

VOODOO

THERE are a great many people who will tell you that Voodoo or snake-worship among American negroes has ceased to exist. This is not true, for within the last year I have been an eye-witness at a secret Voodoo ceremony.

For more than ten years I have attempted to see one of these meetings—the heritage of black Africa and the West Indies. And in New Orleans, among the Creole negroes, this magic has become entwined with a sort of perverted Catholicism, like the Black Mass.

For the last ten years, then, I have tried to see this thing for myself and have always failed. But now I have seen it. And it came about like this:

For a long time I have known Robert, a full-blooded Congo black man. He is very ignorant, very superstitious. At one time he worked for people who were my friends. But Robert was sent away because he upset all the other servants with his charms and spells.

Not long ago, returning to New Orleans after an

absence, I met Robert and talked with him. I led up to the subject so near my heart. I told him of my troubled love-life, of my rival who had stolen a woman from me. I wanted to do away with him, but I was afraid. I urged him to find me a *cunjer* to do this favor for me. After a long time he promised. He knew a woman, he said, who could do any-thing. She could destroy my rival, and even make me "King of the World" if I liked. It would cost me ten dollars and "expenses." I must swear I would not tell the police, nor make a complaint no matter what harm befell me; I must promise to tell no one where I was going. This arranged, he promised to meet me that night.

We met at the intersection of Claiborne and Esplanade avenues, a few squares beyond the border of the Vieux Carré—a hybrid section in which there are decaying man-sions with gardens, small Creole cottages set flush with the *banquette,* and occasionally an old house converted to busi-ness purposes, harboring many families on the floors above. Both streets are wide and lined with trees; it was quite dark, for the arc-lights at the corners lighted but dimly the inter-vening stretches.

Robert came out of the shadows without a word and motioned me to follow him. It was close on midnight and the streets were deserted. Somewhere in the distance I heard a policeman drop his wooden club upon the pavement—a signal that all is well and that he is on guard, one of the old city customs which has survived until now. We had not gone far along a side street when Robert stopped before a gate in a wall. It opened to his touch, and we found ourselves in an alley, narrow and dark, but open to the sky; the alley opened presently into a courtyard which we traversed, and another gate was opened—a gate which led into some inner court, long and narrow and overhung by a balcony. It was evident that this court adjoined the slave quarters of the house, which fronted on another street. There was, even in the darkness, an air of dilapidation about the place, and I thought the house to be untenanted. There were several tight-shut batten doors along the wall of the house, and upon one of these Robert tapped lightly. Almost instantly it was opened, and a dim light shone through the chink. A whispered consultation, and we were admitted.

The room was small, and upon the walls there were shelves bored with holes for holding bottles—the old wine-room of the house. An oil lamp was burning, the wick turned low; by its light I could see a dozen or more bottles on one of the shelves, dark and new-looking against the dusty walls.

A woman and a man stood there. She was a light mulatto of about twenty-five years of age, the man was a very black negro of middle age. The girl would have been pretty had it not been for the deep smallpox scars on her face; she wore a guinea-blue wrapper and was barefoot—a white cloth was tied around her head. The man was a burly fellow, barefoot and wearing only a pair of overalls which left his shoulders and chest bare; his face was mask-like and his eyes half-closed. He stood behind the girl, regarding me narrowly.

After a pause the girl said: "Mamma Phemie's ready fo' de w'ite man now."

Robert took my overcoat and hat and put them upon the shelves with the wine bottles. The girl opened the door in the wall behind her and led the way into the other room.

It was so dark that at first I could see little. A fire was burning in the large open fireplace, and one candle set in a glass of water on the mantel gave a dim light which seemed dissipated before it reached the dark ceiling or the flagstones of the floor. A pot hung on a crane over the smouldering fire; there was a pleasant smell of gumbo in the air, mixed with the musty smell of unused rooms, and the sharp salty smell of unwashed negroes.

In the shadow beside the fireplace an old woman sat huddled on the floor; her head was covered with a white *tignon,* and she wore a wrapper of red calico. Beside her, a small table-cloth was spread on the floor; the candle light fell across it, and I could see that it was stiff and clean; there were still creases in the cloth from ironing. Upon the cloth were two plates, one containing meat and bread, the other banked high with oranges and bananas. Three bottles of wine stood at regular intervals; one in the center and the others at diagonal corners of the cloth. Three black candles, unlighted as yet, stood in glasses half-filled with water. A ladle and several spoons were piled together at one side.

Figures were discernible in the gloom, shapeless shadows sitting against the walls. Here and there one seemed stretched out as though sleeping. The room was very warm.

I went forward with Robert and the big negro beside me, the mulatto girl walking a little ahead. The room—it seemed to me—was filled with tension, nervousness. For some reason I counted my paces; there were ten between the door and the fireplace where the old woman crouched.

As we came close she raised her head and looked at me; a strange, fat face, full of fine lines like crazed china; one eyebrow was higher than the other—a lax, lewd mouth. But there was dignity there, too, and when she spoke her voice was full and husky.

"W'at yo' doin' heah, w'ite man?"

I repeated again the story I had told Robert, of my rival, "a handsome fellow with dark hair who had stolen my woman from me." I wanted him put out of my path. She nodded slowly, reached up and took my hands, drawing me down beside her. There we squatted, eye to eye and toe to toe. Finally she let my hands drop and hung her head upon her breast again. I drew the ten-dollar bill from my pocket and handed it to her. She took it carelessly, without looking at it, and tucked it under the edge of the table-cloth beside her.

"Is yo' Cat'lic?" she asked finally.

I answered that I was not a member of any church. She seemed to brood. Finally she muttered something that I could not understand. Robert touched my shoulder and I was led from the room. My clothes, it seemed, were not "right." Things were crossed and buttoned; I wore black shoes and hose. These must be removed before she could "work."

Determined to see the thing through, I submitted, stripping down to underwear. A faded cotton bathrobe was given me and I put it on. Then I was led back to the old woman again—the flagstones gritty and cold under my bare feet.

In my absence, some one had lighted the three black candles, and now the room was fairly illuminated. In the glow I could see perhaps twelve men and women sitting or lying along the walls. I sat down before the old woman, who put her hands upon my head, and with closed eyes began to moan. . . .

"Sperrit comin' on 'er. . ." I heard some one say. But the old woman seemed distressed and worried. She moaned feebly, and her hands closed tight around my head.

"Dere's somethin' wrong, w'ite man," she said at last in her ordinary voice. "Pichotee says so. . . ."

Again her eyes closed and her body became tense. She began to twitch and shake. A low humming came from the negroes along the walls, led by the mulatto girl, who now stood just within my range of vision, leaning against the wall, arms folded under her depending breasts.

"Hit's all jumble' and mess' up . . ." the old woman said at last. "T'ings is tied up in knots."

The big negro came forward, somewhat aggressively, and opened my robe and began examining my underwear. Somewhere at the back of the belt he discovered a knotted tape. Again I was led from the room, and the underwear was taken from me. Now I had only the thin cotton robe left on me.

This time all was well. Immediately the old woman began to twitch and shake. The hand that held mine grew damp with sweat. Her eyes closed, her head fell back, and she began speaking in a high nasal voice: "I see 'im!" And the negroes along the walls began to hum afresh:

"Um . . . m . . . um-um . . . oom. . . ."

"I see 'im! I see 'im!" Mamma Phemie repeated, and then went on to recount some long story of a man standing in my way. He hated me. He would kill me if he had the chance. He might kill me, anyway. I was in constant danger. But she could "fix all dat." Oh, yes. She could "work t'ings

to fix 'im instead." It was very lucky for me that I had come
to her in time.

In the silence of the room, the thing had an air of reality that was amazing. For a moment I forgot that I had invented this rival, and I seemed to see him standing over me, a threatening and baleful figure.

"Plenty, plenty wine!" shouted old Phemie suddenly. There was a stir in the room. The mulatto girl picked up a bottle and held it to the woman's lips. She swallowed some of it, then filling her mouth with the rest, spit it out over the big negro, the mulatto girl, and myself. We were covered with it. Much of the remaining wine dropped down the old woman's chin, staining the white fichu she wore around her shoulders.

Then her voice began mumbling again. "W'at yo' willin' to do to git rid of 'im?" she asked finally. "Anything," I said. Then: "W'at yo' willin' to do fo' dese people who is helpin' yo'?" She indicated the negroes in the room. I was puzzled until Robert whispered into my ear that I might buy some additional wine for them. I agreed to this, and sent him to get what money was left in my clothes in the other room. He brought a five-dollar bill back and gave it to the big negro, who left the room at once. The wailing along the walls began again. Now and again I could hear the snapping of fingers.

Now the pock-marked mulatto girl came forward with a shapeless piece of black wax in one thin hand. The old woman took it and began kneading it between her fingers. Presently it assumed the crude shape of a human figure.

In her mumbled song I could distinguish a few words now and then: "Drop of w'ite man's blood . . . blood.

. . ." My blood, I now came to understand, must animate the image. The big negro had returned and came forward with a steel knife. This was more than I had bargained for and I demurred. But Robert snarled into my ear: "Yo' gotta! Yo' gotta! Else she can't do nothin'!" So I took the knife, held it first in the candle flame and then pricked my forearm. A drop of blood oozed out. A sort of shout went up from those in the background: "O-ou-ou!"

Old Phemie took the knife from me and penetrated the breast of the waxen figure; the image was then pressed against my arm, and the blood shone moist against the black wax.

> "Oh, guilty, guilty my mind is . . .
> Oh, take away de stain . . ."

Along the walls the humming was changing into words. This was a familiar chant called "The Moan after the Prayer," often heard in negro churches as the preacher begins his sermon. Feet were patting on the flagstones, and from a dark corner there came suddenly the soft throbbing of a drum, a definite rhythm:

Zoom-zoom . . . zoom . . . zoom. . . .
Zoom-zoom . . . zoom . . . zoom. . . .

The effect was hypnotic. The humming became louder, more pronounced, but wordless again.

The old woman was still rubbing the black waxen image between her pink palms. A bottle was being passed from hand to hand among those who sat along the walls.

Finally the figure seemed fashioned to the old woman's liking, and she turned and laid it upon the hearth, near the

embers and near the simmering pot. The drum-beat changed
and grew faster:

Zoom . . . zoom-zoom . . . zoom. . . .

Zoom . . . zoom-zoom . . . zoom. . . .

As the heat of the fire began melting the wax a louder
cry came from the assembly: "Aie! Aie! Aie!" Rising and
dying away, rising again. And always the drum as an undercurrent of rhythm.

Only a pool of melting wax remained. The old woman
began to pray: "Mary, Jesus, Joseph . . ." on through the
Act of Contrition of the Catholic Manual. Then stopping
she cried aloud, sharply: "Maron!"

Immediately the cry was taken up by the others:
"Maron!" It was repeated over and over. The big negro
came forward carrying with him a tawdry statue of St.
Anthony, such as is found in any store selling religious
articles. He placed it upon the table-cloth beside the old
woman. "Done set de table, St. Maron . . . now what yo'
goin' to do?" And instantly the phrase was repeated in
chorus by the others:

"W'at yo' goin' to do? Oh, w'at yo' goin' to do?
Oh, Maron, oh, Saint Maron,
W'at yo' goin' to' do?"

There was no response from the sad-faced saint. The
old woman began to scream. She hoisted herself to her feet,
aided by the mulatto girl: "Yo' answer me, Maron! What
yo' goin' to do?"

She stamped her foot. She spat upon the image. And
the wailing from the others rose high and clear.

Mamma Phemie was working herself into a frenzy. She

shouted curses, filth, at the statue. She spat wine over its plaster head. Then she flung herself to the floor, beating the flagstones with her fists.

She rose again, saliva dripping from her mouth, staggered, shrieked, and fell to the floor. The negroes rose and swarmed around her, clutching her head, her arms, her legs and feet. She struggled, fought. Her clothes were ripped half from her fat body. She moaned and her eyes crossed. She quivered and ground her teeth together. She frothed at the mouth. Her limbs grew tense. Her heels beat a tattoo on the floor.

It was an epileptic fit, but the negroes cried out in joy: "She done possess! She done got 'er way! Saint Maron done answer 'er!"

The spasm reached its climax. The old woman's tongue, clenched between her teeth, was bloody.

The mulatto girl was sprinkling salt over her. Other negroes dipped their fingers into the salt and then put their fingers into their mouths, keeping their hold upon the old woman all the time.

"De sperrit done come strong on 'er!" cried the big negro in a sort of ecstasy. The thin mulatto girl was crying hysterically: "Oh, I jus' can't stand it!" over and over.

The old woman was relaxed now and lay upon her back, her red wrapper pulled over her knees. The floor around her was wet. A stench of latrines filled the room.

The crowd is on its feet now, gathered together in the candle light. One emaciated *griffe*—a light yellow girl— wore only a skirt and a white waist, now open to the waist. Several of the men wore only trousers. All the women had scarves or handkerchiefs tied around their heads. One of

OLEANDERS AND FIGS NOW FLOURISH IN
OLD GIROD STREET CEMETERY

MADISON STREET LOOKING TOWARD
FRENCH MARKET

the men had a bandanna handkerchief tied around his neck, but was naked otherwise except for ragged trousers. All were barefoot. As they moved about, several of them staggered uncertainly. One black woman's nostrils were working spasmodically, as though from cocaine.

The big negro and the mulatto girl that I had seen first now took command. They handed me things that had been prepared for me: a small bag containing ashes, hairs from a white horse's tail, salt and pepper and some crushed dried leaves; a box containing pecans which had been drilled with holes and in which feathers had been inserted; a bundle of feathers, wound around with dried grass. In a whisper I was instructed to throw all of these, one at a time, into the path of my rival. The feather bouquet was to be placed, if possible, in his pillow; the pecans, upon his threshold. When next he left me, I was to throw a pinch of salt after him— then he would never return. An orange from the "table" was given me. This was for me to eat at my convenience, to make me "strong." It could not fail me now, for Saint Maron had blessed it. Had I not seen this miracle?

I withdrew to a corner beside the fireplace, and the mulatto girl removed the cover from the simmering pot which hung over the fire. She began to ladle out the gumbo into bowls handed her by the others. With her large spoon she stirred the pot, and lifted out a snake which had been cooked along with the gumbo. Then she let it fall back into the pot again.

The first bowl was offered to me. I made a gesture of refusal. Robert, at my elbow, urged me to take it. "Tek it! Tas'e it! It ain't goin' to hu't yo'!" To prove his point, he began to drink from his bowl with relish. All the others stood watching me as I mustered all my force of will and put the bowl to my lips. My gorge rose, but I managed to swallow a little. They were satisfied. A black woman took the bowl from me and began to imbibe noisily.

"W'ite man all right," said the big negro, looking at me for the first time without suspicion. Gagging, I slumped down upon the floor again beside the fireplace. Between the legs of the negroes I could see Mamma Phemie, who was moaning feebly now and trying to rise. A bowl of hot gumbo was given her, and she gulped it down. Almost at once she was on her feet again, in command of the situation.

It was time for the dancing. Men were already handling the women, rubbing against them. In the corner the drum was throbbing restlessly. Bottles of wine were passed around. Men and women gurgled as they drank.

Mamma Phemie was shaking her breasts in rhythm with the drum. The circle formed around her, the men and women standing alone, shaking slowly in time with the drum-beats. Hardly moving. A shoulder, a knee twisting. Black and yellow faces were blear-eyed. Sweat shone on black flesh.

Zoom . . . zoom . . . zoom-zoom. . . .

Zoom . . . zoom . . . zoom-zoom. . . .

Now came the "animal motions" that I had heard of. A man fell on his knees; in imitation of a rabbit he munched grass, rubbed his face with both hands at once, shook that part of his anatomy which represented the rabbit's tail. Then he rose and resumed his swaying. A woman followed, imitating a cat in the act of licking itself. . . .

And all the rest swaying, twitching with the drum-beats.

Zoom . . . zoom . . . zoom-zoom-zoom-zoom.

Zoom . . . zoom . . . zoom-zoom-zoom-zoom.

A new rhythm. Hips are shaking now. Men and women tip bottles to their lips as they sway. The emaciated yellow girl tears off her waist with a shrill scream. A man throws himself upon her and bites her breast. The big negro pulls him away and throws him to one side. There is blood on the girl's breast, but she continues to swing her body, uttering now and then a thin, high cry. Another man clutches her. She claws his face.

Old Phemie, eyes glazed, standing alone in the center of the group, screams aloud: "Zombi!"

The dance stops. The drum breaks off short. Men and women fall face down on the floor, lying prostrate, moaning: "Zombi! Zombi!"

And then, after a pause, the drum begins again as before. The dancers rise and begin to sway again. A woman fills her mouth with wine and spews it out into the face and over the shoulders of the man beside her. Others follow her example. Old Phemie, twirling slowly, spurts out wine impartially.

Zoom-zoom . . . zoom-zoom . . . zoom-zoom. . . .

Zoom-zoom . . . zoom-zoom . . . zoom-zoom. . . .

Men and women are like animals now. There are screams and shouts. Men bite. Women scratch. The big negro, quite naked now, catches a thin mulatto girl around the waist and bears her down across the table-cloth, upsetting the candles. The room is almost totally dark. Only the flickering firelight remains.

A woman is picked up and hurled half-way across the room, falling limply upon the flagstones.

Other bodies, seemingly animated with some fiendish

force, crash against me in the dark. Wine is poured upon me. I am tripped, flung to the floor, whether by accident or design I cannot tell.

Robert, almost naked, is beside me, but he knows me no longer. His body is taut. He is jerking about spasmodically, alone, attaining some artificial Nirvana of his own. He shrieks: "Aie! Aie!"

I crawl on my hands and knees along the wall toward the door. A bottle comes crashing against the wall just over my head. Just in time I find the latch, push open the door and pass through.

The wine-room is as I saw it first. My clothes lie in a tumbled heap. I drag them on as a madman would, ignoring buttons, breaking shoe-strings.

The door opens and a strange negro man lurches drunkenly toward me: "Whar yo' goin'?"

"Out! I'm going out!" I answer. "Get out of the way."

Robert comes staggering after him: "Is yo' all right?" he asks, slobbering as he speaks. I motion for them to let me pass, and they do so. Outside in the dark court there are huddled figures, the guards. Some one takes me by the arm. I am led down an alley, a gate is opened and I am pushed through.

Horribly sick, I make for the curb and lean against a post. From outside I can hear nothing of the din from the dancers behind the tight-shut battens of that inner courtyard. . . . Finally the spasm of nausea passes and I stagger along the dim streets, back toward a sane world which tells me that Voodoo no longer exists—if it ever existed!

The sky, back of the closely shuttered houses toward the east, is beginning to turn gray.

Chapter XXXV

A LAST GLIMPSE OF THE VIEUX CARRÉ

THE old buildings are still charming in their decay, but they are sad too. Ironwork hangs rusting against mouldering plaster; window sashes sag; old courtyards—once the center of Creole family life, once gardens filled with palms, cape jasmine, crepe myrtle—are used now as stables for horses or as a parking place for automobiles. Hungry-looking cats parade upon the walls like ghosts of the past, wailing to the moon.

But still, tucked away behind the façades of the old houses there are a few families of the old régime, old ladies and old gentlemen who refuse to desert their homes in the Vieux Carré, old people who prefer to remain shut up within their own four walls rather than move into those palm-bordered drives of "uptown" New Orleans.

If you will call some evening at dusk, you will find yourself in another world, a world of faded elegance and candle light, a world where old customs are still observed and where the simple manners of other days persist.

We will walk—let us say—down Royal Street, once the main thoroughfare of the city. Six short squares from Canal Street—the busiest corner of the new New Orleans—you will come upon a row of three-storied brick- and plaster-houses set side by side, filling the square from end to end. These old houses, like the men and women inside, have suffered from the passage of time. The façades of the houses are flush with the sidewalk, and from the second and third floors, balconies of wrought-iron overhang the *banquettes*. From the first balcony, five or six French windows —sheltered with heavy batten blinds—open into the drawing-rooms. Above are smaller balconies, before the bedroom windows. The ground floor of each house is a shop. The entrance to the house proper is through a large double door, kept always tightly shut. From outside the houses appear to be unoccupied.

Raise the old iron knocker and let it fall—then wait. Presently there will be a shuffling of feet, a click, and one of the doors opens upon its protesting hinges. There stands before you an old negro woman, spotlessly clean, black as ebony, wearing the *tignon* or head-handkerchief. You ask for Madame. You are invited inside.

It seems that you have entered another world. A passage more than ten feet wide stretches before you for sixty or seventy feet. At the end you see large arches. A lantern hangs from the roof, and beyond the arches the courtyard, paved with blue-gray flagstones. Palms are growing high, reaching up toward the sun. An iron fountain trickles. There are wrought-iron benches and tables beside the flower beds. High, high up you see the top of the courtyard wall, iron spiked, and beyond the gables of other houses, the sky.

The old woman stands aside in order that you may mount the stairs first, apologizing that her rheumatism keeps her from being as agile as she would like to be. One of the arches has been glassed in, and behind these glass doors the stairs rise, a graceful curve from the courtyard to the roof. Well built stairs these are, wide and easy to ascend. A mahogany rail is shining in the sunlight which comes into the hall through the glass wall to the court. You mount.

The stairs pause, it seems, at the second floor, and then you realize for the first time that the Creole house is built with its back to the street. The sitting-room, you perceive, faces the courtyard.

The stairs have brought you to the great room on the second floor which forms the keystone of the whole house. Across the side facing the court there are three large fan-light windows, open to the warm air of late afternoon. The tops of the palms are just outside. The room is nearly all doors, double glass doors opening to the inner rooms. There are three of these, corresponding to the three large windows opposite. The stairs pass through this room in a gentle curve and disappear into the shadows of the floor above. The walls are of plain white plaster with a wide cornice. In the center of the room there hangs a large and ornate chandelier upon which cupids, shepherds, and shepherdesses disport themselves, holding up the gas-globes. A few pieces of heavy mahogany furniture stand about—a large sofa, two arm-chairs, a table with a gay scarf. Flowering oleanders are growing in large jars. Ferns hang in baskets in the windows. A green parrot is preening itself on the window-sill in the last rays of the setting sun. There is a feeling of peace, of refinement, of the world shut out.

Here you are asked to wait, while the old negress climbs the second flight of stairs to tell her mistress you are here. There is a short pause and then the tap-tap of a cane. A little old lady, wrinkled, old like the house, comes slowly down the stairs to receive you. You go with her into one of the rooms opening from the room in which you have been sitting.

This is the drawing-room. A rectangular apartment— probably thirty-five feet long and more than half as wide. It reaches from the room overlooking the court to the balcony which overhangs the street. Here you find the same white plastered walls with fading family portraits. The chandelier is of crystal, and has places for fifty candles. Old rosewood and mahogany pieces stand about invitingly.

You are warm. "A fan, Delphine!" and *presto!* the old negro woman produces a large palmetto-leaf fan and presents it to you. You are thirsty, perhaps? Delphine does not wait for your reply but goes out to return presently with a decanter and glasses. Rare old crystal glasses in a lacquer tray that would wring the heart of a collector.

Madame then begins to talk. She does not see you often. You are forgetting your old friends. She feared it would be so. Marie, her daughter, since her marriage has gone to live uptown in St. Charles Avenue. Madame thinks her foolish—but what would you? She—Madame—has not been out lately. Since the burning of the French Opera—"mon Dieu! It brings tears to the eye"—she has not been out at night. Nothing would induce her to attend opera in a theater uptown. Opera is not opera in a barn, says she. *"Non!"*—she will remain at home first.

And the tourists! Ah, Madame is cruel when she speaks of the tourists. She has told Delphine never, never under any circumstances to allow the gate of the courtyard to remain open.

But that Delphine! She went out for a moment—I give you my word it was not five minutes—and while she was gone a horde of those barbarians invaded the court.

"I heard them talking among themselves," Madame continues, "and I leaned from the window to listen. Perhaps they would like my old garden? But no! What do I hear? 'What a funny old place,' they cheep like sparrows. 'I wonder if decent people ever lived here?' Mon Dieu! I was angry. I called to them and asked if they were seeking any one. They laughed at my English, laughed at me in my own house. It is an outrage! I quarreled with Delphine all day about that gate."

Delphine has returned with two tiny cups of black coffee, but Madame waves her aside. She insists that you try her wine. She has plenty, she says—enough to last her lifetime. Prohibition? Pouf! People will come to their senses and allow us our liberty again. She has read in the paper that some great man predicts it. She has forgotten at the moment who it was. But whoever he is, he is a sensible man. She would like to know him.

Candles are brought in. Delphine lights an old lamp of brass and crystal. Madame does not care for electricity— gas, yes, her father installed it, but electricity, no. It is bad for the eyes, she assures you.

You say good-by. Darkness has set in. Delphine has

lighted the lantern in the courtyard. A blue haze has settled in the branches of the palm-trees. The sleepy parrot complains as you pass him nodding on the window-sill. Quietly you descend the stairs and regain the court. Delphine follows to close the gate behind you. You look back as in a dream. It is something too charming to be real.

Outside in the street, ragged children are playing under an arc-light with shrill cries. The dust swirls up. A boy is selling papers. At a corner grocery women with shawls over their heads are buying cans of tinned goods, and bottles of milk. Little barefoot boys stand waiting with baskets. You cross the street and gaze up at the house you have just left. Close-shuttered it stands, keeping its secrets.

You return to reality through the noisy streets.

NOTES

IN THOSE ways that set it apart from other American cities New Orleans changes very little. It is true that the city has grown—in 1949 its population is over 600,000. There are new and flourishing businesses, organizations and clubs, as well as fine airports and a new era of trade with Latin America that is making always cosmopolitan New Orleans more and more an international city. But it is still the fabulous New Orleans of which Lyle Saxon wrote. The French Quarter, with which, as I have stated in the Introduction, he was so concerned, remains the same, as do other old parts of the city. The people also remain the same. The customs and traditions and even the old superstitions do not change.

So, although Fabulous New Orleans first appeared in 1928, few notes are needed to append this book. Yet, naturally, the city does not actually exist in a world apart and there have been a few things that might be noted.

For instance, the so-called "shutter girls" to whom Saxon refers on Page 45 no longer exist. Prostitution, which became illegal in 1917 in New Orleans, continued to exist for many years afterward quite openly, particularly in the French Quarter. It vanished after the Quarter began to become a popular place of residence for some of the city's leading citizens, a process actually begun in the 1920's. Now there are only a few houses and none so open as that conducted by the "shutter girls," almost none in the French Quarter itself.

The neighborhood called the Irish Channel, referred to on Page 53, is no longer a "bad" section. Today it is still a poor one, but relative peace and quiet prevail.

On Page 67 Saxon refers to the meeting of the courts of Rex and Comus on Mardi Gras night at the old French Opera House. The French Opera House was razed by fire in 1919, so the meeting, still a regular Mardi Gras tradition, takes place in the Municipal Auditorium. The Municipal Auditorium, mentioned on Page 283, was completed in 1930, and has since been the scene of most carnival balls, concerts and operatic performances. However many Orleanians find this far from satisfying and dream as Saxon did of the future restoration of the French Opera House. Congo Square where the Auditorium stands is now called Beauregard Square.

Prohibition has of course been long repealed and New Orleans again enjoys all its favorite and famous drinks— and in great abundance. Repeal has made the French Quarter a much livelier place, for parts and streets of it, particularly Bourbon Street, are now filled with bars and night clubs. The scenes described on Page 323, however, can still be found, for those persons who have bought and restored French Quarter houses have done a splendid job in most cases of bringing back an illusion of "a world of faded elegance and candle light . . ." Some of the bars and cafes also preserve this atmosphere.

A few, but very few, of the buildings mentioned in this book are gone, for instance the Union Bank which once stood at the corner of Iberville and Royal Streets and was later known as the Citizens Bank.

The Arts and Crafts Club, mentioned on Page 274, is no longer situated in the Brulatour Court, but has moved to larger quarters at the corner of Royal Street and Orleans Alley. The old Brulatour Court is as lovely as ever, however, and is still open to visitors. The Court of the Two Lions, referred to on Page 275, is also occupied by other tenants, but has lost none of its charm.

These are almost the only differences between what Saxon saw in 1928 and what can be seen now, insofar as the contents of this book is concerned. For he was interested in what was old and timeless in New Orleans, in that which will always be the same as he saw it.

ROBERT TALLANT

BIBLIOGRAPHY

Martin's History of Louisiana.

Gayarré's History of Louisiana.

Fortier's History of Louisiana.

"New Orleans, The Place and The People," by Grace King.

"Creole Families of New Orleans," by Grace King.

"New Orleans, As It Was," by Henri C. Castellanos.

"New Orleans and Environs," Norman's guide for 1845.

"Strange True Stories of Louisiana," by George W. Cable.

"The Creoles of Louisiana," by George W. Cable.

"The Oaks," an article by John Augustin, printed in "The Louisiana Book."

"Standard History of New Orleans," compiled by Edward Rightor.

Jewell's "Crescent City Illustrated."

"The Settlement of the German Coast of Louisiana," by J. Hanno Deiler.

Many editions of "The Times-Picayune Guide Book."

"Social Life in Old New Orleans," by Eliza Ripley.

"Autobiographical Sketches and Recollections," by Theodore Clapp.

"New Orleans Sketch Book and Guide," issued for the exposition of 1884.

"In and Around the St. Louis Cathedral," by the Rev. C. M. Chambon.

"The Creoles of History and the Creoles of Romance," a pamphlet by Charles Gayarré.

"General Butler in New Orleans," by James Parton.

"The New Orleans Sketch Book," by G. M. Wharton.

"Stories of the Crescent City," by Napier Bartlett.

"Society in America," by Harriet Martineau.

"Travels in America in 1819," by the Duke of Saxe-Weimar-Eisenach.

The publications of The Louisiana Historical Society.

The publications of The Mississippi Historical Society.

The Colonial Archives of Louisiana.

The Colonial Archives of Mississippi, Dunbar Rowland's translation.

Scrap-books compiled by Mrs. Cammie Garrett Henry of Melrose, Louisiana.

Files of the following newspapers:

"L'Abeille."

"The Advertiser."

"The Gazette."

"Le Moniteur de la Louisiane."

"The Times-Picayune."

"The New Orleans Item."

"The Daily States."

Various old letters, diaries, records, and legal documents cited in the text.

"Father Mississippi," by Lyle Saxon.

"The Gates of Empire," by Lyle Saxon.

INDEX